An American's
Journey into Buddhism

An American's Journey into Buddhism

ALBERT SHANSKY

McFarland & Company, Inc., Publishers
Jefferson, North Carolina, and London

LIBRARY OF CONGRESS CATALOGUING-IN-PUBLICATION DATA

Shansky, Albert, 1925–
    An American's journey into Buddhism / Albert Shansky.
        p.   cm.
    Includes index.

    ISBN 978-0-7864-3719-1
    softcover : 50# alkaline paper ∞

    1. Shansky, Albert, 1925– .   2. Buddhists — United
States — Biography.   I. Title.
BQ986.A56 A3   2008
294.3'927092 — dc22 [B]   2008007031

British Library cataloguing data are available

Cover photo ©2007 Shutterstock

Manufactured in the United States of America

*McFarland & Company, Inc., Publishers
    Box 611, Jefferson, North Carolina 28640
    www.mcfarlandpub.com*

For the Rev. Daigaku David Rumme,
whose friendship, guidance,
and inspirations made this story possible

Acknowledgments

I should like to acknowledge three people who have helped me considerably by reading the manuscript of this book, making suggestions, and offering constructive criticism. The first is Dr. Morris Grossman, professor emeritus in philosophy at Fairfield University; the second is Mr. Scott O'Reilly, research associate of the International Institute for Field-Being at Fairfield University; and finally the third is Dr. Maurice Siegel, painter, playwright, and chemist. All three gentlemen have considerable past experience in the art of writing and so I have valued and used most of their suggestions in modifying this book. I am extremely grateful for their effort on my behalf.

In addition, I should like to recognize my wife, Pearl Brody Shansky, who has heartened, advised, and inspired me for more than sixty years. Without her guidance, presence, and proximity this book would certainly not have been attempted.

Also, this story could not have been written without the memory of my two brothers, Daniel Shansky and Bernard Shansky. They were my role models in my youth who taught me to cherish scholarship and craftsmanship. It is said that remembering is the hand of God. I remember them; therefore, I make them immortal.

Table of Contents

Preface

This story is about the experiences I had when I followed the tenets of Buddhism and the impact it had on my life. I became interested in Buddhism through my devotion to East Asian art. The image of the Buddha and the many Bodhisattvas were always evident in Asian artifacts and were present so frequently as to arouse in me a need to partake of this culture.

I have always been enamored with the cultural fluidity and the extraordinary range of visual styles practiced by the Chinese, Tibetan, Nepalese, and Japanese artisans. I found that their pictorial, sculptural, and architectural artifacts escape easy analysis and raise questions about the difference between verbal and pictorial description. The ways in which meaning could be embedded in images through juxtaposition and collage and the production of paintings and calligraphy that were intended as supports for practice and not initially as works of art all had a profound impression on me.

The narrative begins in the early 1990s when I began investigating Buddhism as a religion and runs through about a seventeen-year period of learning and participation. But, first, some background of my life seems appropriate.

I was born on March 26, 1925, in Sheepshead Bay in Brooklyn, New York, to a Jewish working-class family. I had two older brothers and a younger sister. I never knew my father, who died when I was four years old. We were a poor family, but as my mother used to say, "It's no disgrace to be poor; it's just very inconvenient."

The meaning of life for me became clear and patent when I was about eight years old. The year 1933 was the height of the Great Depression. I quickly learned the value of work, the ways of survival and the usefulness of self-reliance and independence. A growing consciousness of social inequity was developing during my adolescence until the age of fourteen when the Spanish Civil War ended and World War II began in 1939.

At the age of eighteen, shortly after graduation from Boys High School, I was drafted into the United States Army where I earned two battle stars, Rhineland and Northern France, in the European Theater of Operations. Upon being mustered out of army service in 1946, I immediately took up my college career at Brooklyn College where I graduated with B.S. and M.S. degrees in chemistry. I then went on in 1951 to Illinois Institute of Technology in Chicago to earn a Ph.D.

I worked as a chemist for more than fifty years, thirty years of which I was an independent consultant operating my own laboratory. During my chemical career I wrote and published more than sixty scientific papers and produced eighteen patents.

In 1947 I married Pearl Brody and as of this writing we have been married sixty years. We have four children who have produced seven grandchildren.

I have had a lifelong love for scholarship and in 1978, at the age of fifty-three, I returned to college. I attended Fairfield University where I took a total of fifty-three courses, half in philosophy and half in art history, over a twenty-year period. In 1995 I established a second career by accepting the position of Executive Vice President of the International Institute for Field-Being at Fairfield University on a part-time basis while still pursuing my chemical consulting practice. As of this writing, I have written and presented more than twelve papers on philosophy at various professional and scholarly organizations and conferences.

In Part 1, the account of my life in the monastery, I attempted to examine the tension between life's experiences and narrative creations. The people and places in this story are all drawn from real life.

Part 2 deals with a search for a Buddhist temple to continue my practice.

Part 3 deals with my involvement in the International Institute for Field-Being and how my Buddhist training helped in that venture.

Part 4 explains my involvement with Buddhism as a lonely practitioner.

The story is structured as a patchwork of conversations, recollections, and lyrical encounters. This quietly earnest quest yielded valuable understanding of myself and a deeper appreciation of the mysteries of people connections and disconnections that can never be resolved.

Most of what is written in this narrative is based on memory. But memory is often distorted by events. Nevertheless, memory has a much larger appetite for small things than for anything on a scale not easily managed.

The selected entries gathered herein form a rich spiritual autobiography, allowing readers to eavesdrop on a restless soul in quest of self, God, and home.

PART 1

Life in the Monastery

The First Day

I looked up as I got out of the taxi. There it was — the most imposing and impressive gate that I have ever seen in Japan. It was about thirty
feet high sitting on top of a flight of eleven stone steps. It had a Japanese
slate roof with a stone decoration along the top edge. It was about twenty
feet wide with two massive wooden doors, which were open at this time.

"*Arigato gosai machete*," I said to the driver as I paid him the 500 yen
for the ride from the Obama station.

As I approached the gate, I had a foreboding feeling and yet a certain excitement whelmed up in me. In walking towards one of the buildings, which was designed in typical Japanese architecture, I was met by a
monk quickly shuffling down the pathway in slippers. He was tall, with a
shaven head, horn-rimmed eyeglasses and black robes.

"My name is Ryubu. Welcome," he said in perfect English. He was
obviously an American.

After a minor courtesy struggle I allowed him to take my bag. We
walked to the first of the buildings. "I'll show you to your room, then we
can go and get your bedding," he said. The room was up a flight of stairs,
behind a sliding paper *shoji* screen, in a high ceiling attic over the dining
area. Ryubu laid my bag down. "This is where you sleep. There will be
two others coming to share the room with you. One will arrive tonight.

The other will come tomorrow. Now let us get your bedding. Have you ever slept on a futon?"

"Yes, I have," I replied; thinking about the many *ryokans* I slept in during my many trips to Japan.

We went to a different building and found a storage room with many bedrolls stacked neatly in a corner. I grabbed one bedroll and shouldered it while Ryubu picked up some sheets, a pillow and a pillowcase. We returned to my room.

"I'll leave you now so you can rest from your journey. I'll call you later for the evening meal." In a moment, he was gone. I looked around at the empty room. I suddenly felt very lonely and I was left with my thoughts. Why am I here? How did I get here? I immediately recalled the year I spent in traveling to Minneapolis and attending practice sessions at the Minnesota Zen Meditation Center. It was there that I met Katagiri Roshi, the Zen Master of the center. At the time he was deathly sick with cancer and was not expected to live. He was bedridden most of the time that I knew him but he was lucid enough to advise me of my needs. I became interested in Buddhism as a result of my deep engrossment in Asian art and I felt that studying Buddhism would give me greater insight into the artistic quality of the painting and sculpture of East Asian culture. In those days, I was traveling once a month to Minneapolis on business. One day I came across an announcement for the Minnesota Zen Meditation Center in the local newspaper. It read something like: *GET CALM! PRACTICE SITTING MEDITATION WITH US!* I found the ad very intriguing so I decided to call. They invited me to observe and participate in their practice. As a result, I had spent almost a full year there learning Buddhist ways and participating in Buddhist practices such as *zazen*, which is sitting meditation and Buddhist chanting. I befriended other members of the Buddhist community, all of whom were Americans. During this time I met with the Roshi several times in *dokusan*, which is an interview with a Zen Master. I told him that I was interested in learning the great concepts of Buddhist theology. Even though he tried to explain the essence of Buddhism to me I felt something lacking and somewhat unfulfilled. On the last occasion that we met he told me that if I wanted to continue with Zen in a serious way, I would probably benefit more by spending some time in a Japanese monastery. Several months later on March 1, 1990, Jikai Dainin Katagiri Roshi died and passed over to nirvana. I attended his funeral on April 16, 1990, at the First Universalist Church in Minneapolis. I now had to pursue the possibility of finding a Japanese monastery on my own. I discussed this matter with several members of the Minnesota Zen Meditation Center and almost all agreed that the Hosshinji Monastery was the place to be. Apparently, Hosshinji is one of three great monasteries that go back to the origin of Soto Zen; the other two being Eihei-ji in Fukui and Soji-ji in Yokohama. Since Hosshinji is a training monastery it was thought best for me. In addition, several monks and aspirants who trained there came from the Minnesota Zen Center.

After making arrangements for an extended stay by writing a letter to the Hosshinji Monastery, I left New York City on Sunday, May 11, 1992, arriving in Tokyo on Monday, May 12, 1992. I checked into the Nikko Hotel in the Ginza district for two days until my "biology" came back to normal. I then took the bullet train to Kyoto and stayed overnight at the Ryokan Hiraiwa. The next morning I took the train to Omi-imazu a small town on Lake Biwa. At Omi-imazu I took a bus to Obama and then a taxi to Hosshinji, arriving on Thursday, May 15.

I stretched out on the floor, leaning my head on the rolled-up bedroll. Soon I fell asleep. I dreamt I was standing before a dais behind which was an old man with a long gray beard and a yarmulke on his head. I assumed he was a Rabbi. At least he looked like all the Rabbis I have ever known. He spoke Yiddish in a deep, somber tone.

Was tust du zwischen dieseh goyim? (What are you doing amongst these gentiles?)

"I am still Jewish," I answered him. "I am here to study Buddhist philosophy."

Buddhist philosophy cannot help you. Only God can help.

"Where is God? I cannot see him," I said. "Why is he hidden?"

Have you never felt the presence of something unseen? If you believe, you will feel the presence of God. If you believe deeply and truly, you may even see Him. God's greatness and man's weakness is revealed in Isaiah 40, vox clamantis in deserto, a voice crying in the wilderness. Prepare for the Messiah's coming. Remember no definition of God devised by the human mind could adequately encompass and describe the whole nature of God. One can find the revelation of God in Psalm 19, where the Psalmist recognizes a unity between God's work in the heavens and His revelation of the law of truth on earth. People discover God only when He has cursed them. God doesn't punish the wicked and award the righteous.

In what seemed like a few moments, I heard a voice calling. I shook awake out of an oneiric stupor. "Hey Al, it's time for the evening meal. Are you hungry?"

"Okay, I'm coming," I said. I went down the stairs and followed Ryubu to a small room off the dining area.

"Tonight we shall eat alone because I have to show you how to use *o-ryo-ki* bowls. Buddhist monks eat in a special way. Tonight, I'll demonstrate it and tomorrow morning you may eat breakfast with the others. After we finish eating we'll get you a *samu-e* uniform. It's an everyday work uniform worn by monks. Now, to begin with, you must sit in a *seiza* position, that is, on your knees. If you find this too difficult we can get you a *seiza* bench, which supports you by lifting your butt up and off of your heels. The *o-ryo-ki* bowls are three concentric, nested bowls wrapped in a cotton napkin, including a pair of chopsticks and a small sponge-tipped brush. That's what you have in front of you. Let's unwrap it and get started."

I learned how to untie the knotted napkin and place the three bowls in front of me in a regimental order with the napkin on my lap. In a few minutes a monk carrying two wooden buckets and a spouted pot came into the room, having been summoned by Ryubu's bell. He placed some cooked rice in the largest bowl and topped it with a piece of fish. In the second bowl he placed some cooked, green vegetables that looked somewhat like spinach. In the third smallest bowl he poured some pale yellow-green liquid, which must have been tea.

"This is what we call *udon*, but it is not the fancy variety one gets in restaurants. Tomorrow for breakfast we will serve *congee*, which is rice porridge. We serve *congee* every morning with pickled vegetables or ground sesame seeds. After we finish eating we will go back to your room and I will give you a daily schedule. I know you must have many questions. Talking, as you may know, is not allowed except in your room, at tea or in the bath. Zen is a silent order. But first, you must learn how to clean your bowls."

After I finished eating, Ryubu sounded the bell again; the door opened and the same monk came in carrying a spouted pot, which contained hot water. He poured some into the largest bowl. I then proceeded to scrub down the sides of the bowl with the sponge tipped brush. Upon completion, I repeated this with the other two bowls by transferring the water. When finished with the brush, I sucked the sponge end and drank the remaining water. Thus, there is no need to wash in a sink.

"Every weekend you will be able to wash your bowls with soap and water and get a new napkin. Also, that is the time you can do your laundry. Meanwhile, wrap up your bowls and we can go back to your room," he explained as we proceeded up the stairs to my room.

Upon arrival, I noticed a Japanese boy standing in the middle of the room He had a shaven head, wore thick eyeglasses and was dressed in a black *samu-e*.

"*Konnichiwa*, my name is Hanaoka. I am your roommate," he said in halting, broken English.

Ryubu came over and bowed to him with his palms together. Turning to me he said, "Hanaoka is a long-time resident of Hosshinji. I am sure the two of you will get along very well." Turning back to Hanaoka he said, "You know where to get your bedding. I must tell Al the schedule of daily activities. But afterwards would you help him get a *samu-e*? *Arigato.*

"Now, Al wake up call is at 4:00 A.M. You must be in the *zendo* by 4:20 A.M. for morning meditation. *Zazen*, or what is commonly called meditation, will last 40 minutes until 5:00 A.M. After *zazen* there will be one hour of sweeping and clean up until 6:00 A.M. at which time break-fast will begin. Be sure to appear in the dining area with your *o-ryo-ki* bowls. You will discover the seating arrangement when you get there. Breakfast will last for one half-hour until 6:30 A.M."

Having said all of this, Ryubu left at the end of our conversation, saying that he would see me tomorrow morning to give me further instruc-tions and to meet Doiku, the monk who answered my letter giving me permission to come to Hosshinji.

I turned to Hanaoka and said, "Let's get my *samu-e* and your futon now." We departed for the storage room again; this time to get a futon for Hanaoka as well as a *samu-e* for me. When we arrived we came across a large wooden box containing many different sizes of pants and shirts.

After much arduous searching, I found a pair of pants and a shirt that would barely fit me. The *samu-e* pants have an elastic waist and elas-tic ankles much like ski pants. The pants are called *zubon* in Japanese. The pants and shirt are black. The shirt is really a double-breasted jacket with a side tie. It is called a *hippari*. The problem is that I am rather tall, 5 feet, 11 inches, whereas most Japanese average about 5 feet, 8 inches in height. In any event, I was not disturbed by the outcome since what I selected would certainly be serviceable. In addition, we were given small hand tow-els to be used as head coverings because of the oppressive sun. Hanaoka shouldered his bedroll and we returned to our room.

When we got there I changed into my *samu-e* while carrying on a run-ning conversation with Hanaoka. We each divided the room, leaving space for the third roommate due tomorrow. Since I was the first to arrive, I got the side near the window. I found out that Hanaoka had already spent two years in the monastery and was training to be a monk. He told me that he hopes to be ordained next year. Hanaoka came from an impoverished farm-ing family in central Honshu. His family wants him to become a Buddhist priest and have his own temple. Since he is the second son, he will not be able to inherit the farm. In Japanese tradition this is reserved for his older brother. Hanaoka is being supported at Hosshinji by one of the benefac-tors of the monastery and his father seized on this opportunity.

It was getting late and I was tired from the whole day's events so we decided to go to sleep. I unrolled my futon, put on the fitted sheet and pillow. I then changed into a T-shirt and boxer shorts, which I intended for pajamas and got into the futon with a book. After a while Hanaoka asked to put out the light to which I agreed. My eyelids were getting heavy and I welcomed sleep. In the dark, I looked out the window. I could see the moon bathing the inner courtyard with its silver light. It was a very eerie feeling to see the play of shadow and light on the plants and trees. I imagined they were people sitting and looking at the moon. I felt exhausted but my thoughts brought me back to home where I left my wife, my four children and my six grandchildren (a seventh arrived a year later). Is it reasonable for a 67-year-old man to pursue this quest of the unknown?

Suddenly, I awoke with an urgent need to urinate. I looked at my watch; the time was 1:30 A.M. I had only slept three hours. I got up as quietly as I could, grabbed my flashlight and descended the stairs looking for the lavatory. I found the lavatory next to the bathhouse and urinated into a Japanese-style squatting toilet bowl. On leaving the lavatory, I passed someone in the courtyard that raised his arm in a sign of greeting. I proceeded back to my futon to continue my sleep. I would only get two and a half hours more of sleep. In what seemed a short amount of time I heard a bell ringing loudly. Time to get up! I got out of the futon, rolled it up and ran down the stairs looking for the urinal once again. I then proceeded to the *zendo*.

I went in and looked for my name place. I found it with my name written in *kana*, the Japanese phonetic script, on a wooden plaque overhead. I then sat on my *zafu*, which is a round cushion and crossed my legs by placing my left foot on my right thigh in the half-lotus position. I then placed my left hand in my right hand with thumbs touching on my lap and imagined that I was holding an egg. This is called the cosmic mudra. I placed my tongue against the roof of my mouth and closed my lips and teeth firmly. My eyelids were just half-closed so I was aware of my surroundings. We were all sitting on a platform facing a wooden wall. The monks were dressed in traditional robes, which seemed to get in their way as they sat, leading to a lot of fidgeting. Coincidentally, Hanaoka was sitting next to me. After a while, Hanaoka fell asleep while sitting and dozed forward to bang his head against the wooden wall with a loud noise. It didn't seem to arouse any reaction from anyone.

I should explain that there are two kinds of meditation, apophatic meditation, which is emptying of the mind of all images and thoughts, and kataphatic meditation, which is concentrating on or filling the mind with images. Apophatic meditation is peculiar to Zen Buddhism, whereas kataphatic meditation is usually used by Tibetan Buddhists who might stare at a statue of the Buddha for a while before commencing meditation and so hold the image of the Buddha in one's mind. In addition, Zen Buddhists practice *shikantaza* or single-minded sitting, not *zuisokkan* or following the breath as is common amongst *Theravadan* Buddhists. *Zazen* is never to be used for *koan kufu* known as *koan* solving. The purpose to *zazen* is to calm the mind in a concentrated state and thereby seek enlightenment. There are two kinds of states or vehicles for seekers, *the shomon* or those who seek enlightenment for themselves through study and practice and *the engaku* or those who gain enlightenment through one's own efforts or realization. Zen emphasizes the attainment of a sudden enlightenment, or *satori*, through meditation and the freeing of one's own mind from the phenomenal world and from preconceived notions of reality.

There is no Bible in Buddhism but there are many sutras that are both sacred and secular writings by wise men. In Zen there is a book that comes closest to a Bible. It is called the *Shobogenzo*, which was written by Dogen Zenji, who is also known as Eihei Dogen, the founder of Soto Zen in the early thirteenth century. This book is centered on those essays that generations have regarded as containing the essence of Buddhist teachings. They clarify and enrich the understanding of Dogen's religious thought and his basic ideas about Zen practice and doctrine. Dogen's uncommon intellectual gifts, combined with a profound religious attainment and an extraordinary ability to articulate it, make *Shobogenzo* unique even in the vast literature the Zen school has produced over the centuries, securing it a special place in the history of world religious literature.

From Dogen's perspective, it is possible to authenticate the self by means of *zazen* or motionless sitting in meditation. This method possesses some common features with kenosis or Christian emptiness. Kenosis is a process that empties the self of any intrinsic particularity, as was the case with Jesus when he gave all his love, some say salvific love, to others and thus emptied him of love. This process, however, renders the self faceless, without identity, nonpresent, acentric, and anonymous, whereas Dogen's method of *zazen* helps one to find one's center of being. While kenosis represents the disappearance of the self, *zazen* is the realization and authentication of authentic selfhood and the disappearance of egoism. A major difference between kenosis and *zazen* is intention. Kenosis is an intentional activity performed by a subject, whereas Dogen thinks that a genuine method is intention less in the sense that it is not thought out or contrived. Thus, the concept of intuition proposed for Zen Buddhism becomes unique to Zen and is differentiated from other Buddhist motives.

At the end of the forty minutes' sitting a bell rang and everyone got up to do *kinhin* or walking meditation. We walked a circuitous route in single file around the inside of the *zendo* in *shasshu* position which is a clasping of the hands at one's breast and walking slowly and deliberately. It was now 5:00 A.M. and so I returned to the dining area for instructions from Ryubu.

As we met, he told me, "Let's go over to meet Tenzo-san and register as a member of the monastery."

I greeted Tenzo with a *gassho*, which is a bow with palms together. He responded with a nod. Tenzo's face looked severe with slits for eyes, a nose that was shaped like a reversed number 6 and a mouth without lips. I then signed a guest book and paid my fee.

We left the office and Ryubu began to explain my cleaning duties to me. I was to sweep the dining area and all the walkways to and from the dining area, the *zendo* and the *hatto* or prayer hall. Having accomplished all of this, we all gathered at the dining area with our *o-ryo-ki* bowls at 6:00 A.M. The dining area was converted into a dining hall by the placement of benches along its long axis in the center of the room. The room had windows facing the courtyard, which would be open during the day unless it rained. Otherwise the room was bare except for a Buddha mounted on the wall. Everyone in the dining hall sat in the *seiza* position. Someone, unknown to me, gestured for me to sit at the farthest end. It appeared to me that of the twenty or so individuals seated only four were Westerners. Soon the food was brought out in wooden buckets and placed at strategic places along the benches, which now served as tables. *Congee*, which is the Sanskrit name for rice gruel, was spooned out by individuals into the *o-ryo-ki* bowls. I added some pickled cherries to mine, which gave the *congee* a tart flavor. After eating two bowls of *congee* and a bowl of tea known as *cha* I felt satisfied.

Sitting in the *seiza* position was painful and tiresome and I knew immediately that I would require a *seiza* bench. The bowls were cleaned and the area was quickly cleaned up and restored to its original condition. I had an opportunity to speak with Ryubu once again.

He said, "It is now 6:30; we will meet in the *hatto* for morning prayers at 7:00 A.M. You can use whatever time you have between now and then to straighten up your room. Also, since you can't read Japanese, I shall provide you with a transliterated version of the prayers."

I returned to my room, where I met another new roommate. "Hello," I said with a *gassho*.

He returned the gesture and said in broken English, "My name is Yerney, Yerney Mehle; I am from Slovenia in Europe."

"I am very happy to meet you," I said. "Is there anything I can do to help you?"

"Thank you, but no," he said in an accent which sounded somewhat Teutonic.

Suddenly the *shoji* screen opened and in walked a monk dressed in black robes. He was Western and I knew he was American as soon as he started talking.

He bellowed, "Which one of you is Al Shansky?" Looking directly at me he said, "Ah, so it is you; then the other must be Yerney. Well, Al, my name is Doiku and I want to thank you for your letter. I hope you will be happy with us. Ryubu asked me to give you this prayer book and I wanted to personally greet you. We'll have more time to get further acquainted later on." Turning to Yerney, he said, "Welcome to Hosshinji, Yerney. Please let me know if there is anything I can do for you." With that, he left as quickly as he arrived.

At 7:00 A.M. we departed for the *hatto*. Seating in the *hatto*, in a *seiza* position, much like the dining hall, I was given a distant spot. By now, Ryubu had given me a *seiza* bench, so I was much more comfortable. The seating arrangement in the *hatto* was such that the Roshi was up front with his back to the statue of the Buddha, facing us. The congregation was divided in half with the monks on one side of an aisle and the novices on the other side. The prayers were read from the provided prayer book but were delivered in a chanting style. I admired those who could chant from memory. I really enjoyed the sound from an aesthetic point but to be candid since I did not understand the language it meant nothing to me of an ecclesiastical nature. There is an impoverishment of consciousness when there is a lack of language. The object of Buddhist prayer is *samata* or the sameness of Buddha and man. It was my hope that I could study this concept as well as the other major concepts in Buddhism. My vantage point in the *hatto* enabled me to observe and study the participants and I enjoyed this as much as the chanting. Using a *seiza* bench no longer embarrassed me, since I saw that some of the Western monks used them as well. The Japanese monks seemed at home in that position without the need for a bench.

At 8:00 A.M. the prayers were over and we gathered outside of the *hatto* to take up our assigned task. Ryubu introduced me to another Western monk whose name was Daigaku. He was over six feet tall and looked like a giant compared to the Japanese monks.

"You will work with Daigaku on the vegetable farm," Ryubu said, "until ten o'clock in the morning, and then there will be one hour rest in your room and afterwards lunch at 11:00 A.M."

Ryubu left and I followed Daigaku to the vegetable farm. The farm was up a slight incline along a dirt path about a quarter mile from the *hatto*. I was given a hoe called a *kuwa* and told to till the soil of the furrows where soybeans were growing. I took to the task with relish. I always liked farming and this gave me an opportunity to enjoy that activity. The farm consisted of three separate one-acre plots each growing a variety of vegetables. The plots were separated by rows of tea bushes, which were harvested once a year.

While we were working, I managed to learn several things about Daigaku, whose name means "great learning" in Japanese, even though talking was severely restricted. He has been a monk at Hosshinji for more than twenty years, having started in 1976, and was ordained in 1978. In addition to farming, he is the principal translator for the Roshi. He was forty-two years old and was born in Mason City, Iowa. He came to Japan as a youngster with his father who is a missionary. He attended Japanese schools and became proficient in the Japanese language. I have since found out that he was a graduate of Luther College in Decorah, Iowa. We became immediate friends. At the conclusion of our farming work I was told by Daigaku to report to him every day at the same time.

Returning to my room, I engaged Yerney in an excited conversation, trying to learn as much as we could about each other. While talking to Yerney, Doiku came into the room and told me that the Roshi would like to talk to me after the evening *zazen*. I was also told that Daigaku would be there to act as an interpreter. I looked forward to this meeting with some foreboding because I had many questions about Buddhism. Doiku left and I continued my conversation with Yerney. He told me that he was very poor and his aged father gave him a little money to pursue his dream of learning about Buddhism. He did not know how long he could last at Hosshinji with such a severe lack of funds but he had enough to last him until his 90-day visa would run out. His first exposure to Buddhism came from his interest in martial arts. He was a member of a martial arts team in Slovenia that competed all over Central and Eastern Europe. He spoke several European languages: German, Slovenian, Croatian and Serbian. Like me, he struggled with Japanese.

The bell rang for lunch. We all grabbed our *o-ryo-ki* bowls and headed for the dining hall. We sat in our previously assigned places and large wooden buckets of food were brought out. The meal consisted of green soybeans boiled in the pod in salted water together with small dried sardines wrapped in sheets of seaweed. In addition, there was freshly pickled eggplant and wild yam gruel. What a meal! As they say in Japanese, *oishi*, which means delicious. After eating I returned to my room. I had time off until 1:00 P.M. I decided to write a letter home and then listen to the radio on my headset while relaxing with a book. Japanese radio (NHK) has a wonderful station of Western classical music. I noticed Yerney was writing a letter as well. Hanaoka went to speak with one of the Japanese monks. He apparently has a good relation with the other monks. It was my fondest hope to break down the ethnic barrier that seemed to exist. This, I hoped would come to pass as I learned more Japanese.

There are two Tibetan monks in the monastery named Piyadassi and Sumano. They are both from Ladakh and were ordained in the Tibetan sect at the early age of 12 years. They became interested in Zen and decided to become ordained as Zen monks and bring the discipline back to Ladakh. This explained their presence in Hosshinji. Ladakh is a tiny landlocked state high in the clouds of the majestic Himalaya Mountains. Geographically, Ladakh, or Land of the Passes, is the western extension of the Tibetan plateau; it is now administered by India, but culturally Ladakh has been part of the Tibetan sphere of influence. The religion in Ladakh is Tibetan Buddhism, which combines Buddhism with ancient shamanistic beliefs. I was anxious to speak with them and hoped I would have some time tomorrow.

At 1:00 P.M., we all assembled in the courtyard and Doiku, now dressed in work clothes, started to assemble cadres to work in the bamboo forest. Our work consisted of cutting down slim bamboo trees, removing the branches and the nubs and piling them on hand carts. These bamboo trees were used for fencing in various parts of the monastery compound. This was very hard work and caused me to sweat profusely. We continued this work at a very steady pace until teatime at 3:00 pm.

At the sound of a bell, the work stopped and we all assembled in the dining area for tea. Talking is permitted at teatime and I looked on this as an opportunity to become further acquainted with some of the others. At teatime there are confections such as cookies, little cakes and candy available. Of course, most of the workers drank copious amounts of tea in order to quaff their thirst. It was here that I met Taizan, the monastery carpenter and general handyman. He told me that he came from the Minnesota Zen Center where he studied for two years and had been living in the monastery since then for three years. He was ordained as a monk last year. I regarded him as a kindred spirit because we both had Minneapolis in common. All that time he was renovating those areas where there was rotted wood. This must have been a full-time job since all the buildings are made of wood and are very old. The monastery is more than two hundred years old. It was a former carriage house of a lord who lived on the hill above us. The hill overlooks the city of Obama, which is located on Wakasa Bay just north of Kyoto. There is a graveyard attached which is administered by the monastery and serviced by the monks. The graveyard is located up the hill a short distance from the monastery grounds and located next to the vegetable farms. This is a good source of income for the monastery. Many of the laity comes to the graveyard on special occasions to offer prayers for the dead, in which case a monk is provided to officiate. In speaking with Taizan I was able to learn more about the monastery and its activities. Shortly after we started talking he introduced me to Piyadassi and Sumano, the Tibetan monks. We had a pleasant chat and I began to learn more about their home in Ladakh. Sumano asked if I would teach him English. His English was very faulty and required a lot of guidance to improve it. But, I agreed on the condition that he teaches me Ladakhi.

Ladakhi is classified as a dialect of Tibetan, but though the two are very closely related, they are sufficiently different that Ladakhis and Tibetans often speak Hindi-Urdu with one another. Sumano spoke Ladakhi, Hindi-Urdu and Afghan-Dari fluently and struggled with English and Japanese. We arranged a time during one of our rest periods to accomplish this. It was now 4:00 P.M. and I returned to the farm to help Daigaku once more for an additional hour. At the end of this hour he asked me to pull out a goodly quantity of mustard greens from the ground and take them to the kitchen where I was told to wash them and prepare them for boiling for dinner. According to the schedule 5:00 to 6:00 P.M. was clean-up time.

Dinner was at 6:00 P.M. This evening we were given a treat, dumplings made of buckwheat flour and taro. This was accompanied by fish cakes and boiled mustard greens and, of course, the ubiquitous boiled rice. I should like to explain that the largest meal of the day is lunch whilst dinner is usually an exiguous meal of scanty fare. But this evening for some reason unknown to me a big meal was served. In a Japanese monastery, the evening meal is called *yakuseki*, and a dish often made at this meal is called *zosui*. This is a mixture of rice, leftover soup, and assorted vegetables, served like a soft porridge. At the conclusion of dinner, we adjoined to the bathhouse, which was next to the kitchen. The bathhouse has a wooden paneled anteroom where monks bend over in obeisance with their forehead to the ground in front of a statue of the Buddha. Then they proceed to disrobe and go into the tiled bath house where they sit on a very low stool in front of a hand held shower spray and soap up using a large wash cloth and bar soap.

There are about twelve shower spray stations. I started to rub the bar soap directly on my skin without the need for a washcloth.

Doiku, who was next to me at another shower spray, started to yell, "Don't do that. You must use a washcloth. I know that rubbing the soap directly on the skin is done in the States, but it is not allowed here."

I felt terribly embarrassed and proceeded to use the washcloth. I don't know why it bothered me. I knew that yelling by monks to novices is done without rancor to jolt their minds. One must get over such a minor incident. However, I was to learn much later on that Doiku had a drill sergeant's attitude to all the novices.

After soaping and rinsing soap-free, one proceeds to the large tub almost the size of a small swimming pool to soak in very hot water. The tub could hold about five or six people at maximum, all wallowing in the hot water. It was almost automatic and spontaneous that as soon as a new person wanted to get in the tub, the earliest one in the tub got out. This gave each one in the tub about 15 minutes of soaking. The temperature of the water seemed to melt away any aches or cares one might have. To me it was the most enjoyable part of the day.

After a quick towel rub, I got dressed and made ready to go back to the *zendo* by 7:50 P.M. for forty minutes of *zazen*. I knew I had an appointment with the Roshi after *zazen* at 8:30 P.M. for what is known as a *dokusan*. The interview took place in a small room behind the *zendo*. This room contained a Buddha in the corner and had no furniture except for a small table next to where the Roshi was seated. When I arrived, I made a *gassho* to the Roshi and then to Daigaku who were already seated. I then sat down in half lotus position and waited for a response from the Roshi.

He greeted me in a very kind and congenial way. "Welcome to Hosshinji. I hope you will be happy here. Please forgive the need for me to speak with you through an interpreter. My English is very poor."

I responded, "That makes two of us; my Japanese is very poor as well."

He looked at me with his large almond shaped eyes as black as coals and heavy, black eyebrows and said, with much choreography of his eyebrows, "Do you have any questions or are there any problems I can help you with?"

For a moment I became very pensive and then began to speak cautiously. "My interest is to learn the great concepts of Buddhist philosophy and theology. Will being a member of Hosshinji provide that?"

In a very slow and solemn voice he answered me, "Buddhism has the concept that a human being exists, at one time or other, in one of the ten realms of delusion and enlightenment. In other words, depending on various conditions, one lives as a sentient being in one of these ten realms. There are six realms of pain and delusion which are: heaven, human beings, hell, hungry ghosts, animals, and fighting devils or *asuras*."

He continued in a deliberate manner, while his face was expressionless, "In the realm of heaven there is only happiness. The realm of human beings is a condition in which there is constant change between satisfaction and dissatisfaction. Beneath the realm of human beings is the realm of hell. Life in this realm is the exact opposite of heaven. The realm of hungry ghosts is one in which it is impossible to become satisfied. The realm of animals is one in which the beings there cannot understand reason. Finally, there is the realm of *asuras*, or fighting devils, the world of anger." He stopped his bantering for a moment and looked at me quizzically, then continued, "We are continually migrating through these six worlds. Even while we are practicing *zazen*, we are living in one of these realms. During *sesshin*, though the different conditions that we come in contact with are relatively few."

Then he leaned forward, his eyebrows and nostrils quivered like wings when he spoke. He looked me straight in the eye and said, "Apart from these six lower realms there are four higher realms of *sravakas*, persons who have unshakeable confidence in the teaching of Buddha, *pratyeka-buddhas* or self-enlightened buddhas who do not attempt to save others, and *bodhisattvas*, and *buddhas*. Buddhism teaches that to become happy, greed, ill will, and delusion must be transformed into their counterparts: generosity, compassion, and wisdom." I nodded to the Roshi but felt somehow that he did not quite answer my question.

He then leaned back to relieve the discomfort in his sitting position and started to speak again, "*Sesshin* are held at Hosshinji six times a year; the first seven days of April, May, and June; and of October, November, and December. Since it is now the middle of May our next *sesshin* will begin June first for one week. I think you will find some of your answers during *sesshin*. Before you leave, may I give you a *koan* to work on?"

He waited for a moment, then in a slow, deliberate voice he said, "It is as follows: A buffalo passes by the window. His head, horns, and four legs all go past. But you can't see the tail. Why can't you see the tail? You should work on this *koan* in your spare time but not during *zazen*. Also, do not reveal it to anyone. If you like, you may discuss your answers or any other problem with me during *dokusan*. Now, I would like you not to simply understand Zen or the Buddha-dharma conceptually. It is fine to investigate what others have said or written in books. But to say, "*I've understood something that I didn't understand before.* That is not Zen practice." I left him with bewilderment and confusion. I retreated to my room. It was very late so I got under my cover and fell asleep. Thus, the first day at Hosshinji ended.

The Next Day

The next day during the morning break at 6:30 A.M., I went to the tool house to look for Taizan, whom I found at work amid the scent of fresh lumber. I wanted to get a straight opinion of my talk with the Roshi the previous night and I also wanted a full explanation of the purpose and meaning of *sesshin.* Taizan seemed to me to be the proper person to help me. He was tall but not gangly yet gentle and his demeanor was guileless and reticent. His humility prevented him from lording it over anyone and he always expressed a willingness to help. By the way, his name Taizan means "peaceful mountain" in Japanese.

As I approached him, I saw his blue eyes dancing in anticipation.

"Hi, Al," he said. "How're you doing?"

I told him about my meeting with the Roshi last night, without revealing my *koan* to him.

"He gave you a *koan?*" Taizan said in an incredulous voice. "That is very unusual so early in the game. *Koans* are usually only given to people who anticipate being ordained. Whatever motivated the Roshi, you must understand that *koans* are conundrums designed to jolt your mind. My advice to you is not to attempt a rational or logical answer but to focus on the *koan* as a metaphor. The trap most people fall into with *koans* is the readiness to give an intellectual answer or explanation. Your answer to the Roshi, during *dokusan,* will only be accepted if it coincides with what is in the Roshi's mind."

I thanked him for the suggestion and then asked him about *sesshin.*

"What is *sesshin?*" I asked. "The Roshi said that much would be revealed to me after I completed *sesshin.*"

Taizan looked at me in disbelief and said, "I don't know what the Roshi meant by that. Sitting *zazen* requires eliminating thoughts from the mind and emptying the mind of all cogitation. It is single-minded sitting, which usually develops into a trance-like condition. *Sesshin* is for those who aspire to sit quietly and practice *zazen* in order to awaken to the true Self.... It was Descartes who proposed that the Self is not identical with one's body, or indeed, with any physical thing. Instead, he famously concluded that the essential self—the self one means when one thinks, "I exist"—is a nonphysical conscious thing. That is why I say *sesshin* is a method of focusing or unifying the mind. Better yet, it is a way of putting the mind in order. This implies that there is a part of the mind that is not in order. Therefore, the aim of *sesshin* is to realize that this is our condition now. *Sesshin* is used to resolve your questions and doubts about the present, the moment right now. You see, Buddhism is a self-reliant religion. For this reason, Buddhism has been called a noetic activity because it is a purely intellectual apprehension or perception. Don't be put off by people who claim derisively that Buddhism is atheistic just because it has no God in the Western sense."

I thanked him for his help and said I had to get back to go to the *hatto* for Morning Prayer service. I hurried off and took my place in the *hatto*. I noticed Sumano and greeted him with a blink of my eyes; he returned the acknowledgement. We all began our chanting. After prayer service, I whispered to Sumano that I would meet him at break time at 10:00 A.M. for an English lesson in my room. In the meantime, we gathered outside, where Doiku was assembling a cadre to dig for wild mountain yams. We had to climb the slope up to the mountaintop above the monastery. This was difficult trekking and I was out of breath when we reached the summit.

We broke the soil with a bamboo stick and recovered any tuber roots we found. These were put in cloth bags to be brought down to the kitchen for part of the evening meal. I dug all morning by bending over until my back was breaking. Some of the others dug while on their knees. Most of the Japanese monks sat on their haunches while digging. As I moved from place to place, I became entangled in a very large nettle bush and couldn't get out. I called out to Yerney to help me. It was very frightening to be caught that way but he was able to eventually free me. Afterwards, we brought the bags of collected yams downhill. Yerney and I were assigned the job of cleaning and peeling the yams for the cook.

The cook was a monk known as a *tenzo* who prepared all our meals. He got help from the other monks who took turns in food preparation and from novices who washed utensils. These assignments were given out in fair turns. Indeed, sanitary clean-up and bath preparation were also part of this scheme. Right now, Hanaoka was on bath duty, which required making the fire for hot water, cleaning the tub and bathhouse and making sure the tub water was the right temperature at which point a small sprig of a pine leaf is introduced into the water for fragrance.

It may be of interest to note that the fire for the bath is made with discarded refuse whereas all edible or decomposable garbage is added to the compost pile near the vegetable farm. The decomposed compost is eventually added to the soil of the vegetable farm. In addition, the fecal waste from the toilets is collected as a liquid and heated to remove bacteria and odor so it can be used as fertilizer on the farms as well. The monastery is rather self-sufficient. It grows all its own vegetables except for rice, which is donated in large hundred-pound bags by local rice farmers. This rice, however, contains a very large portion of hard inedible kernels, which must be removed by hand-picking. The monks and laity accomplish this task at leisure time. The hand-picking is used as a device for introspection and silent musing.

After performing our "yam task," Yerney and I went to our room where I met with Sumano for his English lesson. He was waiting with a notebook in hand in which he intended to write useful English words. Sumano was a diligent student and made remarkable progress even in our first meeting. I learned a few words in Ladakhi such as *jule*, which means "hello," and *nga*, which means "I" or "me" and *nyerang* which means "you." From then on I always greeted Sumano and Piyadassi with a hearty *jule*. After this lesson the lunch bell rang and so we all grabbed our *o-ryo-ki* bowls and proceeded to the dining room for lunch.

Lunch consisted of grated radish and roasted yams, which had a white dusting of taro and a boiled eel glazed with hoisin peanut sauce known as *una don.* I could not eat the eel and gave it to the monk sitting next to me. I had plenty to eat with the addition of *gohan* or boiled white rice. After lunch, I returned to my room where I engaged Yerney in conversation. He told me he was going to partake in *takuhatsu* next week. *Takuhatsu* is a group of monks going into the community from door to door to ask for food and alms in exchange for good wishes. The monks dress in special robes, wear a peasant hat and straw sandals and carry a bowl in which are placed the offerings. Unfortunately, this is often referred to as "begging" by the Western uninformed masses. I thought I might like to try *takuhatsu,* too. So I arranged with Yerney to go with him next week. Of course, this must be approved by Tenzo-san but there would probably be no problem.

The grounds of the monastery were dotted with many trees known as *shikiji* trees. These trees ceaselessly dropped their leaves all year long, resulting in an unsightly accumulation. In order to remove these leaves groups of monks and laymen swept the leaves up and placed them in the compost pile at the farm. The brooms for this sweeping operation were made of bamboo poles around one end of which was tied thin twigs and branches. Myoku made the brooms. She was a female monk who resided with two other female monks on the distant side of the *hatto.* There are usually a minimum number of female monks in Zen monasteries, who are often called "nuns" by Westerners. This is a Christianization of which I disapprove. Female monks are not nuns in any sense of the word. They are monks who have gone through a period of learning equal to their male counterparts. To call them nuns is to display a lack of understanding.

Myoku is a German national who practices as a psychotherapist in an urban setting in Germany. She has lived in the monastery for many years (about three) until her ordination. She received her dharma name, Myoku, on ordination.

Myoku had invited me to visit her during rest time. She was a woman in her mid-thirties with piercing brown eyes and a ruddy complexion. She also spoke fairly good English so there was no trouble communicating. I often watched her squatting on her heels as she made the brooms. After lunch, during break time, I ran up to my room to retrieve the fruitcake my wife gave me when I left home. I brought it for the tea with Myoku. When I arrived in the female compound I discovered that all three female monks were there to greet me. We sat around a low table and began to consume the fruitcake, which I brought together with unusually dark green tea. The tea was served in bowls over a small amount of rice.

In conversation, a mixture of German, English and Japanese, I discovered that Myoku was a psychotherapist in a village near the city of Bonn in Germany. She was looking for more meaning to her life and so found solace in the Soto Zen tradition. She was amazed at my age and the fact that I had such a large family in America. The other two women, who were Japanese, barely spoke English and when I spoke Japanese they giggled while covering their mouths with their hands. In traditional Japan, the teeth were considered ugly bones and should be covered. In the old days the teeth were often blackened to prevent visibility. This can be seen in many *ukiyo-e* woodblock prints of beautiful women. Nevertheless, I knew that my accent must have seemed comical to them and was not offended by the laughter. Even though they lived separate for propriety reasons they partook in all the activities and meals with the men.

At the conclusion of our repast, I returned to the courtyard, expecting to work with Daigaku on the farm. Instead, Daigaku told me that we would be going into the dense forest of *hinoki* trees to collect *hinoki* berries. A group of us consisting of two more Japanese monks and Daigaku and me carried wooden buckets and went into the forest to collect berries. The two additional monks were Japanese with whom I had a fleeting acquaintance. After a two-hour period we all had relatively full buckets and were told to bring them down to the kitchen. As I have indicated previously, it was an unpretentious kitchen, the sort of place where mushrooms, beans, peppers and herbs could be found hanging from the rafters and drying. We were told to wash the berries and then spread them out on large trays to dry in the sun. After about a week of this treatment they would turn into raisin-like peas.

We then assembled in the dining hall for teatime. Doiku who spoke with me at length about life in the monastery approached me.

I asked him, "Where is Ryubu-san? I haven't seen him lately."

"Ryubu," he answered, "left the monastery. He's on his way back to Long Beach, California. I think he is getting married so he will probably not return."

"Why not?" I naively asked.

"Well, for one thing, you cannot train as a monk while married. After ordination, marriage is permitted. Buddhism comes in many forms, but in Japan it stands apart from all the rest in one most striking way, the monks get married — it is an openly married clergy. I might as well tell you that I have a Japanese girlfriend in another town and we will probably get married some day soon." I thanked him for confiding in me and promised to be faithful to his secret.

At the conclusion of our talk I bumped into Daigaku, who told me that there was a small library in the room behind the *hatto* where I could find some interesting books on Buddhism. I hurried over to the room and found, to my delight, a glass-doored cabinet in English traditional style sitting on Queen Anne legs with much ornate marquetry, which contained many interesting books on Buddhism. Not all were in English; there were many in various languages such as German, French, Spanish and, of course, Japanese. In addition, I found some popular authors such as D. T. Suzuki, Alan Watts, and John Blofeld. There was a worn, dog-eared copy of Philip Kapleau's two-volume treatise on Zen but most of the books were classical works. I found a *Shobogenzo*, the book written by Dogen Zenji, the founder of Soto Zen. In looking around the room, I could see how the cabinet seemed out of place with its ornate structure compared to the austere character of everything else. The adjacent wall was covered with framed pictures of soldiers and sailors in uniform. Most of the pictures were yellowed and sepia-toned indicating age. I assumed they were fallen warriors of World War II. The opposite wall contained a pedestal of a bronze Buddha, about eighteen inches high, sitting in the cosmic mudra position. In front of this statue was a narrow table on which were two brass candlesticks with melted candle wax and a censor containing a burned-out bundle of incense; next to this in front of the Buddha was a brass platter containing a pyramid of apples and oranges. To the right of the Buddha was a vessel with water and a wooden ladle for pouring water over the Buddha's head. I could see that the Buddha was still wet. From all indications the room was recently used. I could still smell the sweet odor of the incense. I brought the *Shobogenzo* back to my room to read in the evenings just before lights out. I was to learn later from Daigaku that previous tenants left most of these books.

I then returned to the farm for one more hour of farming; then clean-up and dinner. Tonight we were getting a light supper of boiled buck-wheat noodles. These are eaten wet by fishing them out of the water in the buckets and placing them in one's bowl together with a piquant soy sauce. Soy sauce, in Japan, comes in various styles and grades and is purchased with almost the same attitude as wine is purchased in the West. There are even soy sauce tastings arranged at various venues. After teatime, I went back to the farm to work with Daigaku.

When I arrived at the farm, I found two other Japanese monks there. One named Shozan, which means "Laughing Mountain" and the other named Unzan, which means "Moon Mountain." It would seem that most monks are named after mountains. The reason is that mountains are considered sacred in Japan. We all did a *gassho* and then Daigaku gave us instructions.

"Let us go to the number 2 farm and harvest the adzuki beans. After you have filled up the two wooden buckets that each of you have, we'll take them to the forecourt of the kitchen and wash them."

It was backbreaking work, pulling out the plants and removing the beans. After a while we were finished and brought the eight buckets of little red beans to the kitchen area. We then washed them and packed them tightly in a wooden barrel. Sugared water, known as *ama-natto*, was added to the barrel until all the beans were covered. A muslin sheet was used as a cover and was secured on top of the barrel. This was to be left to ferment for about two months during which time a mold grows and eventually covers all the beans. When eaten the beans and the mold are both consumed. It has an extraordinarily sweet taste with a very unusual flavor. I was told that this is the most popular flavor for ice cream in Hawaii among the Japanese community.

I then went to clean up and prepare for dinner. Tonight we were given *hachihai-dofu*, which is bean curd or tofu cut into small pieces and stewed in a sauce of 4 parts water, 2 parts sake, and 2 parts soy sauce. This was eaten with the ubiquitous bowl of cooked rice. After dinner I bathed, then went to the *zendo* for *zazen* and finally to my room for sleep. The next day was Sunday and we were allowed to go into the town. I looked forward to this break.

Sunday in Town

On Sunday morning we didn't get up until 5:00 A.M. and started *zazen* at 5:20 A.M. Breakfast was at 6:00 A.M. as usual and the *hatto* service was at 7:00 A.M. Sweeping was at 8:00 A.M. and room clean-up and laundering was included at this time until 11:00 A.M. At 11:00 A.M. a light lunch is served at the conclusion of which almost all go into town. Some take the bicycles, which are kept in the tool shed; others simply walk. I looked forward to walking in the cool mountain air. As I left the main gate known as a *Mon*, I saw the mountain of abandoned gravestones in the front plaza. This was a pyramidal structure of headstones and gravestones left in the graveyard and abandoned by families that have disappeared. They were removed from the graveyard to make room for new gravesites.

I continued to walk down the driveway passing a field of azaleas and begonias of myriad colors on the right, which was planted by the monks of the monastery. Finally, I came to the end of the driveway across which loomed a giant *Torii* gate. On the left was a Shinto shrine. I climbed up to the platform and grabbed the heavy knotted rope and shook it until it made a dull sound on striking the gong. At a left turn there was a small

residential neighborhood of wooden houses with the typical Japanese architecture. I greeted people as I passed them and then went across the road
to walk on the dike, which separated the rice paddies. Eventually, I came
to the railroad station. I went into the station and obtained a JNR
timetable. I knew I would need this for future trips around Japan.

After arriving at the intersection where the two main streets fanned
out to cross the town, I decided to use the southern street in one direction and return on the northern street. The first store I passed was a photography shop. I had my camera and film with me so I went in and started
to talk in my broken Japanese. The proprietor recognized me as a member of Hosshinji because I was wearing my *samu-e* uniform. I gave him a
role of film for processing and tried to tell him I wanted immediate service. I kept saying *hayai* to him, which means fast.

Apparently he understood me and replied, "*Kore wa hiru desu. Koko
okaeri go nanji,*" which means something like "come back about 5 o'clock."
We both laughed after that exchange. After that struggle I thanked him
and went next door to the ice cream parlor.

I ordered an *icecreamu tempura*, which is a bar of vanilla ice cream,
dipped in batter and deep fat fried quickly. It tasted wonderful: the batter gave a nutty flavor to the ice cream. The play of the hot surface outside and the cold ice cream inside in one bite was startling and surprising.
I really enjoyed it. I proceeded up the street to the bank, having previously enquired of the ice cream vendor, "*Ginko wa doko desuka?*" "Where
is the bank?"

Upon entering the bank, which looked very much like an American
bank, I was greeted by a young, pretty girl who said in English, "May I
help you?"

I was startled but asked her how to cash travelers' checks. She led me
to a window and spoke to the teller in Japanese. She remained next to me
until the transaction was over. I asked her where she learned to speak
English. She replied that she learned it in school but also practices it with
foreigners she meets in town. I realized then that the Europeans and other
visitors who don't speak Japanese must speak English to be understood.

She was kind enough to give me a fairly good layout of the stores along both streets. There was a very large food store up the block where I stopped next to purchase a loaf of packaged bread and a jar of strawberry jam to keep in my room as a supplement to our scanty meals. I also bought three Fuji apples to share with my roommates. The apples were gigantic. They were almost the size of melons, pale yellow with a slight blush to the skin. I have never seen such large apples.

After the food store I stopped at the post office to buy some stamps. We could mail letters from the monastery but we had to provide our own stamps. The post office was only a few blocks from the harbor so I decided to walk to the end before turning back on the northern street. At the end was a long esplanade where there were many restaurants and summer homes. By walking along this esplanade one could see the calm water of Wakasa Bay broken by the wake of fishing boats coming in to the piers. At the piers it was reminiscent of a Turner seaport painting. Straight out as far as the eye could see was the misty water reaching Korea.

To the left the esplanade curled up to the top of a mountain over-look. I decided to do that trip some other time. I turned back and crossed over to the right to see the large fish market on the pier. It was a massive place with many stalls containing the day's catch. The parking lot was crowded with people who had driven to Obama to buy the freshly caught fish. I went inside and partook of the sounds and smells. I found some of the women haggling and some of the men inspecting the fish displays in an authoritative manner. The din was breathtaking. This place reminded me of the *tsukiji* fish market in Tokyo, a shutterbug's haven. Many of the people, particularly the children, looked at me quizzically. The children giggled and held their hands against their mouths. I had become used to this after traveling to Japan for so many years. I must have seemed strange to them with my round eyes, long nose and bald head, dressed in a *samu-e* uniform.

After leaving the fish market I headed up the northern main street. I came across an antique shop that had many ceramic artifacts displayed in the window. I went inside and looked at the many beautiful objects.

There was a studio in the rear where the ceramist worked. I purchased a very lovely *sake* bottle as a souvenir. I was so impressed with the merchandise that I knew I would return in the future. I kept walking for a little while until I came across a small store that sold little snacks, candies and cookies. I bought a bagful of rice cookies and went across the street to a little park and sat on a bench.

I started to munch my cookies when I suddenly saw Yerney on a bicycle.

I called out to him, "Yerney, Yerney!" He saw me and came over. We shared the remainder of the cookies and started talking hastily.

He asked, "Are you going with me tomorrow on *takuhatsu?*"

I said I was and he clapped my back in approval. I then asked him what he intended doing with Buddhism after he left Hosshinji. He said he was going to write a book on the importance of life. I did not understand him but did not pursue it further since I felt he might be embarrassed.

He said, "There is going to be some entertainment after dinner tonight."

"What do you mean?" I said.

"Well, a musician who comes to the graveyard on some Sundays has offered to entertain the monks tonight. The Roshi gave his approval," he said in a matter-of-fact way.

After a while we parted company and I went on to the photography store to pick up my pictures. "Okaeri nasai, you have returned," the photographer said. I picked up my pictures and headed back for the monastery.

When I arrived in the monastery I had just enough time to clean up and get ready for dinner. At 6:00 P.M. the bell rang and we all went into the dining hall. Upon arrival I noticed that the Roshi joined us at the head of the table. Through Daigaku he announced that Minamoto Murayama, an exponent of *Kiyomoto*, who sat at his left, would entertain us on his *samisen* and sing some traditional songs.

A *samisen* is a Japanese string instrument that looks like a guitar or a lute. A *plectrum*, a spoon-like instrument, is used to pluck the strings.

Kiyomoto is a school of singing to a *samisen* accompaniment that arose in the early nineteenth century. It is distinguished by its constant revisions of repertoire in order to stay in the forefront of popular taste and for its high pitched, ornate, and strongly nasalized vocal line.

Since this was a special occasion the cook prepared a gourmet meal. I was really hungry and looked forward to the various dishes. We started with Miso soup made with wakame seaweed, tofu, and shitake mushrooms. This was followed by a salad made of greens with hijiki and Miso Dijon dressing. Next there came cold peanut soba noodles with shitake mushrooms, tofu and spinach. Also present, of course, was the inevitable cooked rice. It was a great meal. We quickly cleaned up and restored the room to an auditorium. Murayama-san sat in full lotus posture and began playing and singing. He played one of my favorite Japanese folk songs, *sakura* (cherry blossom). It was very melodic and I enjoyed it very much. He played for about an hour then we all went into the *zendo* for evening *zazen*. When I got back to my room I checked with Yerney about preparing for *takuhatsu* tomorrow. Then I got into my futon with my book and quickly fell asleep.

Takuhatsu

After *zazen*, sweeping, breakfast, and prayer service, we prepared for *takuhatsu*. There was a small anteroom in front of the dining hall, which had hooks on the wall containing the robes, hats, and straw fiber slippers used by the monks for *takuhatsu*. Yerney and I took a complement of items to our room. We changed and immediately went downstairs to congregate with the others and get last-minute instructions. The following was the group of monks who were going:

Shozan, Laughing Mountain; Kiho, Strange Peak; Unzan, Moon Mountain; Gido, Truth Hall; Muhan, No Precedent; Keigan, Moon Tree Cliff; Ninzan, Lover of Mountains; Zuizan, Joy Mountain; Heizan, Flat Mountain; Hogai, Beyond the World; Tenzo, Chief Cook; and Taizan,

Peaceful Mountain. This made twelve monks and two novices with Yer-ney and me, a total of fourteen. Taizan told us to put on our hats and pick up our wooden bowls and file out through the great wooden gate. A gaunt-let of the remaining people was waiting in *gassho* position outside of the gate to wish us luck. We then moved into the neighboring residential area loudly chanting sutras.

Takuhatsu is a Japanese word which literally means "request (*taku*) with the eating bowl (*hatsu*)." In *takuhatsu* the monks generally go in groups of ten to fifteen, one behind the other, and recite sutras in front of houses for the benefit of the residents. Believers and well-wishers, when they hear the sutras, make donations, either in the form of money, which they toss into the monks' wooden bowls, or of uncooked rice, which the monks collect in a sack, or any other foodstuff such as canned goods or packaged food. Recipient and giver then bow to one another in mutual gratitude with humility and respect. The frequent translation of *takuhatsu* as "begging round" is not accurate, since here both parties are recipients. The notion on which *takuhatsu* is based is as follows: The monks, who are guardians of the dharma, offer it to the public by means of their own example; in exchange for this they are supported by those who trust in the truth of the dharma. In addition, from the traditional Buddhist point of view almsgiving is considered a virtue, which increases good karma. The monks through *takuhatsu* provide the public with an opportunity to prac-tice this virtue. According to Dogen, there are three types of "pure food": that which comes from trees and plants, that obtained from *takuhatsu* and that donated by supporters. Anything that is given is purified by the act of giving, provided it is pure giving, done with an open heart, with no strings attached. And so it is with all things. The purity of the thing is determined by its origins, how we come by it.

As I approached one of the houses an elderly gentleman came out and started talking to me in rapid-fire Japanese.

I said to him, "*Chotto matte*," which means "just a minute" in Japa-nese. I then ran to get Tenzo-san to translate.

Tenzo-san said that the old man wanted to give us a wooden box of salted mackerel but it would be too heavy to carry. I volunteered to go back to the monastery and get Doiku with his motorcycle. Doiku kept a motorcycle in the tool shed covered with a tarpaulin. He got it out and I climbed on the back seat.

We then returned to the house of the elderly gentleman. Two of us lifted the box onto the back seat of the motorcycle and Doiku drove off to the monastery. Taizan told me there was enough fish in the box to make several meals for the monks. Taizan also told me that the elderly gentleman had given large contributions of food in the past. His son was buried in the monastery graveyard and often visited to converse with him at the gravesite. Yes, he really speaks to the headstone in a conversational tone. I returned to my sutra chanting and after about two hours we returned to the monastery where the remaining residents greeted us resoundingly. The experience was quite invigorating and I could see that Yerney really enjoyed himself. He was dancing and whooping like a giant crane. After his quixotic behavior we all simmered down and Tenzo-san offered our accumulation to the Buddha in the dining hall with a prayer. It was now time to change into our *samu-e* and hang up the *takuhatsu* clothing in the anteroom.

It was 11:00 A.M. and time for lunch. For lunch we had green peas, onions and green and red peppers mixed with cooked rice together with tofu fried in a curry sauce with bean sprouts and cucumbers. After lunch and a shortened break period I was assigned the job of placing some of the mackerel into a large tub filled with running water. The salted mackerel had to remain in the water for a whole day in order to remove the salt. This was done by occasionally adding running water to the tub. It was obvious that we would have mackerel for lunch tomorrow.

I then went to the farm to work with Daigaku. While I was there Daigaku told me he had a small lump behind his right ear and may have to go to the hospital to have it removed. I asked when this would take place but he was not sure. This bit of news put a pall over the day's activities. He had a biopsy some weeks ago which proved to be non-malignant and he did not seem to be too worried. We then returned to the dining hall for the tea offering (*fusa*). I then had an opportunity to speak at length with Daigaku. He told me he noticed the lump during the past winter. It was a particularly cold winter for the monks who slept in the *zendo* on the wooden *zazen* platforms known as *tan*. Their only source of heat is a kerosene heater placed in the middle of the *zendo*. The bedrolls or futons are kept in built-in cabinets overhead and are put away every morning before *zazen*. When he discovered the lump he had to go to Kyoto for a medical examination. Monks are given free medical treatment by the Japanese government. After he learned of the diagnosis he was told to consider surgery to remove the lump but had not made up his mind when he would consider doing this.

We went back to the farm to do more work then clean up, dinner and bath and off to sleep. The next day we had to make preparation for the onslaught of people to arrive for *sesshin* next Sunday, June 1. There was a large hall in back of the *zendo* where visitors for *sesshin* were housed in dormitory or barracks style. This had to be swept and cleaned. Some came a few days earlier but most arrived on Saturday. About thirty additional people were expected. They come from all walks of life, most are Japanese but a few will come from Europe and America. Their motivation was uncertain to me but I suspected that they all had some need to do Buddhist practice. Still it was necessary to lay out futons in a livable manner.

All day long I seem to have been overcome by ennui and thought it best to have some time to myself. I went to the kitchen and requested an *obento*, which literally means "a lunch" but is any kind of food taken as a lunch to be eaten away from home. The cook was very kind and gave me some of the green peas and cooked rice of yesterday's lunch in a bowl with a pair of chopsticks. I thanked him and as I started to leave he reached over and put a pomegranate in my hand. I was overwhelmed by his kindness. It seemed that he was very aware and prescient of my condition. I put the items in a bag and headed for the mountain. I found myself thinking about my wife and children back in the States. Whenever the loneliness became unbearable, I climbed to the high ground in the monastery where I could see the town of Obama and Wakasa Bay below. The cawing of the crows and the screeching of the gulls was a reminder that I was near a seaport.

After I finished my lunch I picked up the pomegranate. This immediately brought to mind the kindness of the chief cook. The *tenzo* or chief cook in a traditional Japanese Zen Monastery is second only to the abbot (Roshi), according to Dogen. The chief cook's job is first and foremost to nurture the monks and to ensure their well-being and peace. Dogen calls it the act of "nourishing the seeds of the Buddha." The cook is fully responsible for the monks' nourishment, not just physically, but morally and spiritually as well. He's not just a dietician in the modern sense, but more like a religious teacher. Therefore, the chief cook's job is usually given to a very mature monk. I began to peel the pomegranate with much difficulty until I exposed the inner seeds. As I ate the seeds, it reminded me of the haiku poem by the writer Usuda Aro:

> *Hitotsubu hitotsubu*
> *Zakuro no akai*
> *Mi wo taberu*

> One by one
> I eat the red seeds
> Of a pomegranate

The Japanese word for pomegranate is *zakuro*. This is also the word for the autumn season and once again I thought about home. The author composed this poem shortly after his wife's death. Therefore, the poem takes on a deeper meaning. The poem conveys the sadness of the poet, at a loss and unsure what to do, eating the seeds of a pomegranate one by one. Thus, with me not knowing what to do to overcome my feeling of weariness and dissatisfaction, I ate the seeds one by one.

Suddenly, I was brought out of my languid state when I saw Myoku, the female monk, approaching. After a *gassho* to each other she sat down next to me and started to talk.

"Hello, Shansky-san. How are you?" I offered her part of my pomegranate, which she accepted graciously.

"I am not very cheerful today," I said.

"Yes," she replied, "I can see you are very dejected; what's wrong?"

She started to extract the seeds one at a time from the pulp and delicately placed them in her mouth. Not having an adequate answer, I just shrugged my shoulders.

"I think I know what is bothering you," she said. "You are at a point in your monastery life when you now question whether all this trouble is leading anywhere. You are wondering whether all of this is worth it," she said boldly.

She then stopped speaking for a moment and then with a curious smile on her face she resumed. "After living on this mountain for the past four years, I can't help but realize that my body is completely integrated with the body of the mountain. Every time I drink the water that spills out of it into the mountain stream, my body assimilates it. My body is now largely composed of water that comes from this mountain. We grow our food in the mountain's soil. The plants start out as a single seed and by taking water, light and minerals from the mountain, eventually manifest themselves as fruits, vegetables, and flowers. Thus, we take the mountain into our very being; we consume it. Our septic system even returns our waste to the mountain. How could we feel separate from it? Speaking metaphorically, you must take the mountain into your very being or more specifically Zen must become a part of your very being. You must consume it until it becomes a part of you indistinguishable from your very being. I suspect you have too many doubts and you are influenced by other belief systems." She stopped talking and looked at me enigmatically.

For what seemed the longest time nothing was said. I slowly retorted, "I think you are right." She dropped her head but I hastened to add, "You are very wise."

She said, "Give it some time; I know you are searching for answers and I also know that you accept many of the Buddhist concepts. Eventually, the answer will appear like a *fata morgana*—a mirage rising out of the desert clouds." She got up to leave and I rose as well and made a deep bow and *gassho*.

"Thank you very much for all your help. I feel much better now." I said. "It's almost 1:00 P.M. and I am due at the farm."

I accompanied Myoku down the mountain and we parted company as I reached the farm. Daigaku was waiting for me. As I approached him, I remembered his affliction and was embarrassed at my own minor problems.

"Hi there, Al; how're you doing? We have to plow under the mustard greens in the third farm. Would you go down to the tool shed and get the roto-tiller? You can drive it up here by the handlebars but be careful not to engage the clutch since that would make the blades turn. We have over-produced mustard greens and need the area for planting the eggplants," he said.

I spent almost the full two hours tilling the soil and planting the eggplant seeds. I then went down to tea when suddenly it broke out in a warm rain, which undoubtedly would soak the newly sown fields and cause them to germinate. I was exhausted from the day's work and was glad to sit and watch the rain.

In a few minutes I was aware of Doiku sitting next to me. "A person who suffers develops great forbearance," he said by way of an introduction to conversation. I sort of laughed with a little bravado.

He eventually told me that he was born in Chicago where he grew up and worked as a short-order cook in some of the jazz joints on Rush Street. Then his family moved to Minneapolis. It was in Minneapolis where he joined the Minnesota Zen Center and eventually came to Hosshinji. He was ordained as a monk six years ago. His sister owns a bed and breakfast in Minneapolis with her husband. While here he learned to speak and read Japanese fluently. I asked him about the organizational set-up of the monks.

He told me that there was no real head monk but that Tenzo-san probably came closest to that description since he ran the office and is the contact person with the outside world. Apparently, the Roshi preferred the competition amongst the monks. However, there never had been any problems except for assigning responsibilities. Even this was accepted in good humor. He further told me that he shared a small room with Daigaku, where they write letters and read, but they sleep in the *zendo*. Daigaku practiced calligraphy and he, Doiku, listens to jazz on the radio. He then told me that after dinner tonight I must accompany him in the kitchen and wash the pots and leftover dishes. I agreed and returned to the farm to finish up my work and return the roto-tiller to the shed where I bumped into Taizan.

"Well Al, how are you? How's it going?" he asked.

"It's funny," I said. "The Americans all address me as Al and all the Japanese address me as Shansky-san."

"Well, that's the tradition in both countries," he said.

"Tell me, Al, have you had a chance to practice your *koan*?" he questioned.

"I struggle with it from time to time and I feel I am making some progress," I said.

Suddenly the bell rang and we both left the shed to clean up for dinner. For dinner we had a mixture of rice gruel and vegetables and a bowl of miso soup. When dinner was over I went into the kitchen to help with the dishes. Doiku told me to use the soap very sparingly because we did not want to pollute the water table. As it was it was diluted to an almost non-foaming product. While washing I dropped a dish, which cracked into several pieces. Doiku got very angry.

"You must be more careful. Now take the broken pieces outside and bury them in the soil so they can return to the earth."

I apologized and did what he said. When I returned someone else had taken my place. I then cleaned the sink. Doiku told me to remove the strainer with the accumulated rice kernels and feed it to the koi fish in the pool in the forecourt. I approached the pool with the strainer and stood on a rock at poolside. The fish immediately swam to me in hope of getting the rice. I found this very touching. I must have passed this pool a hundred times and only thought of the fish as something decorative. Now the fish and I had a living partnership and a real connection, much like a Buddha connection to living beings. I finished work in the kitchen and went to bathe and prepare for *zazen* and bed. The next day, Saturday, was the last day of May and the great influx of people would take place.

The Last Day of May

At breakfast in the morning we had compote of mixed fruit in addition to the usual *congee*. It was very refreshing. After prayer service in the *hatto* we all went about our usual tasks of cleaning and straightening up. I then had time to help Sumano with his English lesson.

It was at this time that Piyadassi approached me with a request. "I wonder, Shansky-san, if you would do me a kind favor. In Ladakh the ground is very rough and full of stones. This makes it very difficult to walk in these simple slippers. Could you send a pair of work shoes for Sumano and me when you return to America?"

"Of course," I said. "But first I must make a template to gauge the proper shoe size. Why don't you and Sumano stand on this piece of paper and I will draw an outline of your foot?" I tore a piece of paper from Sumano's pad and made a template of each of their feet.

"I am returning to America in September. That's when I'll buy the shoes and send them to you." I folded the piece of paper and put it in my pocket.

After our break it was time for lunch. Just as I predicted we got mackerel for lunch but to my surprise it was made quite differently. The mackerel were roasted on skewers on a hibachi. This was served with pickled radishes and roasted chestnuts mixed with cooked rice. Chewing and crunching the bones of the small fish was part of the pleasure of eating. After lunch the new guests started arriving. Each of us pitched in to help the new arrivals with bedding, registration and layout information. They all had a myriad of questions and despite the silence ordinance there was a constant buzz in the atmosphere. Doiku assembled some of the newcomers into weeding gangs to keep them occupied. This did not sit well with some of them who retreated to the dormitory.

For the remainder of the day we were busy orienting the newcomers to the monastery and its workings until dinnertime, which was served in the *zendo* so that all could become familiar with seating arrangements. After dinner, Doiku gave instructions for *sesshin* the next day. Dinner this evening was a treat, which would not be repeated in the future. It consisted of chilled tofu with fresh ground ginger and green shiso. There were also sliced cucumbers and freshly pickled eggplant. The monks served all the meals and this arrangement was carried out through the entire week of *sesshin.*

After dinner the newcomers walked around the grounds inspecting the farms and the graveyard. Some hiked up to the mountain to enjoy the view of Obama below and the evening sunset over the calm waters of Wakasa Bay. I made for the bath and then my room to talk with my roommates. The next day was sesshin.

Sesshin

Sesshin is a Japanese word which means, "collecting (*setsu*) the heart mind (*shin*)." *Sesshin* is considered the high point of Zen training in which one is devoted exclusively to meditation (*zazen*). Long periods of *zazen* are interrupted only by a few hours of sleep at night, *teisho* recitations and rest breaks during meals. Special inspiration and incentive during the days of *sesshin* are provided by the *teisho* (talks) of the Roshi. The schedule is as follows: Every day we awaken before dawn at 3:30 A.M., make our way to the *zendo*, and commence sitting *zazen* at 4:00 A.M. until late in the night at 9:40 P.M. This gives 17 hours of meditation according to the following schedule: At 4:00 A.M., sit *zazen* for forty minutes until 4:40 A.M. This is followed with *kinhin* walking for twenty minutes until 5:00 A.M. This, then, is repeated hourly, with forty minutes sitting and twenty minutes walking until 6:00 A.M. Breakfast is served until 7:00 A.M. The process starts again at 7:00 A.M. until 12:00 noon when it is time for lunch. At 1:00 P.M. the cycle continues until 6:00 P.M. when it is time for dinner. After dinner at 7:00 P.M., the cycle of *zazen* and *kinhin* continues until 9:40 P.M. At this time, one has twenty minutes to wash up before lights out at 10:00 P.M. This dogged regimen is repeated daily for seven days.

As I said, the monks serve meals to the participants who remain seated comfortably in their places. Meals are very frugal, usually consisting of *congee* for breakfast and some variation of rice gruel with vegetables for lunch and dinner. I performed *sesshin* during the first week of June. *Sesshin* is not performed in July and August during the hot, sultry weather of summer. *Sesshin* is intensive Zen meditation specifically designed for those ready to do serious work on their selves. It is a time devoted to the single-minded realization of the Way. Characterized by an atmosphere of deep introspection, the *sesshin* emphasizes *zazen*.

Dawn. The sound of the drum and bell, and the timekeeper's steps through the hallway as the wake-up bell is rung. First thing: roll up my futon, water on my face and was in the *zendo* for dawn *zazen*. There was complete silence, stillness, darkness, and the cold dawn air. Then I began concentration. Early morning light began to fill the hall and yet I continued with deep concentration focusing on emptiness. Thoughts came into my mind but I did not focus on them. I allowed them to pass through as I focused on the space between the words. I met myself as I went deep into my practice, taking a chance at being truly honest with myself. Who am I? I maintained my concentration. Then the darkness of night crept in. The day was hot and torrid and I awaited the approaching coolness of evening. I had a pain in my legs and shoulders. This could only be cured by a whack from the *kyosaku*, a long flat stick wielded by a passing monk monitor as I sat in the *zendo*. An expression of compassion, the *kyosaku* is used only when the sitter specifically requests it for relief of shoulder, back or neck tension. To make such a request, one puts his hands in gassho as the monitor nears the seat to let the monitor know one would like the shoulder acupressure point struck. The sound of the *kyosaku* also serves to keep the atmosphere in the *zendo* crisp, awake and alert. By the time I returned to my futon, I was completely debilitated from this eerie and enervating experience. Could I keep this up for six more days?

The next day I came to the *zendo* with a shawl because of the morning cold, which made me shiver. By the time the day advanced, the temperature in the *zendo* kept rising until it was so brutally hot that even the crickets began to sing in the stonewall outside. Even though I was bone-weary and exhausted from my day's work of sitting *zazen* I kept at it because I discovered a strange euphoria coming over me. I finally realized that a self is only a set of perceptions. After the third day of sitting it became easier to do the routine. Perhaps, I had escaped from the world of illusion.

The essential art of *zazen* consists of thinking of not thinking, which is accomplished by non-thinking. One must cease the following: involvement in worldly affairs; all movements of the conscious mind; and making distinctions. The aspirant must simply sit silently and immobile and think of non-thinking, which is the essence of *sammai* in Japanese or in Sanskrit is called *samadhi*, the word for concentration. Non-thinking, a mode beyond thinking and not thinking, functions by realizing both thinking and non-thinking. It is thinking of emptiness, a thinking of the unthinkable, which implies that non-thinking is objectless, subjectless, formless, goalless, and purposeless.

By the end of the seventh day I was ready for my regular life. On Sunday, June 8, the visitors started leaving the monastery. I made no friends amongst them, which I found very sad. However, the opportunity to do so was hardly available. By the end of the day they were all gone.

What kind of people were these participants in *sesshin*? In my estimation, only about 70 percent of them are serious candidates in Zen practice. Most have taken one week off from work or their daily activities to participate in this religious practice. I think about 20 percent are curiosity seekers who are testing to see if Zen practice has any greater meaning for them than their present religious involvement. Lastly, I believe a small 10 percent are people who are fascinated by exotic religions, particularly religions of the East. They flit like bees from flower to flower to become exposed to the latest religious fashion and to talk about popular Eastern concepts such as T'ai chi, Feng shui, Yoga or TM (transcendental meditation). They are interested in the allure of such unorthodox practices as energy healing, therapeutic touch and the real meaning of such esoteric terms as the subtle body, psychic energy, auras, chakras, prana, and chi which have become deracinated in the Western world. Maybe I am being too skeptical but these are my observations.

Yerney and I decided to take a walk around the graveyard. After seven days of concentrated effort it seemed strange to come alive again. We were so intent on conversation it seemed that we were ceaselessly babbling. A sudden shower came up and the conversation was cut off. The two of us ran for the shed of discarded flowers and sat inside watching the rain pour into the rear garden. Tomorrow started the usual routine again. I for one was looking forward to it.

Dokusan

After about a week of routine daily activity, I joined a line up of those seeking *dokusan* with the Roshi. It took about twenty minutes of waiting in line in seated position until it came to my turn. Doiku was there to act as my interpreter. I entered the room with a lot of nervous trepidation and sat in front of the Roshi with a *gassho*. I felt my legs quaking and my body trembling.

Nevertheless, I began to speak, *"watakushi namae Shansky."* [My name is Shansky.] I am here to give you my answer for the *koan."*

In a soft voice, he said, "What is your *koan*?"

I replied, "The *koan* is: A buffalo passes by the window. His head, horns and four legs all go past. But why can't you see the tail?"

He looked at me with his dark, brooding eyes and cherubic face. "What is your answer?"

I began to speak slowly and deliberately, "The head, horns and four legs represent the three characteristics of conditioned existence for an individual: the first is *dukkha,* which is suffering or unsatisfactoriness, the second is *anicca,* which is impermanence or transitoriness, and the third is *anatman,* which is ego-less-ness or no-self. As for the tail, it is true that you cannot see the tail but you know it should be there.

"Everything, every item around you, has its roots in the unseen world. The forms may change, yet the essence remains the same. The source of the unseen tail is eternal. It is continuously growing and giving new life.

The source is within you and everything is springing up from it. The unseen tail represents Buddhist salvation.

"Buddhist salvation is the coming to understand that the forms are structures subject to decay, and that nothing is transmitted but an impulse, a push from behind, and dependent on the heaping up of the past. It is a man's character and not a self that goes on."

The Roshi looked at me with his dark black, penetrating eyes as if he could look directly into my mind. His eyes burned with a tiger-like gleam. I felt like a fly in a bottle. After what seemed like several silent minutes, he began to speak. "I can see that you have given this *koan* deep thought and consideration. But I do not accept your answer. You are trapped in a net of logic."

Then there was a long period of silence. I was so sad I could not respond. My throat choked up. There was a smirk on Doiku's face. Suddenly, the Roshi continued speaking, "You are not ready to receive the precepts."

I could not answer. I looked at Doiku for help and he said, "This means that you will not be ordained as a lay monk."

I immediately turned to the Roshi and said, "I thank you. I shall continue to work on my *koan*."

The Roshi said, "That is good."

I arose from my seated position, made a *gassho* and left the room. My whole body was sweating. I was morose beyond description. As I left the room, I encountered Myoku and told her the whole story without revealing my *koan* or my answer.

She was very sorry for me and said, "Anyway, you will need a new *samu-e*. What you are wearing is too small. Let me accompany you to a woman I know who can make the *samu-e* for you. Her name is Myojo Myozaki and she lives just down the road from the monastery entrance. We can go there Sunday if you like." I thanked her and went to look for Taizan. I knew I would find Taizan in the tool shed.

As I approached him he seemed to know what I would say. "You look like you are ready to cry. What happened?" he asked.

I couldn't contain myself. "The Roshi did not accept the answer to my *koan*."

"He didn't? Well, that's too bad," he said with a low bow and *gassho*. "All is not lost. You can always try again in the future. To be a Buddhist does not require ordination. All you must do is accept and abide by the precepts. Of all the Buddhist sects, Zen is the only one that gives lay ordination. In any event you do not have a *rakusu*. By the way, what will you do about a *rakusu*?"

"What do you mean?" I asked.

"Well, Al, ordinarily a *rakusu* is sewn by the candidate. It took me three months to make mine," as he took his off from around his neck and handed it to me.

I looked at it and answered rather meekly, "Myoku has offered to take me to a seamstress to make a *samu-e*. I think I will have her make a *rakusu* for me. By the way, what is the significance of the *rakusu?*"

He started slowly saying, "The *rakusu* is a rectangular piece of fabric composed of 'patches,' which is worn by hanging around the neck. It symbolizes the patchwork robe of Shakyamuni Buddha and his disciples and is worn by monks and lay followers of *Mahayana* Buddhism. The *rakusu* is conferred upon one during the *jukai*, the initiation into Buddhism in which one takes the Buddhist vows known as *jujukai*.

In the *jukai* ceremony one receives the precepts, in addition to the *rakusu*, as well as a Dharma name, and a circular chart of the Dharma lineage from Shakyamuni through the successive generations to the Roshi and then back to Shakyamuni. There will be a *jukai* ceremony next week for Sekkio. That's when you will see the whole ceremony happening."

I thanked him for his help and good wishes and went up to the farm to speak with Daigaku about the coming ceremony for Sekkio. I came upon him resting while sitting on a flat rock.

"Hi, Daigaku. I understand that there will be an ordination for Sekkio next week. Would you tell me about this? I am interested in the format that will take place." He seemed very tired from his work. He looked at me with a broad smile on his face and began talking slowly trying to recall all the necessary information.

"The ceremony of the reception of the precepts is performed in the *hatto* as follows: The Roshi will be seated in front of the Buddha and Sekkio will be seated facing the Roshi. The entire ceremony will be in Japanese and the entire membership of the monastery will be there. The Roshi bestows the sixteen Bodhisattva Precepts, *rakusu* and *kechimyaku* or lineage paper on Sekkio." He stopped for a moment, looked up and then continued.

"The ceremony has several parts. At the beginning of the ceremony the Roshi, Sekkio and the *Sangha,* that is the congregation, invoke all Buddhas and Bodhisattvas, requesting their presence. The Roshi then will give Sekkio the *rakusu,* the miniature monastic robe. Sekkio will then acknowledge 'all the karma' that he had 'ever created' and declare their repentance. The Roshi then bestows upon Sekkio the Triple Treasure: refuge in the Buddha, Dharma, and Sangha. The Roshi then gives the three Pure Precepts: to abstain from the unwholesome, to do the wholesome, and to benefit all beings. Finally, he gives Sekkio the ten Grave Prohibitory Precepts: abstinence from willful killing, from stealing, from misuse of sexuality, from lying, from taking harmful intoxicants, from speaking ill of others, from promoting oneself while slandering others, from being sparing in the bestowal of teaching or materials, from harboring ill will, and from denouncing the Triple Treasure. Then Sekkio will receive a lineage paper bearing his Buddhist name and showing his direct historical connection through the Roshi with the Buddha. The ceremony concludes with prayer and the Roshi's instructions to Sekkio."

I stared at him with great incredulity, saying, "It sounds overwhelming and all in Japanese as well."

He looked at me as if to scribble on my brain. "Try not to be concerned; there will come a time when you will be ordained," he assured me and then continued. "Please let me give you some advice. Lay ordination doesn't mean that you will become a Buddhist. To behave like a Buddhist, you must adopt a definite way of life. You should never take any action when under the following four states: impulse, fear, hate and delusion and there are three deludic passions — anger, greed, and ignorance. Also, to be a Buddhist you must practice and abide by the Precepts."

I acknowledged the seriousness of this advice by nodding and bending my head closer to him. He continued, "Never do anything impulsively or on the spur of the moment, always think before you act, never do anything out of fear, always let things simmer down until you have a clear mind, never do anything when you hate, always avoid this feeling until it goes away, and as for delusion, nothing is accomplished when you act out of anger; it can only lead to displeasure and further antagonism and greed is nothing more than avarice and leads to reprehensible acquisitiveness mostly of things not needed. Most importantly, do not act out of ignorance since this usually leads to intolerance and a lack of understanding of the arts and ways of civilization. Always remember that Buddha-nature is obscured by ignorance." I thanked him for his help and left with a head swimming. I now felt that I had the proper covenant for being a Buddhist. I vowed silently to continue seeking the way of the dharma.

Myoku and Myojo

On Sunday after the morning tasks, at about 10:00 A.M., Myoku came to me to ask if I was ready to visit with Myojo Myozaki the seamstress. I agreed and we started off together down the road toward the Torii gate. While walking we had a lively conversation about the *jukai* ceremony for Sekkio. It seemed that everyone in the monastery had been talking about it and was looking forward to the event. Myoku told me she felt honored to accompany me to the seamstress, especially since she could help me with communicating to Myojo. In about five minutes after we left the Torii gate, we arrived at Myojo's house. There were little pots of flowering plants on the windowsills and surrounding the door.

Myoku knocked and the door opened. There before me was the smallest woman I had ever seen, no more than 4½ feet. Not only was she small but she was also bent over with a slight "widow's hump" so often seen in older generational women in Japan. There was an exchange of greetings and after a formal introduction I made a *gassho* and her old face creased into a very broad smile. I asked her to make a *samu-e* and a *rakusu*. She nodded affirmatively and started to measure me at various bodily places with a cloth tape measure.

She was talking incessantly with Myoku while doing her work until finally Myoku turned to me and said, "Myojo has told me that she deals in used clothing and has several items that may be of interest to you."

I perked up and asked, "What items does she have?"

Myoku said, "She will make the *samu-e* for you but that she has a robe and a kimono which will fit you."

I asked to look at the used items and the old seamstress shuffled away to retrieve the items. When she returned carrying the robe and kimono I felt a certain excitement. The robe was beautiful, made of shioze habutae silk, I was told by Myoku. The robe and the kimono seemed in excellent condition and so I agreed to buy them. While I was there I decided to order two styles of *samu-e*, one in black and one in grey, both with pants and *hippari*. In addition, I selected two used *haori*, which are like short coats to wear over a *samu-e* in cold weather. The whole cost came to $320 and I was extremely satisfied.

She told me her nephew would deliver everything midweek in about three days. Thanking her in my faulty Japanese, which made her smile broadly, she bowed to me in a very low way. Myoku and I departed with courteous repetitive bowing and finally walking back towards the monastery.

I said, "I'll be glad to get the new *samu-e*. This one I am wearing barely fits me and I shall be able to return it to the monastery."

"Yes," she said, "Your ankles are protruding and it gives you a comical look. I am glad you are getting new clothes."

After we left Myojo-san's house, I suggested to Myoku that we take a walk to the esplanade and watch the boats on the bay. On the way, we passed a large parched lentil field surrounded by several sissau trees. The weather had been very dry and hot and probably accounted for this condition. There had been occasional cloudbursts but not enough rain to soak the fields.

She asked me, "What is an esplanade?"

I told her, "In my youth the walkway along the bay where I grew up was called an esplanade and I have never forgotten this word."

When we arrived the mist was still rising off the water making it look alive and active instead of its usual mirror-like placid appearance. We continued walking up the winding path to the top of the hill where we found an overlook with some benches.

We sat on one of the benches for a while in silence watching the water. Suddenly I said, *"Usuyuki."*

She looked at me quizzically so I explained, "It looks so ephemeral like a light snow."

Myoku laughed and said, "You are very poetic."

I quickly answered, "There is an old Chinese saying: *when one lacks a sense of awe there will be disaster.*"

She laughed loudly, covering her mouth with her hand while rocking back and forth with shaking. I looked up and noticed a white crow. Could this be the same white crow that had gone away somewhere during the winter and returned to the great camphor tree near the shore? The water was moving. The crow must have been flying.

I was jolted out of my musing by her next question, "Tell me, Shansky-san, what have you learned about Zen?"

It seemed that I, without knowing it, had become for her an object of sympathy and admiration. I looked at her for a long time before answering. I became slow and indecisive. There passed the longest and most terrifying minute of my life.

"Your question is as daunting as it is profound," I said shyly in a contemplative manner. It also conjured thoughts of the philosopher, Michel Foucault, who asks a similar question in his *Guide to Living*, "How do we live as against how we ought to live?" I responded slowly, "I can only tell you that I have learned much from the effect Zen is making on my life."

She fixed her eyes in a steady gaze and repeated, "What I mean is, what is there about Zen that really impresses you?"

I hesitated for fear of saying something ridiculous. "Well, I am really impressed with the Zen attack on reason and the fact that this occurs within a religious discipline. In fact there is an air almost of cool rationality in the mounting of the Zen method. I always ask myself the recurring question; can such religious practice make people better? Certainly it may make them calmer, more collected, less given to egoistic passions, in many ways more unselfish. But when you are back again with rivers and mountains are you more able to understand and care for other people? What about love as it is understood by Plato and in the Judeo-Christian religions? What Christians and Jews call love may on closer inspection appear to be shot with egoisms and delusions? Perhaps Schopenhauer followed a Buddhist path in making compassion, not love, the prime virtue. Here, it may seem, in no idle way, a matter of concepts. But equally, ascetic disciples cannot easily be judged from the outside.

"Zen may seem cold; yet Zen art lovingly portrays the tiny things of the world, the details, blithely existing without intelligibility; this too for me has become moral training. I think I have learned that what is important is that we now can take in conceptions of religion without God, and of meditation as religious exercise. There is, just as there used to be, a place of wisdom and calm to which we can remove ourselves. We can make our own rites and images; we can preserve the concept of holiness. This is because in Zen believers seek enlightenment through introspection and intuition rather than through interpretation of a text or scripture." Finally, the problem, which had long been troubling me, like a bone caught in my throat, now found expression.

"Yes, I see Zen has changed you and I am very happy for you," she said. "Why don't we celebrate your pending departure with lunch? I know a very pleasant restaurant that has marvelous food." We started to walk down the hill and continued along the esplanade until we came to a side street of a residential neighborhood. After one or two more streets we came to an entrance, which was draped with a split curtain on which were Japanese characters. We were led to a secluded spot inside with cushions for seats and a very low table for our food.

We started with oyster menchanko, which is a miso broth with lamen

noodles, thick with fat, tender oysters, chunks of tofu, vegetables and bil-
lowy sheets of soymilk skin that look like handkerchiefs but are soft as
bean curd. We finished with yuba chakin, crisp tofu purses stuffed with
vegetables and crabmeat. All of this was accompanied with copious
amounts of green tea. I must confess: I was stuffed and very satisfied.

While eating and talking, I deduced more about Myoku's life and
aspirations. Myoku's life as a woman had until her entrance in Hosshinji
turned out very unhappily. She was not pretty. Her face was ruddy com-
plexioned as if afflicted rosaceously and was spoiled by a nose which was
too long. Her head was shaven bald as befits a monk. She was not just
small — which enhances a woman — but excessively small; she was more
like a schoolgirl than a grown woman. I suspect this may have contributed
to the difficulty she experienced as a psychotherapist for troubled people.
So, at thirty-five, probably no one had paid court to her, no one had
embraced her, no one had kissed her. In the end she found solace in pursuing the life of a Zen monk.

The Jukai Ceremony

At 10:00 A.M. during the rest period of the following midweek, I was
told that a young man was waiting for me in the reception room outside
of the dining hall. I went down the stair ladder and found that Myojo's
nephew was waiting with a large bundle. I greeted him with a low bow
and *gassho*, which he returned.

He said in broken English something to the effect, "My aunt (*obasan*)
wishes you much luck and happiness in the future."

I thanked him as he handed me the bundle. I quickly went upstairs
and opened the bundle to find all the items I had ordered. In minutes I
changed into my new *samu-e*. It fit me like a glove. I was very pleased.
Now, I had to wash the old *samu-e* and return it to Tenzo-san. But first I
wanted to show my new *samu-e* to Daigaku. I also was curious about the
jukai date and time for Sekkio. I found Daigaku in his room. The door

to his room was half-sized and I had to bend down to my knees as I knocked. The door slid open and Daigaku appeared.

I was not invited in as I showed him my new *samu-e* and said, "How do you like my new *samu-e*, Daigaku? I think I am all set for life in the monastery."

He looked me up and down as if it had sacred qualities and replied, "Okay, you look great." Obviously, I interrupted him at some busy work. "Okay, I'll let you know sometime today when *jukai* for Sekkio will take place." He closed the door and I left with a somewhat vacuous feeling.

After lunch Daigaku approached me and said, "The Roshi has designated that *jukai* will take place Saturday at 7:00 in the morning during prayer service in the *hatto*." I thanked him and then went on my way.

I returned to my room to find Yerney writing a letter. I told him about the cold, standoffish attitude of Daigaku.

He shrugged and said, "Monks do not like people to visit them in their rooms."

As I thought about this for a while, I realized that the only time I ever talked to a monk was in some place other than their living quarters. Of course, the only exception to this was Myoku. Why was that? I surmised it had something to do with the feminine proclivity for hospitality.

At 1:00, I went to the farm to work with Daigaku.

As I approached he said, "Al, I need a check to send away for a solar heater. If I give you the money could you give me a check made out to the mail-order place?"

"Of course," I replied. I saw immediately a change in demeanor. He was back to his original friendly self.

He said, "I think you should know that I am scheduled for surgery to remove the lump behind my ear the first week in September."

I looked at him wide eyed, not knowing what to say. "Where will it take place?"

He turned to me and said, "It will take place in the Prefectural Hospital in Kyoto." We both then went about our farming tasks.

On Saturday morning I got up as usual and went to the *zendo* for *zazen*, I did my usual sweep-up and then I got dressed in my new *samu-e* and went to the dining room for breakfast. Everyone was looking at me with curious eyes and smiles on their faces. I was terribly self-conscious. I didn't like being the center of attention. After breakfast I went into the *hatto* with Daigaku who told me where to sit. In a few minutes the Roshi came in and sat facing Sekkio. The Roshi was wearing his robes with a gold damask cloak and a *rakusu* made of a silvery cloth. There was a small lectern in front of him on which was several open books. Daigaku sat to my side. The congregation was divided into two bodies: the monks on one side and the laity on the other.

The service began with a chant called the *sandokai*, which is a celebration of the enlightened state of mind that transcends all duality. At the conclusion the Roshi looked at Sekkio with his piercing eyes and said in Japanese, "Are you ready to accept the precepts?"

Daigaku translated for me. Sekkio responded affirmatively (*hai*). And so the service proceeded until conclusion at which time Sekkio was handed his *rakusu*, which was hung around his neck. Then Sekkio was handed the lineage paper, which contained his dharma name. Daigaku leaned over to me and whispered the translation of everything that transpired between the Roshi and Sekkio. I looked at him with a broad grin. It seemed a very satisfying time for me.

After the service we all went outside where everyone came over to Sekkio with deep bows and *gassho* and congratulated him on his ordination. After a while Taizan took me aside and said, "Well, Al, are you happy now that you have seen how to become a lay monk?"

I smiled and looked him straight in the eye and spoke slowly and deliberately. "The very concept of happiness is conditional, a fiction. The transitory nature and unreality of the concept are implicit in the word itself."

Taizan looked at me with a scowl on his face. "Hold it. Hold it. Are you going to deliver one of your philosophical sermons?"

I was stunned by his reaction. "I'm sorry. I didn't mean to be pedantic."

He said, "Okay, anger was uncalled for, continue please."

I explained, "The word *happiness* is derived from the word that means this hour, this moment. According to Vladimir Dahl, the Russian philologist, happiness comes from a word that means one's fate, one's lot, what one has managed to hold on to in life. The wisdom of etymology gives us a very mean version of happiness. I developed the melancholy notion that there is no such thing as happiness, that it is either unattainable or illusory. In order to understand the nature of happiness we must understand the nature of satiety. When things are going very well, that's happiness. Happiness doesn't depend on how many external blessings we have snatched from life. It depends only on our attitude toward them. There's a saying about it in the Taoist ethic: *Whoever is capable of contentment will always be satisfied.*

"I draw this conclusion not from philosophy I've read but from stories about real people that I've heard all my life. You might say that I am satisfied and content but I believe strongly that I would have felt the same up to this point without witnessing an ordination."

"I see what you mean. I am sorry to have come on so strongly," he muttered with a lowered head. "I know Zen has a different meaning for you than it does for me. My interests are strictly religious whereas I suspect your interests are philosophical. I just want you to know that when I accepted the precepts in Minneapolis I was delirious with joy. It was like a baby taking its first step. I should not have transferred this feeling to you."

I interrupted him, "Oh, let's forget it. I know we are good friends and I would not want anything to spoil that."

Since it had become generally known that I would be leaving the monastery very soon, people started coming over to where we were standing and talking. I never cease to be amazed how quickly information and rumor runs through a small community like a monastery. They were all expressing good wishes to me and some even brought gifts. Daigaku gave me a calligraphy, which said, *Beginner's Mind.* It was beautiful and I immediately thought of where to hang it in my house when I got home. Tenzo-san gave me a pair of wood carved chopsticks (*hashi*). Hanaoka gave me a small ceramic bowl, which I later learned came from the ceramic shop that I frequented in town. Finally, I received a small *Daruma* statue, showing him having meditated into himself, from Taizan. I thanked them all individually with a *gassho* and a deep bow. Suddenly, the outer court was vacated as everyone went on with his or her life.

At lunch, I found that my seat was moved closer to the monks. Actually I sat directly across from Myoku, which made me very happy. For lunch we had cooked snails much smaller than the escargot of French origin. In addition, there was a medley of okra, carrots, mustard greens, mushrooms and tofu together with the ubiquitous cooked rice (*gohan*). As we were eating, I noticed that Myoku was placing several snails in my plate. I thanked her with my eyes by winking. I sucked the meat out of the shell and then returned the empty shell back on her plate.

Piyadassi, who was sitting next to her, shouted, "No. No. Don't do that."

Once again, I suffered embarrassment because of a *faux pas*. Myoku was laughing as if to forgive my mistake. I then reached over and tried to retrieve the empty snail shell with my chopsticks but it fell and bounced along the table to the utter consternation of both Piyadassi and me. I was so dismayed that I decide to overlook the incident altogether as if it never happened. In the meantime, Myoku was having a good laugh at my expense and even Piyadassi was laughing uncontrollably.

After lunch, Piyadassi came over to me and said in an apologetic tone, "Do not be angry with me for reprimanding you in front of the others. I am sorry. I did not think of how it would affect you."

I accepted his apology and told him it was unimportant.

He said, "Anyway, we had a good laugh."

Myoku came over and said, "Would you like to see the azaleas and begonias that we have planted along the entrance path to the monastery?" I agreed and we started walking down the path. There were flowering shrubs of every color and variety. The azaleas were white, pink, purple, red and variations of a salmon color. The begonias were blood red. In between the shrubs were some raceme flowers, which appeared to be lily of the valley. It looked like a pointillism painting with dots of color occupying the area. Myoku said that the shrubs were all pruned to keep them small and that this contributed to a longer flowering season. I was quite impressed with such beauty, which I have never seen in such abundance anywhere other than in a botanical garden.

On the way back, she said, "Do not be angry with Piyadassi. The incident was my entire fault for trying to be generous. I should not have interfered with your lunch."

I replied, "Please don't be concerned. I am curious; however, what caused Piyadassi to say what he did?"

She replied, "He probably thought you were refusing my gift. He might not have known that you had finished eating the snail."

I raised my arms in despair, "It's all like a tempest in a teapot. There is no purpose in pursuing it any longer. I wish we would all forget it."

After returning to the outer court, I was told by one of the Japanese monks that a young man was waiting for me. Myoku and I went over to the anteroom of the dining hall. There was the nephew of Myojo waiting with a package in his hand. Through Myoku's translation I learned it was a gift from Myojo for my pending departure. I opened the package and found a very lovely *obi*, which is a sash for my kimono. I thanked him profusely and conveyed my regards to his aunt. Then Myoku and I parted company with a very low bow and a *gassho*. And so it was back to our regular routine course of quotidian activities.

Independence Day

I found myself repeating the same conditions of *zazen*; getting up before dawn and sitting in a rigid position. By this time, I seemed to accept the inevitable. My body did not seem to ache as much and I did not resist the boredom as I had previously. Indeed, there seemed to be an alleviation of anxiety and sitting became a source of relief and consolation.

Daigaku approached me and said rather quickly, "Saturday is July 4 and I am trying to get Doiku, Taizan, me and you to meet in the library room after *zazen* on Saturday to celebrate American Independence Day." I agreed but wondered how we would celebrate.

We gathered in the library room and sat in a circle facing each other. Daigaku suggested that we sing *America the Beautiful* and he gave a paper to each with the complete lyrics. We sang our hearts out reaching the highest crescendos. We were like a choral group singing a harmonization of a traditional melody. It sure made me feel good. But as I looked at the others I realized that I was the only one going home. Daigaku and Doiku were expatriates and Taizan would probably be away for many years. Still, they were Americans and this was their way of expressing love for American civilization and culture.

We parted with regular handshakes instead of the usual *gassho*. I was exhausted from the whole day's activities and literally crawled into my futon. I had a troubled sleep and thought about the past few days. It occurred to me that the state of non-thinking which I was experiencing during *zazen* was a way of authenticating *shunyata* commonly known in Buddhist mysticism as emptiness.

I was restless and couldn't sleep thinking about it. *Shunyata* is one of the most important concepts in Buddhism. It is a religious/philosophical concept, which is central to much of Buddhist thought. It is employed in numerous contexts by different thinkers and schools, with a variety of meanings. The second-century Indian Buddhist thinker Nagarjuna first expressed the philosophy of emptiness. He came to be known as the founder of the *Madhyamika* School, a school that was particularly influential in Tibetan and Chinese *Mahayana* Buddhism.

Ancient Buddhism recognized that all composite things are empty, impermanent, devoid of essence, and characterized by suffering. In the *Hinayana* emptiness is only applied to the person; in the *Mahayana*, on the other hand, all things are regarded as without essence, i.e., empty of self-nature. All dharmas are fundamentally devoid of independent lasting substance, are nothing more than mere appearances. It does not mean that things do not exist but rather that they are nothing besides appearances. *Shunyata* is without duality and empirical forms. *Shunyata* carries and permeates all phenomena and makes their development possible. Thus each thing is interconnected, fundamentally united, unique, and shares the same basis as everything else. This is made possible by its grounding in the field of *shunyata*.

Indeed, it is possible to deepen our subjectivity and freedom by practicing *zazen*, which will help us to become aware of the reality of *shunyata*. All the schools take as their point of departure Nagarjuna's thesis of the two truths: (1) the apparent truth—which ordinary people take to be real—fundamentally it does not exist since it only appears through "interdependent arising"; and (2) the supreme truth, the emptiness of all phenomena, which cannot be expressed in words but only directly experienced. It seemed in my mind that this turned into a quodlibet exercise as I dozed off. After a while I fell asleep only to be woken up in a few short hours to continue *zazen* on the next day.

At breakfast I noticed a new man sitting next to me. He started talking to me with a slight cockney accent.

"My name is Oscar and I come from Johannesburg," he whispered.

I acknowledged him with a *gassho* and replied, "My name is Al." He told me he was a pilot for a small aviation company in South Africa and probably could best be described as a "bush pilot."

We became rather friendly and I learned that he spoke several European languages, including French and German. He has a girlfriend in Johannesburg with whom he was having some domestic problems. He thought by getting away for a week at Hosshinji he might be able to solve his problems. I guess the Chinese saying *there is no rose without a thorn*, is very apt. Anyway, he was the first visitor that I was able to speak with during my stay. Little did Oscar realize that his problems will be waiting for him when he returned to Johannesburg. I invited him to visit with me in my room after lunch since we were not really allowed to carry on a long conversation at the dining table.

After lunch, he followed me up the ladder stairs to my room. I asked him to be seated and offered him some tea, which he waved off cordially.

He leaned over to me and whispered with a smile on his face, "Do you think I am becoming enlightened?"

I whispered back, "I doubt it, unless you remember the Four Noble Truths spoken by the Buddha."

He straightened up and looked forward as if in a trance and mumbled, "All life is pain and suffering. Pain and suffering comes from desires, craving, clinging and attachments. In order to stop pain and suffering one must give up desires, craving, clinging and attachments. The way to give up desires, craving, clinging and attachments is to follow the Eightfold Path."

"That's right." I replied.

He giggled under his breath, "What is the Eightfold Path?"

I looked at him in disbelief. "Do you mean that you do not know the Eightfold Path?"

He turned towards me and said in a dejected way, "Well, I did know them but I forgot how they go."

I looked at him with a steady gaze and began to recite in a very low voice, "First, right view, i.e., the view based on understanding of the four noble truths and the nonindividuality of existence; second, right resolve, i.e., resolve in favor of renunciation, good will, and not harming sentient beings; third, right speech, i.e., avoidance of lying, slander, and gossip; fourth, right conduct, i.e., avoidance of actions that conflict with moral discipline; fifth, right livelihood, i.e., avoidance of professions that are harmful to sentient beings, such as slaughterer, hunter, dealer in weaponry or narcotics; sixth, right effort, i.e., cultivation of what is wholesome and avoiding what is not wholesome; seventh, right mindfulness, i.e., ongoing mindfulness of body, feelings, thinking, and objects of thought; eighth, right concentration, i.e., concentration of mind."

He seemed stunned by my commentary and said, "Did you memorize the whole thing?"

I smiled and said, "That's basic Buddhism; you must remember the

Eightfold Path does not actually represent a path on which linear progress is made, since in practice the first to be realized are stages 3–5, which belong to the *shila* (morality) phase of the threefold training, then stages 6–8, the *samadhi* (consciousness) phase, and then finally 1–2, which belong to the *prajna* (wisdom) phase."

He seemed rather taken aback but with an incredulous look he said, "It all seems very difficult."

I turned to him and said, "It's not difficult if you live that way. You don't have to memorize anything."

He then looked at me with a startled expression and said, "I thought meditation would give me enlightenment."

I could not believe what I heard. Can this man be so uninformed that he doesn't understand basic Buddhism? I told him very squarely, "*Zazen* is not the same as meditation."

"What do you mean?" he asked.

I went on, "There seems to be a common misunderstanding about *zazen*. *Zazen* is usually translated as 'Zen meditation' or 'sitting meditation.' More and more, in contemporary usage, *zazen* is considered one of the many methods from Eastern spirituality traditions for attaining objectives such as mind/body health, skillful social behavior, a peaceful mind, or the resolution of various problems in life. *Zazen*, as understood by Dogen Zenji, is something different, and cannot be categorized as meditation. For Dogen, *zazen* is first and foremost a holistic body posture, not a state of mind. *Zazen* goes beyond mind/body dualism; both the body and the mind are simultaneously and completely used up just by the act of sitting.

"While most meditation tends to focus on the head, *zazen* focuses more on the living holistic body-mind framework, allowing the head to exist without giving it any pre-eminence. If the head is over-functioning, it will give rise to a split and unbalanced life. But in the *zazen* posture it learns to find its proper place and function within a unified mind-body field. Our living human body is not just a collection of bodily parts, but is an organically integrated whole. It is designed in such a way that when one part of the body moves, however subtle the movement may be, it simultaneously causes the whole body to move in accordance with it."

I hesitated for a minute then continued, "Dogen Zenji said, 'When you sit *zazen* do not think of either good or evil. Do not be concerned with right or wrong. Put aside the operation of your intellect, volition and consciousness. Stop considering things with your memory, imagination, or reflection.'"

I continued, "Following this advice, we are free, for the time being, to set aside our highly developed intellectual faculties. We simply let go of our ability to conceptualize. In *zazen* we do not intentionally think about anything. This does not mean that we ought to fall asleep. On the contrary, our consciousness should always be clear and awake."

I reiterated, "The body does not move in *zazen* posture. The mouth is closed and does not speak. The mind does not seek to become Buddha, but instead stops mental activities of thinking, willing, and consciousness."

He seemed somewhat surprised. "I guess I have a lot to learn."

I put my hand on his shoulder and said, "Oscar, nothing will come overnight. It will take a long time until you learn to do *zazen* properly. It may take years."

He turned to me. "I had no idea, but I am grateful to you for your explanation." He rose and left the room. I only saw him fleetingly from then on. In a way I was sorry, for a while, to have been so forthright with him.

The next day Doiku assembled everyone in the forecourt and announced that everyone would be needed to harvest the tea. I should explain that the three vegetable farms vary from ½ to 1 acre each in size and that they are separated with a living fence of tea shrubs. These shrubs are of the variety known as Japanese green tea, which actually, after infusion with boiling water, yields a yellow liquid. Authentic green tea in Japan comes from the city of Uji and is the variety used in the tea ceremony because it froths when beaten with a bamboo whisk. Be that as it may, Doiku divided the people into three groups of about ten each to be single-filed along each periphery of the three farms. He then gave instructions for picking.

The weather was extremely hot and sultry. The sun beat down on each person at a station as each picked the young leaves, leaf buds and internodes of the plants. These pickings were placed in pouches, which were strung over our shoulders. The older leaves were avoided in order to keep the plant alive and in continuous growth. The work was backbreaking and intense. I was dressed in my work pants, a T-shirt and a towel covering my head. Despite these precautions the heat and sun bore down on us and this required drinking copious amounts of water, which was supplied from a ewer that was kept nearby. Sweat was pouring down the bodies, arms and brows of all the crew. After a few hours a bell rang and the cook with his helpers wheeled out a cart containing large buckets of cooked rice and cooked vegetables for lunch. We all had brought our *o-ryo-ki* bowls on the earlier instructions of Doiku.

We filed past the cart to fill our bowls with food and eat lunch picnic-style. However, before this happened we had to empty our pouches unto a tarpaulin spread on the ground. One person was assigned to the job of culling out inedible items such as twigs and weeds. After I got my food I sat down to rest. I was fatigued by the heat of the seventh month. I was so exhausted I could hardly eat; but I forced myself because I knew I would get hungry later. I was tired and completely depleted. However, after a much needed rest, I rallied.

By late midday the picking was completed and the filled tarpaulins were brought to the forecourt where the leaves were stuffed into large plastic bags. The filled bags had to be sent to a processor for steaming in order to remove bugs, cobwebs and other debris. The thusly-cleaned tea leaves were then subjected to immediate curing by firing and withering. This is the point at which tea assumes its characteristic aroma. Freshly picked tea leaves have no aroma. The processed tea leaves were then returned to the monastery the next day in the same large plastic bags.

Each person was given a small plastic bag filled with withered tea leaves and the remainder was placed in storage. In order to make the beverage one must crush the withered tea by hand into the course powder distinctively found in tea bags. It is then placed in a bowl to which boiling water is added. I should mention that each room is supplied with a Thermos bottle and each person in the room takes a turn at filling it with boiling water from a large pot in the kitchen, which is kept fired all day and banked at night.

By now it was 3:00 P.M. and time for tea. I washed up and met with Yerney in the dining room. I asked him how the picking went on his farm. He was at a different farm than me. As usual he was very enthusiastic, whereas I was still feeling the effects of the day. I told him I was going upstairs to our room to rest before going to the farm and work with Daigaku. He decided to join me and we took our tea and a small cake up to our room. It was then that he told me that his visa would be running out and he would have to leave the monastery and go to Korea to renew his visa and thus return to Hosshinji legally. I told him I was only staying in Hosshinji until the end of August and would probably leave Japan the middle of September. He thought of going to Korea the end of September.

We exchanged addresses and vowed to keep in contact with each other. After a while I went to the farm to work with Daigaku. After working on the farm for an hour and resting for an additional hour, I went to dinner, which was at 6:00 P.M. We had the leftovers from lunch supplemented with noodles. At 7:00 P.M., I went to the bath for a thorough scrub and a relaxing dip in the hot tub. I then sat evening *zazen* and thence went to sleep in my futon.

The next day everyone had to bring out his or her futons and bedding for the monthly airing. The futons were placed on the roof of the main building exposed to the hot sun. The sheets were washed in the washing machines behind the kitchen and hung to dry on makeshift lines held aloft with long bamboo poles. The sun dried them very quickly.

On Sunday, the monks shaved each other's heads and we all did laundry. After I was finished with my laundry I took a bicycle from the tool shed and went to town. On my way into town I stopped at the Shinto monastery and inspected the grounds and buildings. There was a bronze statue of a horse almost life size on the plaza of the entranceway. Shinto is an animistic religion and usually has statues of animals on their grounds such as horses and badgers.

In Japan questions of origin and local tradition are assigned to Shinto, whereas problems connected with living in society are usually given over to Confucianism. But those connected with death and the hereafter is assigned to Buddhism. It is said, married by Shinto; buried by Buddhism.

The shrine was closed but next door was a primary school and even though this was not a school day, there were children playing in the playground on the swings and seesaws. I approached them and started speaking in Japanese, which brought forth giggles and laughter. I expected this response because of my accent. They were nice kids and I waved goodbye as I left. They all gathered and followed me for a little distance waving their hands and shouting *sayonara*.

I pedaled all the way to the harbor and entered the fish house but there was very little activity since I came a little late in the day. I then went to the market and left my bicycle outside while I bought a loaf of sliced bread and another jar of strawberry jam as well as a bag of apples for my roommates.

When I left the market I discovered I had a flat tire. I knew of a bicycle shop on the north street. I was on the south street so I decided to cut across by going through one of the narrow alleyways. I found I was in a residential area with doorways dotting both sides of the street. In some case there were old people sitting in front of the doorways all of which greeted me with very friendly remarks. There were little pots of flowering plants all along the street in front of the houses. In one instance a middle-aged woman was watering her plants. It was strange that I found no men on the street. Perhaps, they were off in their clubhouses or partaking in sporting events. I continued until I came out on the north street.

I headed for the bicycle shop. I entered the shop and motioned for the proprietor to come out and look at the bicycle. This was a case where language was unnecessary. Everything was symbolic and instead of speech there were gestures. I did greet the proprietor with the normal expected cordiality. He went about the task of fixing the bicycle tire.

When he finished I wanted to pay him *haraimasu.* He was immediately taken aback and shook his head from side to side and waved his hands rapidly. He then pointed to the small plate on the rear of the seat. It said in Japanese characters, HO SHIN JI. I then understood that this was an accommodation for members of the monastery. I thanked him profusely with a *gassho* and several bows. I offered him one of the apples, which he took with gratitude. I departed knowing that I made one more friend amongst the merchants in town.

O-Bon Festival

Myoku came to visit me one day as I was working at sweeping the entrance to the *hatto.* "There is going to be an O-Bon festival at the water's edge near the large fish house in town would you like to go?"

"Of course, I would like that very much."

"Well, when you finish we can go into town."

Preparations were being made for the O-Bon ceremony, which would take place on Saturday, August 15. One of the most important events in Japan is the annual O-Bon festival. O-Bon is a traditional Japanese holiday, which remembers and honors those who have passed away. That year O-Bon was held on Saturday, August 15 through Sunday, August 16. People prepare a paper lantern for the deceased. In the evening a ceremony is performed by a local priest. O-Bon culminates with the lanterns floating on Wakasa Bay. A morning service is held Sunday.

The following excerpt is from *Zen Seeds: Reflections of a Female Priest* by Shundo Aoyama. She is a Soto Zen Roshi and chief priest of a training temple for women in Japan.

> *In relation to our ancestors, we are like the apex of a pyramid. The levels of a pyramid ever widening toward its base represent past generations of ancestors. Our present existence is the sum of all they did, and we are the starting point for our descendants. All that our ancestors did reflects on us, and all that we do reflect on both our ancestors and our descendants.*

One's life is not entirely one's own; it contains the past and conceives the future, and should therefore be lived with great care. This is the teaching of the O-Bon Festival.

That is the purpose of O-Bon in a nutshell. It is a very solemn occasion and yet is a happy celebration. Local residents are invited to join the monastery residents on all aspects of the occasion. Many will come to pray at the gravesite of their ancestors and so a whole crew was assigned the job of cleaning up the graveyard. Withered flowers had to be removed, items left on the gravestones had to be removed, the area had to be raked and all decomposable items had to be placed in the compost pile.

Suddenly, I discovered Myoku approaching me. She made the comment "Would you like me to show you how to make a paper lantern?" I grabbed on this immediately.

"Yes," I replied.

"Well then come to my area and we can work on it together after clean-up time."

I was grateful for her offer since I had no idea how to make a paper lantern. We worked most of the day on clean-up, including raking the fallen *shikiji* leaves all the way down to the road to the entrance. Another group was busy weeding and straightening flowerbeds. After clean-up time, I wandered over to the female area and met with Myoku. The other female monks were there but were busy with their own activities. They did, however, acknowledge my presence with a wave of the hand. Myoku took a large sheet of paper and began folding it much like an origami exercise. She demonstrated quite deftly how to make a paper lantern that could carry a small candle and yet be floatable on water.

After a few days of constant work in cleaning up and preparation, it was the beginning of O-Bon. People would be arriving in mid-morning to attend the special service, which would be mostly chanted in Japanese. The *hatto* would be crowded to accommodate all the outsiders but there were special places provided for sponsors and supporters. Indeed, for those wanting special prayers at the gravesites, monks were provided to render this service. This consisted of chanting and the pouring of water from a spouted can over the gravestone of the departed while the participant spoke words to the departed and placed flowers in the attached vase. In addition, some services were to take place in the library room where a Buddha is ensconced. This area is probably reserved for those who are the descendants of the fallen warriors.

At 6:00 P.M., the evening meal was served to all participants. The monastery residents and some select outside people ate in the dining room. At the conclusion of dinner large groups gathered in the *hatto* for prayers and to listen to the Roshi give his dharma talk. When the Roshi was finished people started streaming out of the *hatto* to make the walk to the water's edge of Wakasa Bay.

By the time of arrival it was dusk and the candles were very visible. The participants then floated the paper lanterns with the inserted candles on the water. The lanterns floated off on the tide and gave a wondrous sight as if stars were sparkling on the sea. After a while they looked like a long string of shining pearls on the water. Finally, one by one they disappeared. Most of the participants ambled off in different directions, talking as they walked. However, some of the participants returned to the monastery for evening service in the *hatto* followed by *zazen*. It was interesting to see some people sitting *zazen* outside. Of course, the weather was warm enough to permit this.

The next morning on Sunday, we, of the monastery, started with a new wake-up time of 5:00 A.M., *zazen*, clean-up and then breakfast. Some overnight people went back to the graveyard but most expressed gratitude with many bows and left the monastery grounds. After a busy morning of cleaning up and putting things away, I hooked up with Yerney and we decided to take a walk towards the esplanade.

"Al, do you know how the O-Bon stated?" he inquired.

"As a matter of fact, I do," I answered. "I don't want to sound like a know-it-all but it is steeped in Buddhist mythology," as I related the story.

"The term 'bon' derives from the Sanskrit *ullambana*. It means 'rescue from the torment of hanging upside down in hell.' The O-Bon festival originates in the story of Moggallana saving his mother from one of the Buddhist hells, the realm of hungry ghosts, where she was hanging upside down. A major disciple of the Buddha, Moggallana was known for his supernatural powers. He asked the Buddha how she could be saved and the Buddha said that if Moggallana gave alms to fellow monks, he would earn merit that would liberate her."

He turned to me and with his usual puerile, wide-eyed wonderment, he said, "That's an amazing story. Where did you learn so much about Buddhism?"

I blushed with embarrassment and said, "Actually, I read it in a book and I don't really know very much about Buddhism. That's why I am here, to learn about the great concepts of Buddhism." We continued walking until we reached the esplanade. While looking at the water of Wakasa Bay, I said, "Yerney, if you could put me on a paper lantern I would float all the way to Connecticut where I live."

He laughed and said, "If you put me on a paper lantern I would float to Korea where I will get my new visa."

As we headed back to the monastery, I realized that time was drawing nigh for both of us leaving the monastery.

The Taizan Incident

After sitting *zazen* and clean up, I went to breakfast with Yerney and Hanaoka, my roommates. As we sat awaiting our food, Tenzo-san started to speak very forcefully with intermittent translation by Doiku.

He said, "There is a monk outside at the gate. He is not allowed to come in. No one should speak to him or give him food. He eventually will go away."

I was stunned and puzzled. I immediately looked around and after examining all the faces; I was startled to find that Taizan was missing. My eyes returned to Piyadassi who some how confirmed my suspicion that it was Taizan outside the gate.

Breakfast became a solemn occasion. Everyone looked at his or her food without the usual eye blinking and under tone whispering. I could hardly wait to finish my meal. It seemed an eternity but when I finished I went to my room to put away my *ory-oki* bowls and said to Yerney, "I am going to see if it's Taizan at the gate."

Yerney looked at me cautiously and said, "Be careful, Al; Tenzo-san is in a black mood for some reason."

I went around the backside of the lavatory so as not to be seen on the major walkway. I came to the gate and sure enough there was Taizan sitting on the ground. He was a sad-looking character with his head down. He was dressed in mufti and he had a duffle bag at his side. "What happened to you?" I questioned in disbelief. He gestured expressively with his hands and said nothing. I put the query to him again.

"I can't talk about it now, Al," he said. There was such grief in his voice it was as though he were saying goodbye forever.

I then questioned him, "Are you hungry? Should I bring you some food?" He nodded in assent so I made off to my room and retrieved the package of sliced bread and the jar of strawberry jam and brought them back to him.

He thanked me profusely but it was said with pain in his voice. "Thank you, Al. I'll call you and explain all in a few days. I had a run in with Tenzo-san concerning one of my restoration projects. He is a real marplot, always interfering and making mischief. I am afraid we had bitter words. So he evicted me. You should leave now or you may get into trouble. Thanks again. I'll call you at the pay phone in the anteroom."

I left with a completely dejected feeling. What could have happened to cause such a severe punishment? All day I pondered and wondered what could be transpiring with Taizan at the gate. How long does he intend sitting there? That night it started raining rather heavily. I ran down to the gate with a poncho for Taizan. He was gone. Where could he have gone?

The next day at Sumano's English lesson, Piyadassi told me that he and Sumano and Taizan made arrangements to go to the Buddhist Convention in Vancouver in September. He expected to hear from Taizan soon but in the meantime he knows that Taizan will be staying at Ryosen-An in the Daitoku-ji Temple complex in Kyoto. The promised telephone call never came from Taizan so I made up my mind to seek him out when I arrived in Kyoto next week.

At the end of August, I made the usual departure overtures to the monks whom I befriended. I gave my work clothes to Yerney who would need them for his next 90-day stay. I shook hands with Doiku. Daigaku was in a hospital in Kyoto and I expected to visit him there.

Strangely enough, Tenzo-san approached me and put an *Ojusu* string of beads in my hand and said in broken English, "Goodbye, Shansky-san. May you have good fortune in your new life. Remember to take the benefit and burden both." My eyes filled with tears. This was the man who vanquished my friend saying goodbye to me with a gift. I found it perplexing and disconcerting. I made up my mind to find Taizan and unjumble this matter.

As I looked up, I saw Myoku approaching in the distance. I waited a while and then proceeded to meet her. She made a *gassho* with a very low bow and said in her high-pitched voice, "May all good fortune come your way, Shansky-san. I hope that one day we shall meet again. Goodbye." I returned the bow and thanked her. I made a *gassho* and held it an additional thirty seconds. It was a heart-rending moment. I felt a lump in my throat and could not speak. Was it Shakespeare who said, "Parting is such sweet sorrow?"

Kyoto

I got off the train in the massive Kyoto Railroad station. Ah, Kyoto — city of temples! I've seen this city grow since my first visit in 1973. After many visits since then it has grown from a rather small village to an overpopulated metropolis. But some things never change. I am referring to the section east of the Kamo River, which is still relatively unchanged and is a neighborhood of indigenous people. That is where Ryokan Hiraiwa is located.

I headed for the ryokan which was a short walk from the station but stopped on the way at a flower shop *(hanaya)* to buy three red roses for the *Okusan* (mistress of the house) whom I knew quite well, having resided there many times previously. We greeted each other with deep bows. She could not know I was now a Buddhist since I was dressed like any other tourist. But tomorrow, I would change into my *samu-e* when I went to Daitoku-ji in search of Taizan. In the meantime she showed me to my room and provided me with fresh sheets for my futon, which was rolled up in the closet.

I placed my bag on the floor and sat down to partake of a cup of green tea, which was traditionally provided with hot water *(oyu)* in a thermos bottle on the small stand in the corner. I then started to make plans to try to find Taizan starting tomorrow. But first, I had to go out and seek food for dinner. There is a wonderful Western bakery across the street from the Higashi Hongwanji temple where I headed. I had not tasted bread in three months and my mouth watered at the prospect. I bought a large French baguette and a container of the newly devised yoghurt aptly called Fuji Yoghurt.

The next morning, I took the number 206 bus from the train station to Daitoku-ji. I alighted at the last stop and walked to the temple complex looking for Ryosen-An. When I found it, I was told to wait outside until the head monk Matsunami Taiun would arrive to greet me. He was an affable, average-size man wearing black robes. He spoke perfect English. I was invited into an anteroom and we sat on cushions while sipping tea. I inquired about Taizan.

"Yes, he was here but left yesterday for Tokyo. I am not sure but I think he will return next week," he said in a matter-of-fact voice. "May I help you in any way?" he offered. "I am leaving for America at the end of the week; but I would be most grateful if you would give him this book and I shall write him a note." The book was the one I brought from home, *The Master of Hestviken* by Sigrid Undset. It gave me much pleasure reading it before sleep. I hoped he would enjoy it, too.

I wrote the note and left it in the hands of Taiun, the head monk.

We then had an interesting conversation. I told him about my experiences in Hosshinji and he told me that the Ryosen-An monastery accepted wayward monks without question. It also was a center for foreign scholars interested in Zen practice and learning the Japanese language. I thanked him and left to explore the massive complex of Daitoku-ji.

Daitokuji

Daitoku-ji is known as the Great Virtue Temple and was started in 1319 with the first building erected and dedicated to the Zen sect. It was officially sanctioned in 1342 and was dedicated a place of worship for the Imperial court.

The temple prospered until 1453, when it was damaged by fire. Then in 1468 it was completely destroyed in the Onin War. It was restored in the 1470s with backing from the Emperor.

During the sixteenth century Daitoku-ji was patronized by the prominent warriors of the time. It was in this period that most of its numerous sub-temples were founded. At present Daitoku-ji has more than twenty sub-temples on its grounds. The monastery possesses one of the finest collections of art treasures in Japan. It is, without doubt, one of the great Zen monasteries.

I am one of those who have enjoyed the immortal Heian period novel, *The Tale of Genji*; therefore, a short walk to the tomb of Murasaki Shikibu was in order. It is close to the bus stop east of Daitoku-ji.

I walked all around the grounds and enjoyed looking at all the temples, gardens, bell towers and gates. The temples were rather small but had room for at least fifty people inside. All temples were equipped with a Buddha and a small table for religious implements. The architecture was typical Japanese style with slight variations to give each an individual identity.

I then took the bus back to the train station. It was a short walk to my ryokan from the train station and I was anxious to avoid the hustle and bustle of the city. I was finding it difficult to adjust to a leisure life.

My energy seemed to be on constant activation for work. Also, I kept getting up very early in the morning. I couldn't sleep after 5:00 A.M., at which time I sit *zazen* for at least an hour until my calves ached. I knew this was only temporary and I expected to revert to my usual 40-minute *zazen* soon. When I got back to my room I made a cup of tea and made plans for visiting Daigaku tomorrow.

I was very disappointed not to have found Taizan and could only hope that I would hear from him before I leave or after I get home. The note I left with the head monk, Taiun, contained my ryokan as well as my home address and phone number.

After a short rest, I went out to purchase some food for lunch and dinner. I found a small store just around the corner and bought a bunch of bananas, a loaf of bread, and a jar of peanut butter. I brought the comestibles back to my room and left again to explore the neighborhood. I walked to the Kamo River where I discovered a man fishing off the embankment. He had a long pole with a reel for the line. I greeted him. He spoke no English but I was able to communicate with my faulty Japanese. He had a continuous laugh, which I found somewhat infectious.

After a while, I left him and walked along *Go* (Fifth) Street. I passed a large stone building which had a Latin inscription carved into its frieze. It read: *Omnia Vincit Amor—Vitae Sal Amicitia* that translated means: "Love Conquers All—Friendship Is the Salt of Life." I was a Latin scholar in my youth and laughed on reading this inscription. The more I thought about it the stranger it became. Probably no one, passing by, could understand the inscription and was the equivalent of someone inscribing a building on Fifth Avenue in New York City with Japanese characters.

Daigaku

The next day I took the bus to Sanzen-In on Mt. Hiei, the present location of Kyoto Prefectural Hospital. Sanzen-In is an abbreviation form of *Sanzen-Daisen-Sekai,* which means "3000 great thousand worlds," or the greater part of the Buddhist Universe times a thousand cubed, which was the vast system to which Buddha directed his ministry. The universe was divided into three worlds, six paths, and myriad subdivisions that found a system with no fewer complexes than that of Dante. Only its four highest heavens were not in the *Sanzen-Daisen-Sekai* ministered to by Buddha. The site was on the east side of *Kawara-machi* where the Prefectural Hospital now stands.

When I entered the hospital, a nurse all dressed in white greeted me. She spoke passable English and helped me locate Daigaku. I went to his room and found him sitting in a lounge chair reading a book. His head was swathed with bandaging and he was dressed in what appeared to be a chenille robe. I approached cautiously and said, "Daigaku, how are you?" He looked up with a surprised look on his face.

"Al, it's so good of you to come."

After an initial exchange of pleasantries, I explained that I left Hosshinji and was now residing in Ryokan Hiraiwa in Kyoto for a few days before going home. He told me that the removed lump was biopsied and proved to be benign.

He then rose to offer me a seat and handed me a large tin box containing cookies. I took one and sat in the chair next to him, at which point I handed him the bunch of flowers I bought on the way. With a very slight smile on his face he said, "So you are on your way home. In some ways I envy you. I haven't been home for almost a year. At that time I went to visit my mother who now lives in Asheville, North Carolina. It is very beautiful being near the Great Smoky Mountain National Park."

I agreed with him and offered to call his mother when I got home to relieve her anxiety at his operation. He was pleased with this gesture and gave me her telephone number. I then told him about the problem between Taizan and Tenzo-san.

"I'm not surprised because I've had my differences with Tenzo-san also. He is very ambitious and is jealous that I am so close to the Roshi. Most of the monks rally around him," he said in a straightforward manner. He continued, "Every profession has its aspirants who make up the cortege of those who are at the summit."

At first there was prolonged silence. "Who said that?" I inquired.

"I don't remember," he replied. "But St. Augustine said every cowl may dream of the tiara,"

"What's a cowl?" I asked.

He replied quickly, "It's a Benedictine monk's hood."

He then continued, "I was told by the Roshi that I will not work on the farm when I return. He wants me to edit the Newsletter and to take care of his correspondence as well as translate his book, *The Essence of Zen*, into English."

"Gee, that's great," I blurted out.

He said, "I am sad about leaving the farm but I understand that it is bad to have such attachments. I will look forward to my new responsibilities with increased vigor," he continued. "As for Taizan; he is his own worst enemy. If you beat on a wall your fist is going to hurt."

After a while he leaned back and said pensively, "Tell me, Al, is there such a thing as Buddhist thinking?"

"What do you mean?" I asked.

"What I mean is do you find yourself thinking in a different way now than you did before you entered Hosshinji?"

The question seemed very obscure to me. I frowned and replied very hesitantly, "I feel different but I am not sure it has involved my way of thinking. Yet the mind must be involved. It is said that there is a difference between Eastern and Western thought processes. Can it be that the way I now think has changed from a Western way to an Eastern way? I really don't know." I hesitated before continuing. I noticed Daigaku seemed very pensive. "Shall I go on?" I asked.

"Please do," he answered thoughtfully.

I started talking slowly without animation. "The Eastern mind thinks in a curvilinear way whereas the Western mind thinks in a rectilinear way. To a Buddhist the circle is a symbol of perfection. It is seamless continuum. In Zen the circle is known as an *enso*. It is a teaching tool for

Japanese monks in monasteries who attempt to make a perfect circle with one stroke of the brush during calligraphy. The circle as a Buddhist symbol is also evident in the use of the wheel with eight spokes representing the Eightfold Path. These things we both know, Daigaku. The Western mind, on the other hand, thinks in terms of triangles, squares and lines as demonstrated in the art movement known as cubism instead of smooth, flowing curves and circles which the Eastern mind captures in the flow of the watercourse way and the movement of rivers and waterfalls."

I stopped for a minute as if to conjure my thoughts, "I remember quite clearly one of my philosophy teachers lecturing on this subject. He claimed this referred to the concept of the *actual indefinite*, which may be a contradiction in terms because if something is actual it cannot be indefinite and if something is indefinite it cannot be actual. But, he said, this contradiction is accepted by the Eastern mind because it is nonsubstantial, that is, it is not fixed, not being and has no boundaries. It is becoming, still growing, still changing and still moving. It is flexible and able to bend and with no entities."

I reflected somewhat and then continued, "As an American, more so a Westerner, I am surrounded by the Judeo-Christian schema of a dichotomous universe. Yet, I am beginning to be uncomfortable with dualistic doctrines. Indeed, the ideas that there are some entities that embody goodness and others that embody evil that these exist in eternal conflict with each other, with good almost inevitably winning at the end, are ones that I am now questioning. According to an ancient Buddhist expression, *Knowing is illusion, not knowing is indifference*."

I stopped for a minute to collect my thoughts and then continued.

"Most Americans are probably familiar with the famous yin-yang icon of Chinese origin — a circle containing dark (yin) and light (yang) shrimp-like figures, forming a circular whole. Any radial line intersects both yin and yang, and the amount of whiteness or blackness depends on where one draws the line."

I stopped once again but continued.

"In Hinduism as well, the concept of the continuum of good and evil, rather than categorical states, is inherent in the dominant philosophical school of *Advaita Vedanta*, literally meaning nondualism. Unlike Judeo-Christian philosophy, there is no Satan figure in Hinduism or for that matter Buddhism. There are numerous characters that are evil, but no centralized figure that embodies evil and who is in dynamic opposition to the good that is God."

I felt a need to continue. "There is no eternal struggle; instead good and evil coexist in a less than perfect universe. The great conundrum that seems to occupy Judeo-Christian theologians — if God is perfectly good, why did he create Evil and permit its continued existence — does not puzzle Hindu or Buddhist philosophers at all. Since good and evil are two aspects of only one reality, neither has any existence apart from the other."

I observed that Daigaku was looking at me with an intense stare, "I notice that your answer is in terms of philosophical analysis. To be sure your interests seem to be centered on philosophy. But, I found it very interesting nevertheless. They say that Zen is based on intuition and that this makes the difference between Zen and other Buddhist sects. Do you believe that?"

Hesitating I articulated slowly and deliberately, "Alongside the capacity for conceptual thought, there exists in man a capacity that Henri Bergson, the French philosopher, called intuition. Both capacities are the result of evolution, but the second is derived from instinct, the type of biological activity most elaborately manifested in the 'social' insects as described by E. O. Wilson, the Harvard biologist."

Once again, I reflected on my thoughts and then continued slowly, "Instinctive activity has consciousness slumbering within it, and evolution has awakened the consciousness in man. Intuition for Bergson is 'instinct that has become disinterested, self-conscious, and capable of reflecting upon its object and of enlarging it indefinitely. Since it is disinterested or free of bias, the capacity is detached from the demands of action and of social life. It is like a painter's power of seeing the world just as it is presented to him in pure perception. But instead of yielding an aesthetic experience, intuition yields knowledge. Hence, it is of profound importance for the philosopher."

"I understand what you are saying, Al, and am duly impressed with the extent of your knowledge." He hesitated for a minute and then seemed to stutter, "Let's keep in touch after you get home." He seemed tired after a long afternoon so I bade him goodbye with the promise to correspond with him. I was a little sad at leaving him but hoped on my return to the ryokan there might be a message from Taizan. There was none.

I then roamed around the neighborhood, greeting people and exploring the neighborhood stores. I went into one store that sold candles and incense and bought a supply for my shrine at home. My shrine at home has a zafu and a zabuton plus a table on which there is a Buddha, a censor, and a candlestick. I expected to display some of the presents that I received from my friends at Hosshinji.

Kabuki

On Friday, September 4, I decided to pursue my favorite entertainment in Japan-Kabuki. Kabuki was, during the Edo Period (1615–1868), the theatre of the people. It was to its time what television and the movies are to the present. It was thought of not as a classical theatre, but as the theatre that mirrored the fears, aspirations, and beliefs of the average man. Late in the nineteenth century, however, a new attitude arose. The people's subjective love for Kabuki slowly began to turn to objective appreciation. Awareness of Kabuki's uniqueness became prevalent, and, for the first time, this artless form took on the aura of a serious art form. Kabuki never recovered from the blow. In this regard it seems to parallel Shakespeare and Elizabethan theatre in the English-speaking world.

I have attended Kabuki performances at the Kabuki-za, the National Theatre and the Shinbashi Embu-jo Theatres in Tokyo over a thirty-year period. That day, however, I went to Osaka for Kabuki. I boarded the train at Kyoto station for Osaka to attend the Kabuki Theatre on Dotonbori Street. The play being presented was "Shisenryo Koban No Ume No Ha," with my favorite actor Danjuro Ichikawa. A literal translation of the title is "Leaves of (Japanese) Apricot on 4000 Gold Coins" but is usually simply referred to as "4000 Gold Coins" (*Shisenryo*).

It was a wonderful romp about a masterless samurai, Tojuro, who is infatuated with the courtesan Otatsu in the pleasure quarters, and Tomizo, once a lackey, who succeeded in robbing 4000 gold coins from Edo castle. But Otatsu has a lover by the name of Tokutaro. The stolen coins are hidden for the moment in Tojuro's home.

Tojuro turns into a moneylender while Tomizo leaves to see his mother in Kaga. Otatsu and Tokutaro plan to commit a lover's double suicide. The authorities catch Tojuro. Tomizo, too, is arrested in Kaga and transported to Edo in a wicker basket. The final scene is the prison in Denmacho in Edo. Tomizo gives testimony to clear suspicion that had befallen Tokutaro. Otatsu and Tokutaro become man and wife. Tojuro and Tomizo are sentenced to death after being paraded through the streets, a ritual before execution.

There are hundreds of plays like this one as well as classical dances and musical revues presented at Kabuki theatres. I usually buy a "libretto" but I believe some theatres provide a simultaneously translation headset. I really enjoyed spending the day there. I am always fascinated by the sets and costumes. It transported me out of my cares. I bought a box lunch of sushi and a glass of cold tea from the theatre vendor.

I returned to the ryokan very late and encountered the *Okusan* who invited me to eat *yakatori* (roast chicken) with her. I was grateful for the invitation. She had a small kitchen next to her living quarters. She served the roast chicken with boiled turnips (*kabu*) and boiled rice (*gohan*). It was delicious and even though our conversation was labored, it was delightful. I departed for my room after bowing and saying, "*Gochisosama deshita,*" which means, "Thank you for dinner." I then went to my room to prepare for the bath. One of the great luxuries in a ryokan is the bath where one can soak away all pain, care and concern.

The next day, I arose, had a breakfast of buns and tea and took the Keifuku Railway to the Sagano district. Sagano lies at the foot of the Western hills of Kyoto, an area justly acclaimed for its rural beauty. I explored the district on foot because there is something to see every few feet, whether a lush strip of green bamboo or a brightly painted wooden *torii* marking a shrine. After walking for a rather long period and visiting many temples on the way, I came upon a stone stairway that leads to *Adashino Nembutsu-ji,* a temple that is home to thousands of stone Buddhist images.

Long ago, the dead were buried throughout the foothills of Mt. Atago. The graves of the poor were marked with simple chunks of granite on which crude images of Buddha were carved by hand. About one hundred years ago, these gravestones were assembled and lined up here in the manner of attending a sermon by the Buddha.

Another five minutes beyond brought me to the unusual temple of *Otagi Nembutsu-ji.* On the hilly grounds of this temple I found a wonderful array of carved stone figures, which give lie to the myth of the Japanese as a humorless people. Some of the fanciful carvings clutch babies or children, and even one has a collie. All of the carvings wear the most satisfying facial expressions, in complete contrast to the more orthodox Buddhist figures found at other temples. This is Buddhism in its most approachable guise.

By this time it was becoming dusky, so I returned to the *Adashino Nembutsu-ji* for the evening celebration, which started at 6:00 P.M. More than one thousand candles are offered to these stone Buddhas for the repose of the spirits of one's ancestors. The Buddhist ceremony is called *Sento-kuyo* or the offering of one thousand candles to the Buddha.

The enormous number of candles throws their light on these stone Buddhas in the evening twilight. As time goes on, these stone Buddhas appear to be floating in the waves of candlelight. Sometimes these numerous lights look like flying butterflies in the darkness of the summer night. This is one of the Buddhist memorial services for one's ancestors held at *Nembutsu-ji* Temple. It reminded me very much of the O-Bon festival held all over Japan on August 15.

It was late when I returned to my ryokan but I stopped at the little store around the corner and picked up a "take out" shrimp tempura and a container of cooked rice in hoisin sauce. I brought these comestibles back to my room for a delightful in-house picnic. I was really hungry, not having eaten all day, since breakfast.

The next day, I planned to take the bullet train to Tokyo. In Tokyo, I would stay at Ryokan Chomeikan in the Bunkyo-ku district. This is a very convenient location since it is near the Hongo Sanchome station on the Marunouchi line.

After arriving in Tokyo, I made arrangements to attend Zen services the next morning at 5:30 A.M., at the *Engaku-ji* Temple in Kamakura. This meant that I would have to take the train at 4:30 A.M. in order to arrive there on time. But I was used to arising that early.

I arrived at the Kita-Kamakura station in a dark, misty morning. No one was about and so I had to orient myself to my surroundings. I had a small map of the area and a flashlight and so was able to make my way along a winding path to the Temple of Perfect Enlightenment *(Engaku-ji)*.

I went through the main gate *(san-mon),* which was rebuilt in 1783 after a terrible fire. I then entered the zazen hall *(kojirin)*, which dates from 1928, and sat in a vacant place. There were many monks and some laity already seated. I wore my *samu-e.* The atmosphere was relatively cool despite the warm weather. All was quiet and still to the point one could hear the occasional breathing of the people. After *zazen* there was a charming service, which was quite melodious and rather beautiful.

When *zazen* and service was finished, all were invited to partake of tea and little cakes at a respite in the next room. I noticed at this point that I was the only Westerner. In a moment, I was approached by a distinguished looking monk who asked in perfect Edwardian English with a minor twitching of his nose. "Where are you from?"

I answered, "I am from Hosshinji and I just arrived in Tokyo yesterday."

His eyebrows rose in arcs as he looked across his eyeglasses and said contemplatively, "Ah, yes Hosshinji. I know Harada Sekkei Roshi quite well. He often comes to officiate at my temple, Shoji-ji in Yokohama. Are you American?"

I answered, "Yes, I am."

He looked at me quizzically and said, "What is your name?"

I hesitated for a moment then answered, "My name is Albert Shansky but my friends call me Al and my Japanese friends call me Shansky-san."

He smiled broadly and made a *gassho* as he said, "My name is Kuzan. Isn't it remarkable that we have more than one name?"

I joined him in laughter as I made a *gassho*. Then he asked, "Would you like me to show you around the grounds?" I quickly agreed with another *gassho*.

He took me to the *Shariden*, which is a shrine where some of Buddha's bones are kept. In 1923, it was destroyed by the great earthquake but was repaired later in its present form. He then took me to see various mausoleums and several gravesites of distinguished people. All the time we were observing, he gave a running commentary about each item. We then visited the chief priest's quarters and the Roshi's quarters but did not enter. The grounds were large with many buildings and bell towers dotting the area. It was quite beautiful because of the many gardens and the unique Japanese architecture of the buildings.

When one looked at this, one could feel in imagination the ancient Kamakura temple atmosphere, which has been spoiled by the passing railway trains. Kuzan invited me to stay with him in Yokohama the next time I came to Japan. I thanked him for his kindness and exchanged addresses with him. I would like to see Shoji-ji temple. Perhaps this will happen one day.

Home

On Sunday, September 9, I flew home from Narita Airport. My wife met me at JFK Airport. It was a very joyous moment with many lingering hugs and an occasional kiss. I had a certain reserve, which prevented me from being too demonstrative even though I was naturally given to displaying my

feelings. It was obvious we were both happy to see each other. We walked
hand in hand to the car with occasional glances bringing forth mirth and
laughter. The ride home was uneventful—a few generalized questions—
but nothing profound, such as, how are the children? Is there anything new?

"What will you do now?" she asked.

I pondered for a moment and then answered forcefully, "I must buy
the shoes I promised for Piyadassi and Sumano."

"I don't understand," she said. "What do you mean?"

"Oh, it's nothing important. I promised two monks in the monastery
that I would buy shoes for them when I got home. But I can do this tomorrow."

As she was driving, she glanced to her right and asked in a compelling voice, "I mean, what do you intend doing with your life now?"

I thought about it a moment then said matter-of-factly, "I don't know.
I probably will continue with the old routine, school and work as usual."

After we arrived at home, I decided to take a hot bath. I soaked for
almost a half-hour, thinking sporadically about my past and future life,
until I was aware that the water became cold. I weighed myself after rubbing down with a towel and discovered that I had lost ten pounds. I then
dressed and sat down to a hot bowl of mushroom-barley soup with some
crusty bread. Yes, indeed, it was back to the "old routine."

I had difficulty adjusting to the time-zone difference. I went to bed
early but I slept fitfully, waking up at odd hours until finally I went to my
shrine early the next morning and sat *zazen* for forty minutes. After *zazen*,
I added some of the gifts I received in Hosshinji to my shrine. I began to
wonder about Taizan. Would I ever hear from him?

After breakfast and a long chat with my wife over many cups of tea,
I decided to go to Caldor's Department store to buy the shoes for Piyadassi
and Sumano. My wife said, "I see you are drinking tea now. Have you
given up coffee?"

"No," I answered, "I just got so used to tea that I seem to prefer it.
Doiku, a monk in Hosshinji, told me the one thing he missed most was
a good cup of American coffee."

When I arrived at Caldor's, I sought out a clerk in the shoe department. "I have two templates of my friend's feet. Would you help me select work boots for them?" I said as I held the paper templates aloft.

"Of course," he answered as he began measuring the shoe size with a foot caliper. Then, he brought me two pair of so-called "eight inch" work boots. I told him to stuff each boot with two pairs of heavy-duty cotton socks. I then paid for the items.

After procuring a cardboard carton, I headed for the Post Office. The postal clerk helped me tie the box, address it and apply the customs declaration. "How much will it cost to deliver this package to Japan?" I asked. He answered without hesitation, "By surface mail is the cheapest way. It will take about six weeks and will cost fifteen dollars." I paid him and went back home. I knew, with satisfaction, that my obligation was fulfilled.

I decided to review my future plans and see what order of priorities I had to establish. About sixteen years previously (at the age of fifty-three) I returned to college as a part-time, continuing education student. I attended Fairfield University where I have taken a total of fifty courses to date; half in philosophy and half in art history. This then was my immediate focus — to return to school and immerse myself in philosophy.

Secondly, I must pursue the location of a monastery or a temple where I can practice Zen. The only monasteries I was aware of within driving distance was Dai Bosatsu, a Rinzai Zen monastery in Livingston Manor, New York, Chuang Yen, a Chinese, Pure Land monastery in Carmel, New York, and the Zen Mountain Monastery in Mt. Tremper, New York. Both of the latter two had Zen Activity on Sunday mornings.

There are no Buddhist temples, much less Zen temples, anywhere in my immediate vicinity. I knew of some in New York City and would probably have to investigate those. I also was aware that I must visit my friend Mu Soeng at the Barre Center for Buddhist Studies in Barre, Massachusetts. He is a Korean Zen monk who teaches Buddhist concepts at the Barre Center and has been a reliable and comforting resource for me.

School started in a week and I decided to register for "Epistemology" with Professor James Long and "Heidegger" with Professor Dennis Keenan.

Professor Long has been a cogent friend over the years. I had him for six courses in some version of medieval philosophy and always enjoyed his humor and wisdom. Professor Keenan was a young, new teacher at Fairfield University. I was looking forward to these classes like a young kid. I always have unusual anticipation when it comes to school despite the fact that I spent most of my life going to school.

As I expected, life dovetailed. I became integrated into family life again and had the usual time with my friends as if I was never gone. Somehow, I found all this to be affected with melancholia. Am I different? Better yet, am I not at least a hybrid of my former self? I certainly felt different. I could no longer partake in small talk. I found my interest in everyday matters waning. I did notice, however, that I was more patient and considerate of others and I was not as quick to anger as before. But I attributed this to a residue of my recent stint at Hosshinji and wondered how long it would last. I found solace in zazen and even sat sometimes in the evening before bed as well as morning.

I decide to send a letter to Yerney with a large supply of vitamins in a jiffy bag. I knew he would appreciate them because he often remarked about the non-nutritive value of the scanty meals in the monastery. This, of course, was nonsense but one cannot reason with a fixed mind. I also asked him for some photographs for an album I was developing but did not hold out any hope of an affirmative response.

I called Mu Soeng at the Barre Center and made an appointment to visit him over the next weekend. Indeed, I even decided to sit in the course he was giving at that time. I arrived at Barre on Saturday morning about 9:00 A.M. I had to get up at 5:00 A.M. to sit zazen, shower, and dress and gulp down a small breakfast before the 2½ hour drive to Barre. When I arrived Mu Soeng was waiting for me, but there was something different about him. For one thing, he was not wearing his robes and for another thing — his hair was growing back on previously shaven head. We hugged like lost brothers. I exclaimed, "Sunim, what happened to you?"

He laughed and responded, "Well, I decided to disrobe. After eleven years as a practicing monk I am leaving the Kwan Um order to pursue my present endeavor as a teacher and Director of the Barre Center for Buddhist Studies with extra vigor. So you should not call me Sunim anymore. As you know Sunim is a Korean honorific similar to 'reverend.' How about you, Al? I see you are dressed in a samu-e."

I thought for a moment and then with surprise in my voice I exclaimed, "Well for the last three months I continued my practice in Soto Zen at the Hosshinji Monastery in Japan. I just returned home last week."

He laughed, shook my hand and clapped my back. "I am so glad for you, Al. I wish you much luck."

I presented him with a gray colored sweater as a gift. He thanked me profusely and said, "Come, I'll show you to your room. I prepared bedding and a towel for you. I'll have to leave you now to prepare for my course. Let us have breakfast tomorrow morning at 8:00 A.M. in my quarters. By the way you remember Kathy, don't you?"

I nodded my head and said, "Of course, I remember her. How could anyone forget those jewel-like eyes?" He looked at me and said with a somber voice, "We are now living together."

I slapped him on the back and said, "I'll see you tomorrow morning. Give Kathy my best regards." I thanked him and went about making myself comfortable. I have used this same room several times previously and feel very much at home here. I brought along my headset with a bunch of tapes and expected to use it this evening.

The main building is called the "farmhouse" because it was there when the property was a farm. It has since been optimized and renovated to become a useful and handsome building. I left the "farmhouse" and strolled around the beautiful grounds. There were many flowering shrubs surrounding the "farmhouse" building, which reminded me of Japan.

I attended Mu Soeng's class, which I found interesting and stimulating. Mu Soeng is a born teacher. After the first half of his class, I joined the others at a superb vegetarian lunch. Since it was open-seating, I sat next to a young fellow who immediately extended his hand and inquired, "Are you a monk?" I realized that wearing my samu-e could have produced this question so I immediately responded, "I am not a monk but I wear this costume at Buddhist events. My name is Al and I am glad to meet you."

He asked again, while chewing a mouthful of coleslaw, "What is a Zen monk? I am just curious. I don't mean to pry. By the way, my name is Howard. I am a medical doctor and I am presently pursuing studies in psychiatry."

He was much energized as he extended his hand. I was taken somewhat aback since this was the first time I ever met a physician who showed interest in Buddhism. "A Zen monk is someone who is ordained in the Soto Zen tradition after accepting the precepts. It is very similar to a Deacon in the Christian church."

I reached around my neck and removed my *rakusu* and showed it to Howard with a discretionary comment, "In the Soto Zen tradition all lay monks and fully ordained monks as well as *sensei* (teachers) and Roshi (Zen masters) wear a *rakusu* at Buddhist services and functions. The *rakusu* is symbolic of the tattered robe worn by the Buddha. I wear this one as a sign of respect and commitment to the Dharma."

We continued talking in a discursive way but, inevitably, his interest in Zen brought him back to questioning me in much detail. I was becoming tired of his questioning and excused myself.

After lunch, I attended the second half of Mu Soeng's class and lost sight of Howard who was sitting in the rear. The class was very engaging with a question-and-answer period but I really enjoyed watching Mu Soeng in action. At the end of the class there was a loud, effusive praise for Mu Soeng expressed by the audience.

The class finished in mid-afternoon and I remained sitting on my zafu to allow fatigue to dissipate. I then spent some time exploring the shelves of the library. There were books on every conceivable subject in Buddhism. This library is a real treasure trove and I became convinced that I would return to do research on subjects that I had in mind.

The next morning I went to visit Mu Soeng and Kathy for breakfast. They had an apartment in the section which was an addition made to the sleeping quarters. Kathy was a very beautiful woman with golden hair and green eyes which sparkled like two emeralds. We gave each other a buss and I sat down to a huge breakfast of hash brown potatoes and eggs. Mu Soeng and I told each other about our past experiences in a very lively conversation. I eventually took my leave with a promise to keep in touch with him. Before going, I gave him a check for fifty dollars as a contribution to the Barre Center.

For the next few weeks, I spent time in getting used to my routine of school and work. Nothing eventful happened until I received a letter from Hosshinji.

Misfortune Needs No Witness to Sting

On October 10, I received a devastating letter from Yerney, which I shall reproduce here with all its warts.

8-10-94

Dear All!

Thank you for your letter. And a huge vitamins. It will last for all witer [*sic*], for our room. I am glad you are fine. Here we just finished Sesshin, which I felt was very strong. Today, after one hour Hanaoka-san will become monk. His new name will be Taiki (big ability). Now He is preparing in our room.

And now I must tell you very sad news. Maybe you already know it. In Vancouver, at the night after finishing the Buddhist congres [*sic*], in temple-hotel room, Sumano-san quietly passed away. On the last day, he was very happy, taking the pictures and speaking with friends. On the evening on 27th of Sept., he went to sleep, in the same room with Piyadasi and Amerikan monk Taizan. In the morning he usually waked up the other two, but not that morning. Piyadasi touched his hand and neck — cold. After — doctors, electric shocks and massage — too late. They said — natural reasons. But I think he has weak heart. After Taizan helped very much about all the police-questioning, cremation and so on. Piyadashi send fax to Hosshinji and we were very surprised. He come back May 5th, bringing also one part ashes. Other part goes to Ladak. So, my friend, life is very unexpected. So we must train hard in the aim to know ourselves. Sumano-san was so young and cheerful.

You are asking for some pictures. I will try to find some. You know, it is not easy to picture monks. They don't like it very much. But I will try. I stopped developing my film, because I become very poor. To get another 90-days visa (until Christmas), I had to go to Korea again. I stayed there 3 weeks, in the international Zen Center, very lucky, meeting every day famous Zen master Seung Sahn and having also dokusan with him. After I buyed some ginseng for Roshi and father and I became poor. You were right about that chocolades, but they are soo sweet. Anyway, it is just OK, like it is. I will stay here till middle of December, attending another two sesshins and many takuhatsu. That's great, and that is enough. Now I must to stop, ceremony for Hanaoka is just about to happen...

It was nice ceremony, Taiki-san appeared to be determined firmly. Tomorrow is takuhatsu...

Dear All, that's for today, please, take care of yourself, cold mornings and evenings are coming.

Sincerely,

Yerney

P.S. Excuse me for my written language — many mistakes.

Then a few days later I received a formal notice from Hosshinji, which I shall reproduce here.

IN MEMORIAM

On Sept. 29, 1994, we received the very sad news of the sudden and completely unexpected death of Lobsang Yontan Sumano. Together with his friend and colleague Thupten Rinchen Piyadassi, he was in Vancouver, Canada attending a Buddhist conference at the time of his death.

Beloved by everyone in our community, we will certainly miss his warm friendliness, gentle manner, ever willingness to help, and sincere Way-seeking mind.

Part of his ashes will be interred at Hosshinji.

On reading the letter from Yerney I was stunned. My first reaction was that it has been a dreadful mistake or an awful omission of the facts. Then as it sunk in, I wanted to beat the letter with my fists, kick it, and shout at the top of my lungs — This cannot be true! No! No!

How could it have possibly happened? Sumano was a child, an

innocent. He wanted nothing more than to learn Zen and maybe English. I thought of the shoes I just sent him. No one can possibly fill his shoes. What a silly thought. I kept on thinking that this disaster is a nightmare that will go away. I would wake up and it would be gone. That it was not true and somehow would be corrected.

In the end, I decided to say *Kaddish* for Sumano. In the great Judaic tradition this is the way of confronting God. To the Jews of the world, *Kaddish* has a highly emotional connotation, for it is the prayer chanted for the dead, at the graveside, on memorial occasions and, in fact, at all synagogue services. Yet strangely enough, there is not a single mention of death in the entire prayer. On the contrary, it uses the word *chaye* or *chayim* (life) three times. The *Kaddish* is a compilation of paeans in praise of God, and, as such, it has basic functions in the liturgy that have nothing to do with mourning.

Now that my handkerchief is washed clean by weeping, I am wondering if death is an illusion.

AMEN

PART 2

Search for a Buddhist Temple

Mexico City

As I entered the elevator, I noticed an elderly gentleman following me. He was average height, white-haired with his sparse hair maneuvered to cover his pink pate. He wore a pencil-striped, three-piece suit, which seemed out of place in the warm climate. He wore frameless glasses and stared at me with an uncomfortable intensity. Suddenly, he said, "Why are you dressed like that?" On hearing these words I immediately understood his attitude. I was wearing my Buddhist robes, having just come from a meeting of Buddhist monks in the auditorium below.

"I am a Zen Buddhist and I am wearing my robes," I replied. It should have been obvious to anyone staying in the Hyatt hotel that a convention of Buddhists was taking place.

"How many Buddhists are there in the world?" he inquired.

"I am not sure," I responded, "but I believe there are about four hundred million."

"Wow, that's more than Episcopalians," he said with a loud voice. The elevator stopped at my floor and I alighted with a wave of my hand. It was October 24, 1994 and I was attending the 11th Congress of the International Association of Buddhist Studies in Mexico City.

When I arrived at my room, I began to disrobe and put on civilian mufti. It was a long day, but I really enjoyed listening to Brian Victoria. His paper was titled, "The Buddhist Role in Japan's 'High Treason Incident' of 1910: Buddhist Heretics or Martyrs?" Also he told of his demonstrations against the War in Vietnam on the streets of Tokyo and his subsequent incarceration in a Japanese prison, which was fascinating, to say the least. At the time he was a practicing Buddhist priest with a dharma name — Daizan. He demonstrated in front of the American embassy in Tokyo by carrying a sign and chanting slogans. The Japanese police at the behest of the American officials literally dragged him off to jail despite the fact that he was a Buddhist priest who behaved nonviolently by attempting to deliver a letter to the American ambassador protesting the massacre at My Lai. (People do not realize that the Buddha taught nonviolence, not pacifism.) His treatment in jail was unkind but he was released after a few days. He has written several articles about his incarceration and today gave a lecture on his experiences. At the time he was a professor of Japanese language in the department of Asian languages and literature at the University of Auckland in New Zealand.

That evening we planned to go together to attend a performance of the Ballet Folklorico at the Palace of Fine Arts. I have seen them perform during past visits to Mexico City. I was looking forward to this performance because I enjoy Mexican folk dancing and Mariachi music. Brian speaks fluent Spanish and so we should have no trouble in arranging for our seats, which were generously being provided by the International Association of Buddhist Studies.

It was a warm night and after a small supper we had a leisurely walk to the palace. When looking at the horizon I could see the volcanoes and church towers, which rose above the low roofs like the old temples in the time of the many gods.

Brian told me he was born in Arizona of an American mother and a British father. He was educated in Tucson, Arizona, where he learned to speak Spanish, having mostly Mexican classmates and friends. He and his family are Catholic recusants. He studied Japanese and Asian culture at The University of California at Berkeley. After college Brian decide to study Buddhism in Japan. It was relatively easy for Brian to dovetail into Japanese society since he had a fluent command of the language. He lived in a monastery for many years until becoming an ordained monk. He continued his studies until reaching the high status of priesthood. After his experience in jail, he continued his objections to the War in Vietnam by what is known as "engaged Buddhism." He accomplished this through writing articles to prominent Americans about the immoral and improper status of the American presence in Vietnam. After the end of the Vietnam War, Brian left the monastery to seek work elsewhere. He finally accepted the teaching position in New Zealand.

The ballet dancers were marvelous, with much verve and energy. The company performed with characteristic passion and exuberance. The rhythm and sound were of typical Spanish flavor. There was a fiery yet tender piece by Amalia Hernandez and another by Pedro Ruiz based on a tragic nineteenth-century love story and set to music by classic Mexican composers. Of course, repertory favorites, such as the ribbon dance, highlighted the program. In addition, they had Maria Rodriguez, who sang in the Norteno Tejano style reminiscent of Chicana vocalists. She is the queen of Mexican country music, with tears in the throat and a group of mariachis cooing. I really enjoyed myself. Brian and I walked back to the Hyatt through the dark streets, which gave one a foreboding feeling. When we arrived at the hotel, we bumped into other participants who shared their small talk with us. These participants came from all over the world and I found it particularly strange how all communicated in English. It was getting late so I left Brian and the others in the lounge and went off to bed.

The next morning, I went to a breakfast of hot peanut butter tacos and tea at a small restaurant near the hotel. While walking I encountered the unmistakable Mexico City morning smell of hot oatmeal, orange peel, fresh-baked *bolilio* bread, and the ripe tang of sewer foulness. It was the second day of the conference and I was anxious to participate in the day's program. I was particularly interested in the talk which will be given by Prof. Joseph Wilson of the University of North Carolina. He is an expert in Buddhist — Sanskrit language and is giving a paper on *Yogacara* — the mind-only philosophy. Also, there will be another talk scheduled to be given by a Francis William Paar of the New York Public Library which seemed promising.

I managed to take a short walk around the outside of the hotel before returning to the conference area. The weather was rather cool but refreshing. As I walked I noticed evidence of the devastating earthquake which happened ten years before in 1985. There were filled-in cracks in the streets and some buildings were still shored up with sandbags and braced with timbers. Some of the sidewalks were buckled and crooked. Huge trucks rumbled and belched down the haphazardly cobbled street, contributing to the din. I remembered when the earthquake occurred. It made worldwide news, with much death and destruction.

Returning to the conference center, I decided to sit in on the talk given by Mr. Paar. His paper was entitled, "Buddhist Practice as a Theme in a Book on Neurophenomenology." It was a review of a book, *Brain, Symbol & Experience: Toward a Neurophenomenology of Human Consciousness,* by three authors, Charles D. Laughlin, John McManus, and Eugene G. d'Aquili, published in New York in 1992. Apparently the book is difficult to read and Mr. Paar's explanation and analysis of its contents was very much worthwhile for those who decided to read the book.

After the talk, which I enjoyed very much, I approached Mr. Paar with an outstretched hand. "Hi, my name is Al Shansky," I said as I grabbed his hand. "I enjoyed your paper very much. Is the book you reviewed available in the New York Public Library?" He looked at me quizzically as I felt his hand, which was strong yet gentle.

"Yes, the book is available in the Oriental Division on the second floor, where I work. Are you from New York?" he inquired.

"Well, I was born in New York, but I now live in Connecticut. I go into the City quite frequently," I rejoindered.

"That's good, come and visit me at the Library," he said. We shook hands again and then went our separate ways.

I attended the paper given by Joseph Wilson but I was unsure where Francis Paar ended up. The paper by Joseph Wilson, which was on

Yogacara, turned out to be pedantic and rather boring. According to the central notion of the *Yogacara*, everything experienceable is "mind only"; things exist only as processes of knowing, not as "objects"; outside the knowing process they have no reality. The "external world" is thus "purely mind." This could have been a very interesting paper but Joseph Wilson was not able to get above the didactic approach of a teacher.

There is a dualism between mind and brain. Are minds exempt from the laws of physical nature? The mind's powers in terms of the brain's physical powers are readily evident. We do not think with our brains even though we cannot think without them. Brains are used for controlling the bodies they are perched on. Brains are nothing more than complicated organs which react to a physical change. This is the nature of healing by the mind.

I have always felt that one of the greatest gifts we have is the healing mind. The healing mind can heal one both spiritually and physically. It has been documented throughout the ages that the great leaders, philosophers, artists and inventors created their greatest accomplishments based on their belief in themselves. If you consider the implication of this statement, you will find it monumental, because it implies that we all have the same potential. All minds are equally great — past, present and future. There is no difference. "Know thyself," therefore, is not only a Socratic imperative, but also might be considered a clinical necessity.

The mind's potential is limitless, and becomes even more so when we connect to the spiritual self. Epicurus, the Greek philosopher who lived about 300 B.C.E., believed that people could be happy only if they freed themselves from material thoughts. The healing mind cannot be confined to the elements of the beliefs of the time. The healing mind's basic requirements are that you strive to be pure of mind, to connect your mind with the spirit that takes you beyond the physical, and states, in the words of Lev Shestov, the Russian philosopher, that all things are possible. Then the healing mind can heal. You are what you believe you are.

At lunch time, I decided to buy a corn tortilla and a soda from a local store and eat on a park bench near the hotel. I was startled to find that Francis Paar was of the same mind. I approached him with a hearty greeting and sat next to him on the park bench. He told me that being a vegan he had to be careful where and what he ate. As we sat and munched our food we became more familiar with each other. I found out that he lived in Rochelle Park, New Jersey and only worked twenty hours a week in the New York Public Library, having retired at age 63 in 1978, one year after his wife died of cancer.

He was a 1933 graduate and a 1935 postgraduate student of the University of Lausanne in Switzerland where he was an Asian language major. He spoke Chinese and Japanese somewhat and could manage fairly well in Tibetan and other Asian languages. He also spoke French and German fluently, having been schooled in Switzerland. He was a veteran of the Second World War, as I was, but served in the Military Intelligence Corps. At age 79 (ten years older than me) he was still active at work and with his writings. I was quite impressed with his many activities. He asked of me, "What are you doing this evening?"

I responded, with a shrug of my shoulders, "Nothing in particular. I went to the Ballet Folklorico last night."

He looked at me with a broad smile saying, "That's great, would you like to join me tonight in a small Zen service?"

"Did you say Zen service?" I asked enigmatically. "Where, here in Mexico City?"

"Of course," he responded. "I got the name from one of the conference principals, Victoria Iturbe. It will take place at the Centro Zen de la Ciudad de Mexico on Monte Libarro 1230 Tomas. A person named Luli Albarran will host us there." I was speechless and dumbfounded.

"What a great idea," I explained to Bill. (By this time we were calling each other by our first names.) I told him that I was a Zen Buddhist and was quite familiar with Zen procedure. The thought of attending Zen services in Spanish was very intriguing to me.

I decided to take a short walk before washing up and changing my clothes. I walked along a street to the plaza a short distance ahead. It was the hour everyone in Mexico paraded out into the streets, just as dark comes down and the night air is damp and sticky with the smell of supper frying. Men, women, children, the plaza is bubbling over with people, roiling with the scents of roasted corn, raw sewage, flowers, rotten fruit, popcorn, gasoline, and roasted meat. Streetlights stutter on just as I observe a vendor sprinkling lime juice and chili powder over a huge pork rind. In the gutter there was the bone of a mango with wisps of golden hair and a half eaten corncob. Satellites of green iridescent houseflies swarmed everywhere. It all overwhelmed me and I headed back to the hotel.

After a long walk and a day of listening to papers, I was glad to reach my room for a shower and rest. I dressed in my Buddhist robes and met Bill in the hotel lobby. He exclaimed, "You look great, very authentic. I am proud to be with you."

We took a taxicab to the Zen Center and when we arrived there we were greeted by Luli Albarran. She showed us to our sitting places. These places consisted of the usual *Zafu* and *Zabuton* in a plain, undecorated room. We all faced a seated Buddha, in front of who was a small table, on which was a bowl of oranges and a vase with a single flower. To the right of the Buddha sat a leader dressed in robes. The service began with a chanting sutra, which I found I could follow even though I did not understand the language. At the end of services there was a forty-minute period of silent meditation, which ended with a bell ringing. At the conclusion we were all invited to partake of tea and cakes in the next room. This enabled us to converse with the participants. I recognized some people from the conference and we all greeted each other with gestures of familiarity. I went over to the leader, who is called a *sensei*, and introduced myself. We approached each other with a *gassho* and he spoke to me in broken English.

"Welcome to our center," he said. "Please let me know if there is anything I can do for you." As he started to walk away he suddenly turned around and said, "Please stay for the Tea Ceremony which one of your members graciously offered to demonstrate."

Apparently a Buddhist female monk, unknown to me, would be performing *Cha-no-yu*, commonly called the Tea Ceremony. We all went into the next room which was set up with the Tea utensils on a mat in front of which was seated the host, a female monk. She was wearing gray robes so I surmised she was a Korean Zen monk. On the left and in front of her sat two more female monks acting as the guests, one wearing the gray robes of Korean Zen and the other wearing the black robes of Japanese Zen. All three were sitting in the *seiza* position on their knees. Most of the observers stood around haphazardly watching the demonstration, although some sat on their haunches.

Chado is the ceremony for serving a bowl of tea — but it is a carefully prepared bowl, made with the delicate essence of traditional Japanese hospitality. As we watched we could see the host curiously examine the shape and beauty of the bowl by lifting it gently and turning it around in her palms. She carefully spooned out the green tea powder with a bamboo ladle into the bowl; hot water was then added slowly from a spouted iron kettle. A special wisk was then used in a rapid, circular motion to froth the tea. The bowl of tea was then served to the guest, the monk in black robes, by the host. The front of the bowl is always turned toward the guest, to show the respect that the host has for her. After picking up the bowl, the guest turns the bowl, a quarter circle, before sipping the tea. This act symbolically conveys to the host the guest's feeling of humility for the honor. Before returning the bowl, the guest turns the front of the bowl toward the host, to express both her gratitude and respect. Wordlessly, these symbolic nuances reinforce the mutual understanding between the host and the guest, and intensify their mutual respect and gratitude. The enhancement of mutuality can be considered as the spirit and essence of the tea ceremony. At the conclusion of the tea ceremony people started leaving. Bill and I, together with two other participants, took a cab back to the hotel. We all bade each other good night.

After completing four days at the Buddhist Conference in Mexico City, I had to leave for a stopover in Dallas, Texas, to take care of some consulting business. I said goodbye to Bill Paar with the promise to get together for lunch in New York City. I also bade farewell to Brian Victoria, who told me that he will be going to a celebration of the 50th anniversary of the end of World War II, which is taking place somewhere in Japan the following year. I told him, with enthusiasm, that I would be interested in going too and to let me know the details. We exchanged addresses but I must tell you, sadly, that I never heard from him again despite writing him several letters. I was dismayed for a long time at this unexplained loss.

Finally, I took the subway to the airport and headed for Dallas, Texas. I decided to visit the Dallas Museum of Fine Arts and the Meyerson Symphony Center. I went to the Dallas Museum on Saturday and was quite impressed with the massive sculptures on the ground floor. Indeed, the Richard Serra iron sculpture on the outside plaza was formidable. It consisted of two large shells about 20 feet high and 25 feet long of a curvilinear design, which enabled them to stand upright with incredible stability. They were covered with the usual patina of rust. Walking through the two shells gave one the feeling of entering a cave.

On Sunday, I went to a performance of the Dallas Symphony Orchestra at the Meyerson Symphony Center, a building designed by the architect, I. M. Pei, on Flora Street. The program included Korngold's Violin Concerto, featuring the violinist Ulrike-Anima Mathe and the conductor Andrew Litton. I so thoroughly enjoyed this performance that I bought a CD of the concert so that I could relive that day in the future.

I was very happy and returned home with great satisfaction. After a short respite, I decided to contact Bill Paar. We arranged to meet at Bali Burma Restaurant for lunch. Bill made all the arrangements because the restaurant needed advance notice to prepare their specialty, Rijsttafel, which is pronounced "rice stafel." The restaurant is located on Ninth Avenue and 45th Street in New York City, and is known for its Burmese — Indonesian cuisine. Bill ordered a vegetarian Rijsttafel, which consisted of thirteen exotic dishes plus dessert and tea. The name "Rijsttafel" is a Dutch word which comes from the colonial time that the Dutch occupied parts of Indonesia. The restaurant is owned by a Sino-Burmese and Indonesian, both friends of Bill Paar.

During the meal both Bill and I were busy partaking of the succulent dishes without much talking. After the meal, we were left alone to talk accompanied by endless pots of tea. For one thing, he told me he had a Chinese name, *Shuang Fa-wei*. I am not sure who gave it to him but he did tell me he was a member of the Buddhist Association of the United States (BAUS) and often went to their Temple of Enlightenment on Albany Crescent in the Bronx, New York and also their monastery, *Chuang Yen* in Carmel, New York. It was here that he befriended Dr. Chia Theng Shen, the chairman of the International Association of World Religions and the Wu Joo Library. I believe that Dr. Shen gave him his Chinese name.

Bill is such a multi-talented individual that I was not surprised to learn that he was intensively involved in music. He played a piano and an organ which he had in his house. He also sang in a choral group and maintained a large library of music scores for piano and voice. We made up to attend the Bach Festival at Lehigh University in Bethlehem, Pennsylvania, next May 19, 1996.

Then, in September, he expected to attend a reunion of the Military Intelligence Service which would take place in Seattle. He also planned a post reunion trip on an Inside Passage Cruise on the MS Statendam to Vancouver, Ketchikan, Juneau, Glacier Bay and Sitka.

He confided in me that he was conceived on board a yacht on the Elbe River near Hamburg, Germany, and shortly thereafter his parents moved to the States where he was born, in 1915, in the midst of Yavapai Apache territory in Arizona. He still owns the land and the primitive house in which he was born in Arizona. In all the time he spoke I could see him exhibiting the best combination of exhilaration and humility.

The lunch took all of the afternoon; but before parting we agreed that I would come into the City on April 26, 1995, to attend a lecture, through an interpreter, given by Kenzoburo Oe, the winner of the 1994 Nobel Prize for literature. This was scheduled to take place at the Japan Society in New York City. Bill is a member of the Japan Society and had two tickets to this event.

Sometime after arriving home, I made arrangements to visit Bill at the Oriental Division in Room 222 of the New York Public Library. We decided to lunch at the Star of India Restaurant on West 44th Street right

off Fifth Avenue in New York City and thence to the lecture. I was looking forward to that day with baited breath.

We ate and conversed for about three hours, telling each other about
significant moments in our lives. I found out that he had a daughter named
Andrea who lived in Brooklyn, but worked in Manhattan. After lunch we
walked over to the Japan Society for the lecture by Kenzoburo Oe.

The interpreter of Kenzoburo's speech was John Nathan, a translator of some of his books. He related incidents of difficulties in meaning
during the translation of some of the Japanese *Kanji* characters. This was
a very interesting aspect of books which are written in foreign languages.
Kenzoburo spoke about his son Hirari Oe who, despite being mentally
challenged was able to compose a fairly large quantity of classical music.
I have since purchased one of his CDs of Japanese pop or folk music to
which I listen quite frequently.

At the conclusion of the lecture, Bill noticed some people he knew.
In particular, he wanted to introduce me to Donald Keene, the famous
writer of Japanese literature and language at Columbia University. We
approached him and found him to be somewhat reticent and shy. We shook
hands and exchanged pleasantries but he was anxious to depart. We then
left with the ambling crowd piling into the street and scurrying off in
different directions. I made my way to Grand Central Station after saying
goodbye to Bill on Lexington Avenue.

The Search for a Buddhist Temple

In the late spring of 1995, I was completing a course at Fairfield University called "Bertrand Russell" with Dr. Brooks Colburn. By this time
I had taken about 44 courses, almost half in philosophy and the remainder in Art History. I would go on until the fall of 1999 to take a total of
57 courses over a twenty-year period at Fairfield University before I
finished.

In the summer of 1995 I agreed to volunteer and teach a one-day course in Buddhism and Zen at the Norwalk Community College. This was designed for a class of "Lifetime Learners" and so contained a strange mixture of seniors and adult education students. It developed into a very large class of more than forty participants. The question-and-answer period was very lively and lasted for almost an additional hour. I was surprised to find that some people were very interested in Eastern philosophy and religion. To those people I recommended books and articles for additional reading.

In the meantime, I kept searching for a local Buddhist temple or a monastery where I could practice within a *Sangha* (a Buddhist community). Unfortunately, there was nothing convenient to my home. I could, of course, travel to New York City but this seemed an excessive burden to me on a continuous basis. I hungered to become a member of a Zen temple. To be sure, I did visit the Barre Center for Buddhist Studies which was affiliated with the Insight Meditation Center, on the same property, but they were not Zen. They were a Theravadin sect, called *Vipassana* which is Hinayana, whereas Zen is Mahayana. Besides they were too far away even though I enjoyed visiting my friend Mu Soeng on occasion. My out-of-town business travels brought me to cities where I was able to practice on an occasional basis. I visited the Minnesota Zen Meditation Center in Minneapolis, once again, after returning from the Hosshinji Monastery in Japan. In addition, I had the opportunity to visit the Rochester Zen Center made famous by Philip Kapleau when he was the Roshi. On a trip to California, I visited two separate places, Mt. Baldy Zen Center, made distinctive by the presence of Leonard Cohen, the poet and songwriter, as well as the Kannon Do in Mountain View, California.

Closer to home, I practiced at the Zen Community of New York in Yonkers, New York, the Zen Mountain Monastery in Mt. Tremper, New York, and even a Tibetan Monastery in Wappinger Falls, New York, called Kagyu Thubten Choling. My experience in the Tibetan Temple was very interesting.

I arrived the night before services and arranged for my place in the sleeping quarter. The sleeping quarter was a room behind the dining area.

It was crowded with very primitive, wooden bunk beds. These bunk beds were nothing more than wooden platforms on which a thin mattress was laid. I was told to bring a sleeping bag as part of my bedding needs. There was a separate room for women. After a short walk around the property to explore the facilities, I found the grounds to be very beautiful, with natural plantings everywhere. In the early evening light it was even more beautiful. I enjoy my habit of crepuscular jaunting when all appearances titillate the imagination. I returned to the sleeping quarter and prepared for bed. There were no lights in the sleeping quarter except for a small ceiling night light so I had to accomplish all preparation for bed by flashlight. After getting into my sleeping bag, I attempted to read my book by flashlight. I was reading *Pale Fire* by Vladimir Nabokov. It was very difficult not only because of my circumstances but also because the text was labored reading. The story is composed in a narrative poem of rhyming verse. After a while, my eyelids grew heavy and I soon fell asleep, which was just as well since we had to wake up at 5:00 A.M. the next morning.

However, I got up at 4:00 A.M.before anyone else in order to attend to my toilet and take a shower. There was only one toilet and shower for each gender which is something I could never understand in these domestic monasteries that cater to large numbers of people.

At 5:00 A.M., we all gathered in the dining room and proceeded to eat an American breakfast. The foods were displayed on a sideboard in buffet style and noticeably absent were eggs and breakfast meats. I took my usual corn flakes with milk and a banana, accompanied by a teabag in a cup of hot water. The tables were free seating and this gave an opportunity to speak with other participants.

As I looked around the breakfast table, I noticed most people appeared in a disheveled manner. Some were yawning. All looked confused and sleepy. As the sun was beginning to rise, I knew it would be a beautiful day starting with a lilac morning mist. It seemed the short spring was racing from peach blossoms to wild cherries. As I gazed out of the window, I could see that our building was amid a grayish-green hale of chestnut trees. Suddenly, a voice shook me out of my reverie.

"Good morning, my name is Alice," said the woman sitting next to me who extended her hand in a friendly gesture. As I came out of my languid state, I hastily rose and grabbed her hand, responding with a forthright greeting, "Good morning, I must have been daydreaming. My name is Al."

"Are you a Buddhist?" she inquired.

"Yes," I replied, "I belong to the Soto Zen sect."

"Well, what are you doing here then?" she quickly added.

In a somewhat embarrassed way I responded, "I feel like the Last Samurai who, without a master, is condemned to roam in search of a new master." I continued, "I am on such a quest so I have been exploring various Buddhist venues to fill the vacuum I feel since leaving the monastery in Japan."

"I noticed you were wearing different clothes. Are they Buddhist garments?" she inquired in wonderment.

"Well," I said, "These garments are the work clothes worn by Buddhist monks in a monastery; they are called *samu-e.*"

I then looked at her straight in the eye and asked, "Why are you here?"

She said, with a slight tilt to her head and without hesitation, "I am looking for spirituality."

I was struck mute. As if with ague, I chillingly asked, "Do you expect to find it here?"

She laughed loudly and touched my hand. "Not necessarily; I have been looking for a long time. I have been to many different religious sites in search of a spiritual path. We humans are free from hindrances and have all the necessary conditions for engaging in a spiritual path. If we use our human life to accomplish spiritual realization, it becomes immensely meaningful. By using it in this way, we actualize our full potential and progress from the state of an ordinary, ignorant being to that of a fully enlightened being, the highest of all beings, and when we have done this we shall have the power to benefit all living beings without exception. Thus, by using our human life for gaining spiritual realizations we can solve all our human problems and fulfill all our own and others' wishes. What could be more meaningful than this? That is why I am searching for the source of happiness. Maybe it's here."

I felt inadequate to answer or even to continue the conversation. However, I did feel compelled to say something, so I responded slowly and hesitatingly, "If you are not already familiar with the life and teachings of Buddha, you may find some of the concepts and practices introduced in this monastery a little unusual to begin with. However, if you think about them patiently and sincerely you may discover that they are very meaningful and have great relevance to our daily lives. Although Buddhism is an ancient religion that first appeared in the East, the practices taught by Buddha are timeless and universally applicable."

As she looked at me, I noticed she was a woman in her fifties who had a smooth cherubic face with deep-set eyes and very curly, mousy hair which was once blonde. She had a reddish pug nose and cupid-like bow lips. There were several wild hairs growing out of a mole on her chin, which fascinated me. I had to control the urge to reach over and pluck them out.

"Thank you for your thoughts," she said. As she spoke, a loud gong sounded. It was time, 6:00 A.M., to go into the monastery for morning services. "Maybe we can continue our conversation later," she said as both of us stood up to bring our dirty dishes to the kitchen.

The building we were in was an old farm house which came with the purchase of the property. It was renovated and converted into a guest house and is presently only used for sleeping and eating. An architecturally authentic Tibetan monastery was erected on the other side of an open grassed field. This was to be used for services. The body of the monastery building was painted in a light beige color with red and yellow trim around the windows and doors and along all the edges of the structure. The top center of the building was a truncated roof with what appeared to be a large cupola, more like a campanile, each side of which was decorated with a pair of penetrating eyes giving the building an appearance of being alive. It was the most unusually decorated building I have ever seen in the States. It was reminiscent of temples I have seen in Patan, Nepal.

The inside was even more ornate. Not only was the color scheme of red and yellow carried out within but also there were many wall hangings of *thangkas* and *mandalas*. The prayer hall was a high shining hardwood floor laid out with red magenta cushions and mats for seating. These were assembled in rows facing a front of the room outfitted with a large Buddha and many implements. The alcove surrounding the Buddha was decorated with stalactite-like fretwork painted gold. The large, heavy, gold Buddha stood under the magnificent vaulted ceiling and filigreed dome.

Tibetan Buddhism, also called Lamaism in Western literature, a form of Mahayana Buddhism, is practiced not only in Tibet but also in the neighboring countries of the Himalaya. The specific nature of Tibetan Buddhism comes from the fusion of the monastic rules of the *Sarvastivada* and the cultic methodology of the *Vajrayana*. With the rules of discipline the Mahayana teachings of Nagarjuna, the founder of the *Madhyamika* School and Asanga, one of the founders of the *Yogacara* School, are the great pillars of Tibetan Buddhism.

Close by was a fountain of icy, cold, ferruginous water, which some people accompanied by a monk would go to drink using a metal cup which was attached to a post by a chain. Its real purpose was to rinse out the mouth for purification before chanting prayers.

Upon entering the monastery, we had to remove our shoes and put them on a provided rack. We were given an oblong and narrow booklet which contained a bilingual transliteration on facing pages of a Buddhist-Tibetan Sutra and were told we may purchase them at the end of the service. Having been assigned to a seat near the front, I found myself facing the presiding leader or *Rinpoche*, Lama Norlha. He was surrounded by several assistants, all dressed in magenta red robes, the color of the *Vajrayana* Buddhist monks.

We began our chanting of the sutra and as we continued I noticed the assistants pick up exotic musical instruments, horns, bells, cymbals, and drums and began producing a loud, ear-piercing noise without harmonics or melody and certainly no rhythm — just loud noise. It was nerve shattering; what my brother Danny used to call raucous cacophony. I must admit I found it mirthful but perhaps the accompanying gladness was intentional. In any event, I found it very strange, especially since I come from Zen, a severe and disciplined order without gaiety. This would be analogous to a Catholic going to an Eastern Orthodox service. But as Einstein once said, "The most beautiful experience we can have is the mysterious."

The service took one hour, at the completion of which those of us who wanted to meditate were left for an additional hour. I found it very interesting that a significant number of people left the hall. At 8:00 A.M., the hall was vacated. As I was leaving, I felt a thump on my back and turned my head to discover Alice behind me.

I said, "Hi, Alice, how are you doing?"

She responded, "Although my cognomen is Alice, my friends call me Al."

"That's my name," I quickly retorted.

"I know," she said, "and that causes a problem. How do you suggest we solve it?"

I immediately replied, "You may call me by the name the Japanese Buddhists call me, Shansky-san."

"What does it mean?" she asked after a moment of hesitation.

I responded, "It's Japanese and means, 'Honorable Shansky.'"

She looked at me with questioning eyes which seemed to dance as she spoke, "When I saw you walk *oot* of the *hoose* I caught up so we might continue our conversation of this morning." I stopped walking and turned full face to her.

"Do I detect a Canadian accent?"

"Why, yes," she said, "I come from St. Catherine's in Canada."

"Where is St. Catherine's?" I asked quizzically.

"It's just across the lake from Toronto, next to Buffalo," she responded. "I drove all the way down here and broke up the trip by staying overnight with a friend at Hartwick College in Oneonta," she continued.

"Did you know that there is a Buddhist belt all the way down among the forests of the Catskills?" I said.

"She looked at me with her dancing eyes. "Is that so? What do you mean?"

I related by using my fingers. "Let me see, there is Dai Bosatsu in Livingston Manor, Dharma Drum in Pine Bush, Zen Mountain Monastery in Mt. Tremper, the Karma Triyana Dharmachakra in Woodstock and Sky Lake Lodge, which is the latest edition to approximately more than twenty-five centers. Major Buddhist Centers have spread throughout the wooded hills and valleys of the Catskills. The Buddhist presence is steadily growing, both in the numbers of centers and the increasing variety of their traditions."

"Gee, that's very interesting," she said, as we continued walking. "Do you think my search for spiritually is a fool's errand?" she asked after a few moments.

"I can't really answer that," I said as I looked down at the ground. I felt I was getting myself into an untenable situation. "In my view, man is condemned to suffering because he was born with an unsatisfied nature, so if looking for spirituality gives you solace, then by all means continue. However, I suspect it is the quest not the finding which yields satisfaction," I replied.

She looked up and asked, "But what is suffering?"

I quickly responded, "Buddhism says that all life is pain and suffering which comes about from desires, grasping and attachments." I then decided to continue, "Nothing arouses man's curiosity more than himself. Of course, when I say 'man' I mean it generically and include women."

She was silent and seemed to wait for me to continue, so I spoke rather slowly, "From the dawn of history to this very moment man has addressed himself to two basic questions of human existence: What is man? What is his destiny? Suffering must have significance, even if not in terms of his life. Religion has spent thousands of years seeking the answer. In default of finding one it has found many: Christianity, Buddhism, Islam, Hinduism, Judaism, etc., etc., etc. All agree on the fact of suffering, no two agree on its significance, and, by differing on this, they thereby differ on the nature of man." I stopped with a great sigh, and then I continued,

"Since we have been in a Tibetan temple I suppose it is appropriate to quote the Dalai Lama who said, 'Remember that not getting what you want is sometimes a wonderful stroke of luck.'"

Alice possessed a directness of utterance that has made me wonder where the conversation was heading as she began to exude a dark-hued intensity reminiscent of a Sunday preacher. "Will spirituality prevent the loss of self? Of all the forms of impoverishment that can be seen in the world, loss of self is surely the most devastating. But a transformation is coming. The transformation that is coming invites us to reexamine our own lives. It confronts us with a personal and individual choice: are we satisfied with how we have lived. How would we live differently? It offers us a recovery of self. It faces us with the fact that this choice cannot be evaded, for as the freedom is already there, so must the responsibility be there. At the heart of everything is a change of consciousness. This means a new way of living. This is what I am searching for, and what I have started achieving."

We were still walking as we talked but I was getting tired so I suggested that we sit on the soft, verdant grass. Beyond were the chestnut trees whose branches hung low like small trees and reflected the dappled lights of wind-danced leaves. Beneath their shade, we sat in front of the farm house. The farm house was square-shaped, with two stories and green-painted shutters.

Alice was no more than five feet tall and she was somewhat fleshy and stout. Nevertheless, her plumpness did not prevent her from sitting comfortably in a cross-legged position. After listening to her bombastic ranting, I was reluctant to continue; but I could not restrain myself any longer. I felt impelled to speak of the very important Buddhist concept of self. It was as if what she said invited my response. But I knew I would have to search for the *mots juste* so as not to be misunderstood. This would not be easy, so I began with a simple explanation.

"In Buddhism there are three characteristics of conditioned existence. They are *dukkha* which means suffering, *anicca* which means impermanence, and, of course, *anatman* which means no self. In Buddhism the empirical person is only a bundle of phenomena without something lasting as an essence. Buddhism says there is no self."

She looked at me with a startled expression on her face and exclaimed, "I don't understand that. What about ego and the soul?"

I continued after considering her statement. "No one has ever seen the self. It has no visible shape, nor does it occupy measurable space. It is an abstraction, like other abstractions equally elusive: the individual, the mind, the society. The self is a construct of the mind, a hypothesis of being, socially formed even as it can be quickly turned against the very social formations that have brought it into birth. The locus of self often appears as 'inner,' experienced as a presence savingly apart from both social milieu and quotidian existence. There is probably some continuity between the idea of the soul and that of the self. Both propound a center of percipience lodged within yet not quite of the body. Soul speaks of a person's relation to divinity, a participation in heavenly spark, while self speaks of a person's relation to both others and oneself— though soul may in part serve this function, too. In these ideas of soul and self there is a dualism of self-consciousness. There is a similar link between the idea of self and modern notions of alienation, since both imply a yearning for a fulfilled humanity, unfractured by contingent needs."

Her head was lowered as I was speaking as if to concentrate on my words. For a long time she did not acknowledge my explanation. She slowly looked up and said, while gazing off in a distance, "Your explanation unveils a potent new approach to one of the oldest debates in religious conflict — whether the soul exists."

I was stymied by her remark and being eager to conclude our conversation, I said, "It's almost 10:00 and I was assigned to help in the kitchen. Maybe we can get together at lunch time."

I got up, dusted off my trousers, and began walking off to the farmhouse kitchen. Alice continued sitting and lazily pulled at the grass. She waved her arm in silent acknowledgement.

When I arrived at the kitchen, I reported to the cook. She was a tall, buxom woman in her late forties with heavy arms and close-cropped hair.

She wore a full apron which covered her massive breasts. After a pleasant introduction she asked me to chop the vegetables for a stir fry. Meals in the monastery are vegetarian.

I went over to a table which contained a mass of vegetables and began washing and cleaning them. After cleaning, I began chopping the vegetables into small bite-sized pieces in the following order: bean sprouts, scallions, bell peppers, onions, basil, broccoli, bamboo strips, green beans, potatoes, carrots, eggplant, ginger, and zucchini. I put these in separate plastic containers and then placed them at the stove area awaiting the cook, who would be cooking a stir fry in a very large wok. The cook placed a small amount of vegetable oil and some soy sauce in the wok and began inserting and tossing the vegetables, bunches at a time, until they softened, finalizing with handfuls of lemongrass, mushrooms, tomatoes, and small squares of tofu. The stir fry liquid was thickened with a small amount of cornstarch. When the tofu became slightly browned, the stir fry was placed in a large bowl and garnished with a small dribble of sesame oil, some hoisin sauce and more soy sauce. This process was repeated four times to make sufficient food for the entire complement of people. In addition to the stir fry, fluffy cooked rice was made in a rice cooker and served as well. I was very proud of my participation in making this symphony of vegetables in the stir fry.

Lunch was served with bread and tea. When lunch was over I went outside and saw that Alice was still sitting on the grass in the same spot where I left her. I went over and asked, "Aren't you going to eat lunch?"

"I am not hungry," she said. "I would like to continue our conversation," she added hurriedly. I thought for a little while then said, "Like the Monarch butterfly who migrates south for the winter, I intend leaving here in about an hour."

She answered, "So am I but we can talk for part of that hour."

After approaching her, I leaned over and said, "If I've said anything that offended you I am truly sorry, I am only trying to alert you to commonly encountered obstacles — pride, fear, and attachment, for instance — and the pitfalls whereby a genuine spiritual life can turn into a self-centered preoccupation, one that may end up actually hindering rather than furthering your relationship with God. I am trying to point to the necessity of stripping away the defenses with which we cushion and shield ourselves from the full impact of truth."

I spoke as I began sitting, first on one knee, then in full cross-legged seating. She looked at me with her deep-set eyes and said, "No, no. I am grateful for your counsel. It was the matter of self which I found troubling." As I sat, adjusting to a half-lotus posture, I began speaking very slowly while noticing that she was looking up at me and giving me her full attention, like a child, in anticipation of hearing some Solomon-like wisdom.

"I don't mean to give you advice, it's just that I know that in this culture that bombards us with feel-good-about-yourself spirituality there must be a more genuine spiritual guide to attain truth and peace. Frankly, the components of true peace are the secret of self-sacrifice, the gift of humility, and even long-suffering — unpopular ideas indeed. There is a peace greater than self-fulfillment. But you won't find it if you go looking for it. It is waiting for everyone ready to sacrifice the search for individual peace and discover the importance of living in the present, the necessity of struggle and the value of disappointment."

She looked at me and spoke in a forthright, deliberate manner. "Is there still a God who watches over all, and a stubborn faith that the worst trials of life's difficult hours will one day be overshadowed by his comfort and peace?"

"I don't know," I replied. "Thomas Merton, the trappist monk, once said, 'God is not found in theological exercises, but in the desert of surrender which is entered only when we are willing to let go of our agendas and await the word of God in silence.'"

I took her hand in a farewell gesture, while saying, "It was a great pleasure meeting and speaking with you. I wish you much luck in your quest."

"Hey, wait a minute," she shouted. "Where is the self?"

"I felt somewhat disconcerted. What had I gotten myself into? How could I overcome my reluctance and answer her satisfactorily? I let her hand drop and started to utter words and express myself as best as I could without becoming pedantic.

"The problem of the location of the self can be thought of as being quite independent of any particular body. However, if one accepts this, one needs to wonder whether one needs a body at all to be a self. Dualists may hold that the self is manifested to oneself and to others through the body. Thus the self may even be capable of surviving bodily death. The non-dualist, on the other hand, may argue that a body of some kind is necessary for anyone to be a self because they would claim that one needs to have an identifiable, constant physical location before one can be a self. Therefore, you may make a choice as a dualist or a non-dualist. Now, I really must go. Goodbye and good luck."

I got up and started walking to the sleeping quarters to retrieve my belongings. On my way out I stopped at the small front office and handed the attending monk a check and made a deep *gassho*. "Please visit us again," he said. I smiled and left, carrying my sleeping bag and a small shoulder bag. I looked for Alice as I walked towards my automobile but she was gone. I never saw her again.

One day, some months later, I visited the Tibetan Buddhist Meditation Center, Karma Triyana Dharmachakra, in Woodstock, New York. I spent an overnight retreat there learning "The Two Accumulations" with Khenpo Karthar Rinpoche. The format was the same as Kagyu Thubten Choling in Wappinger Falls. That was my last contact and experience with Tibetan Buddhism.

When I arrived at home from Wappinger Falls, I felt dissatisfied with my latest escapade and sat on my *zafu* to meditate. After sitting *zazen* for one hour, I came to realize that my dissatisfaction resulted from the presence of so many dilettantes at these monasteries and temples that I have attended. Who are these amateurs? Why are they here? What are their motives? In my experience most of them are curiosity seekers who have been greatly influenced by the media and are driven by their promises. There is an ongoing movement from a variety of sources to portray "things of the East" as cogent, fecund, and salutary beyond imagination. In addition, there is a surprising interest in much bizarre New Age, media-driven paranormal belief systems. The hype promotes a mysterious aura which attracts the ignorant to the inexplicable. There are those who believe that practice of Eastern techniques, particularly meditation, will be therapeutic and beneficial to the condition of being sound in body, mind, and soul.

Whilst this may be true, the individuals who practice usually have no appreciation or understanding of Eastern culture and so become selective by trying one or two specific techniques. Many have a discontent with their own indigenous religion and so seek out alternatives. It is interesting to me that meditation and retreats are available in all Western religions and yet this does not appeal to those seeking alternatives. Can it be because in Western religions one is not required to remove shoes and be discalced as one sits on the floor?

Oh well, I still had a few more places to explore before I permitted my present disappointment to influence any decision I may make. For one thing, I intended making contact with ethnic Buddhist centers; those which cater mostly to Chinese and/or Japanese people. I was given the names of two such places in New York City. The first was the Temple of Enlightenment in the Bronx, a pure Land Buddhist Chinese temple, and the second was Shobo-ji temple in Manhattan, a Rinzai Zen Japanese temple.

Being in the Field

As I descended the stairs of Donnarumma Hall at Fairfield University, I recognized a short Chinese man waiting at the base. It was Professor Lik Kuen Tong, one of my teachers in the philosophy department of Fairfield University.

"Hiya, Al!" he lustily exclaimed, "I would like to talk with you for a minute. Do you have some time?"

"Of course," I replied. We both went outside of Donnarumma Hall and he started speaking rather hastily, which made it somewhat difficult for his words to register completely.

"I am starting a new philosophical organization that will be based on the concept of non-substantialism and I am wondering if you would like to join me in this effort," he said in an obscure manner.

"I don't know what you mean," I replied.

"Well, you're a scientist and can certainly understand the Quantum Theory in Physics and the Gestalt Theory in Psychology. Both of these concepts are based on non-substantialism. You see, I have established secretariats some time ago throughout China for the study of what is known as Chang-yu philosophy. Now, what I want to do is expose that philosophy to the international community," he said hastily.

I was thoroughly confused and frankly, could not absorb the significance of what he was saying, so I asked rather timidly, "Why don't we meet in your office next Tuesday at 3:00 so we can review what you mean exactly and how I fit in, okay?"

On the following Tuesday, I met with Dr. Tong in his office. I sat down as he started to talk. "First, let me say that I have decided to call our organization The International Institute for Field-Being. You are about to ask: What is Field-Being? Please, let me explain." He began in his usual didactic manner, "The world is not a collection of independent, substantial entities, nor a definite totality of facts. It is rather an incessant process of activity forming a dynamic continuum, a multi-leveled and multi-dimensional web which refuses to be objectified into definite, divisible wholes and isolated, mutually external individual parts." He stopped talking and looked at me with an anxious expression on his face. "Are you with me so far?" he asked in a professorial manner.

I shook my head affirmatively and said, "Yes, so far."

He continued, "Strictly speaking, there are no 'beings' or 'things' conceived as absolutely self-identical and self-enduring entities. From the Field-Being perspective, shared by the dominant strands of Far Eastern philosophy and the non-substantial orientations in twentieth-century science and contemporary Western thought, the notion of an unchanging substrate or 'thing-in-itself' is a philosophical fiction, a conceptual construction or fabrication of the mind which has no real basis other than the vital-rational demand for simplification and expediency, ultimately dictated by the necessity of human survival and control. The truth is, nothing is self-sufficient or merely itself without reference to other things in the universe — or, as we put it, there is no being other than Field-Being."

"I get it," I said.

"Shall I continue?" He inquired. Once again, I nodded affirmatively.

He started in again in his familiar teaching style. "From the Field-Being standpoint, reality is essentially fluid and ambiguous: nothing has a rigid identity. In the final analysis, the history of civilized thought, as we see it, is simply a history of the dynamic opposition and mutual adaptation between the substantialist and the non-substantialist approach to reality, and not, as the Marxists would have it, a battle between materialism and idealism. In many forms and disguises, the opposition between substantialism and non-substantialism is as old as civilized thought. Indeed, it may not be an exaggeration to say that it defines the very meaning of philosophical wisdom."

I waited for a rather long moment, while looking at Dr. Tong and thought to myself, "this Field-Being is a take-no-prisoners philosophical forced march." I finally said, "I think I understand what Field-Being is. What is it you have in mind for me?"

He said rather succinctly, "I need some one to help me organize our first symposium here on campus."

I replied, "Dr. Tong, as you know, I work as a consulting chemist during the day and I am not sure how much time I can contribute."

He quickly rejoindered, "Why don't you think about it and let me know how we can work out some kind of program?" I agreed and hastened away.

For a few days I thought about nothing else. My consulting practice was beginning to wane and I have thought about doing other things to take up the slack. This Field-Being could be an opportunity. I discussed it with my wife and she asked if it was a voluntary position. I concurred rather sheepishly but I was surprised that she encouraged me to consider it. She said, "Try it and see if you like it. If not, you can always resign."

In a few days, I met with Dr. Tong again and suggested that I start with two days a week. He eagerly accepted and I breathed a sigh of relief. In my zealousness, I decided to contact Bill Paar to tell him of my good fortune but more importantly to get some tips from him on his organizational skills in the philosophical community.

I called his phone number at home and a woman answered. She told me she was Bill Paar's daughter — Andrea.

"Hello," I said. "My name is Al Shansky. Is your father at home?"

"No," she replied. "Are you a friend of his?" I assented. She continued, "I am sorry to tell you that my father had a stroke and is now in the hospital."

I was dumbstruck. I could not gather my thoughts quickly enough to respond properly. I made the usual lame remarks society expects and finally said, "Which hospital is he in?"

She responded, "He is in Pollack's Hospital in Jersey City."

"Thank you," I said. "I shall go and visit him." I hung up, still in a daze.

I hastily called the Pollack Hospital to get directions and the necessary details for visiting Bill Paar. Since he was confined, I knew I would be visiting him as a stranger. After arriving at the hospital in Jersey City, I was told that Mr. Paar was in the "dayroom." In approaching the room I had an overwhelming feeling of foreboding. There he was, propped up in a chair amongst several other incapacitated individuals in front of a blaring television set. He was not watching the daytime soap opera. His head was lowered as if he were examining the design on the counterpane on his lap. I walked towards him very slowly and said, "Hi, Bill." His head seemed to rise up slowly and I could see recognition in his eyes. His face was rigid but I noticed a faint smile.

I repeated, "Hi, Bill. How are you?" He could not answer so I leaned closer to his face and whispered in his ear, "It's me, Al. I've come to visit." He did not respond. But I continued to talk about meaningless matters.

He had suffered a terrible stroke that had frozen him. He was left without words, except to stick the tip of his tongue between thin lips and sputter a frothy sentence of spit. He mumbled in a curious language made up of grunts, gestures, and spit that no one could understand. So much left unsaid. After a while, I found myself laboring to make conversation so I grabbed his hand and kissed his forehead to say goodbye. On the way home I reflected about this man being stuck in an inoperative body like something out of a Beckett play. Poor Bill; is he now confronting his life-long questions about spirituality, mortality, and his own self-worth?

A short time later his daughter, Andrea, called me to say that her father, Bill Paar, died and was buried somewhere in upstate New York. It is difficult to relate my feelings when I heard this devastating news. For some strange and unaccountable reason I thought of that book written about President John Kennedy after he died, *Johnny, We Hardly Knew Ye*. I felt robbed and violated as if an unseen assailant had accosted me. The Angel of Death, the destroyer of life with his scythe, has entered my life once again.

I made a date to visit Andrea in a few days in Rochelle Park. When I arrived I rang the doorbell and there she stood before me dressed in a purple fleece athletic costume. She was a woman of average height and a stature which could only be described as slender. Her face was small and moon-like with rosary bead eyes and a string of soft hair across her cheek. Her hair was combed and plaited as if done with nervous hands. I guessed she was in her early thirties. I reflected that now she would never know what it was to have a father hold her again. Now, there was no one to advise her, caress her, call her sweet names, soothe her, or save her. No one would touch her again with a father's love.

When she spoke she seemed somewhat shy and reserved. "Please come in. Have you had breakfast? Would you like a cup of coffee?"

I refused all with a hand gesture and a negative mumble as I walked inside the house. We sat in the small kitchen and began to talk over a cup of coffee. She told me that she lived in New York City and worked for one of the social agencies.

I asked her, "What will you do with all the furniture?"

She answered matter-of-factly, "Probably give it to the Salvation Army."

I was startled and asked again, "The piano and organ too?"

"Yes," she answered. "I am disposing of everything."

I hesitated but suggested rather timidly, "I have a daughter who is a musician and I am sure she would love to have the piano and the organ. I could arrange for a truck to pick them up and deliver them to her."

She clapped her hands almost child-like in glee and said, "That would be wonderful."

In addition, I suggested that I return next week and pick up some of his books. He had many books on Buddhism, philosophy, and Eastern languages. Some of these I added to my home library, the remainder I sent to Bridge to Asia, a book collection relief agency for the poor Asian school systems.

After a while she said, "I bought some fresh bagels and cream cheese. Are you sure you're not just a little hungry?" Finally, I relented and partook of a delicious breakfast. She went on to tell me that she gave her father's automobile to the next door neighbor in exchange for maintenance of the grounds outside of the house. She was in the process of selling the house and was only living there temporarily until she could dispose of her father's possessions. Inevitably, she intended returning to New York City where she had an apartment.

Then, it was time to say goodbye and I left knowing I would return next week to help with the removal of the books, some musical scores, and an old electric typewriter. Also, I needed to supervise the trucking of the piano and the organ to my daughter's house. I have not seen Andrea since then but we have spoken by phone several times and she did send me some photos of the Lower East Side district of Manhattan where she has some interest.

The following week I received a call from my best friend Maury, whom I affectionately call Mushka, which means "little fly" in Russian. We have been friends for almost a half-century and have an empathetic relationship like brothers. He told me that after three decades of mental abuse, he and his wife were separating. He continued that he is now living in New York City and wondered if we could get together. Of course,

I agreed and made up to meet him. I was stunned by this turn of events and was anxious to be of help.

We met in Grand Central Station at the information rotunda, approaching each other with outstretched arms, and finally locking in a bear hug embrace and thence a reciprocal kiss on the cheek. I always feel good when I am with Maury because of his risible manner, but now seemed a special occasion for sobriety, requiring some chary thought and grave concern. He had that look people have when they've experienced a disappointment in life. I looked at him and saw what seemed to be a watering of his eyes. What were most striking about Maury were his eyes — all blueness with hardly any white showing, like the eyes of horses, and it was this that impelled the world into believing him a sensitive and tender soul. He said with a quick riposte, "Would you like to see my new apartment?" I nodded in acknowledgement and we walked to 43rd Street near the Hudson River. He was talking incessantly about his current situation revealing many surprising things that were obscure to me over the life of our friendship. Finally, I understood his dilemma after many years of a laborious and troublesome marriage.

It was January 1996 and the weather was chilly and blustery but the walk was refreshing. He continued explaining his marital difficulties, some of which I was aware. He then expounded his decision to separate legally from his wife, but I could see the past inevitably continued to haunt him. It is not so easy to escape the burden of one's heritage.

The apartment was lovely within a somewhat luxurious building. I could see the apartment reflected some of his best virtues. Maury was always clean, punctual, organized, precise, and expected no less from everyone around him. I turned to him after expressing my approval of the apartment and said, "We are all born with our destiny, but sometimes we have to help our destiny a little." I think he understood the meaning of my words.

After inspecting the apartment we decided to have lunch. Lunch with Maury is actually telling of our friendship. We really dovetail at this accommodation. Maury has a very small appetite, whereas I have a very large appetite and inevitably he gives me half of his fare. In addition, he usually orders two appetizers and I usually order one entrée, so that, in this way I get to eat a complete meal. After lunch I left for home with the promise of returning next week.

The following week, I called him and arranged for us to attend a performance of a dance company at the Joyce Theatre in Chelsea. We saw Merce Cunningham, one of the pioneers, along with Martha Graham, of modern dance. Maury has a strong aesthetic sense and he enjoyed the performance very much. By now he was peeling back the obfuscatory portion of his life and we began to see each other almost fortnightly. We usually went to a museum together or attended the theatre. A novel routine which evolved from this occurrence was eating lunch at the Metropolitan Museum of Art and then viewing the galleries of paintings afterwards.

He is the ultimate portmanteau friend. He was overcoming his personal problems but I knew that I could always count on his help with my own problems, should the need arise. This is a very comforting feeling indeed. As I've told him, the art of life is the art of avoiding pain. I know I've used the word "empathy" before but in this case it is an appropriate word. Empathy means feeling what others feel, and acknowledging what they are experiencing. This concept is very important in terms of our relationship with other people. I really feel what Maury feels. If I can actually feel the experience of Maury; it is inconceivable to be inconsiderate in my dealings with him. If I am empathetic, but decide to ignore it, then I would have chosen a path which knowingly disrupts the harmonious feelings of Maury. If I do this, then I would disrupt my own harmonious feelings.

In Buddhism, the concept of harmony is to create unity, balance, trust, and oneness with all things. When we do not tune in to our true identity of understanding all things, we ignore the natural state of being. To be one with all things is to be conscious of the feelings of those we touch through our daily experiences. Because I feel what Maury feels, I am kind, considerate, and humane in all my dealings with him.

Back to the Field

The first symposium of the International Institute for Field-Being was scheduled for May 1997, so I found myself very busy with making preparations and arrangements for this conference. I had to contact participants and request abstracts of papers. Papers had to be read and juried. Arrangements had to be made for room and board for the attendees. Transportation requirements had to be made for people from all over the world. It seemed to be endless work and drudgery. In addition, I was plagued with feelings of not belonging amongst these people. Was I really qualified to stand toe to toe with philosophers?

Each of us, myself included, experiences periods in our lives in which we feel overwhelmed by our difficulties. At such times, it's all too easy to become depressed, viewing life's problems as simply too momentous to be solved. But this viewpoint is completely inaccurate. I am absolutely convinced that our personal setbacks have the potential to emerge as our most positive motivators. Let me give you an example.

I was told by Dr. Tong that I would be chairing the session on the *I-Ching* at the symposium. Immediately all the old fears whelmed up in me. Was I up to the task? I balked and stated that I may know something about Buddhism but I was very weak in Daoism and I had only a superficial and limited knowledge of the *I-Ching*. He in turn told me to bone up with the statement, "A chairman doesn't have to be an expert."

Coincidently, I had to drive my wife one day to a gathering of her friends in New Jersey close to the Princeton University Campus. At the Princeton book store I bought a copy of the *I-Ching* and the *Dao De Jing* and began a serious learning process of the material. The result was that I not only performed well as a chairman at the symposium but also I became more familiar with Daoism as a religion.

Because every crisis is an opportunity in disguise, it becomes an opportunity to learn from the experience and to grow as a person. I discovered that many times I was tempted to give up because of the stress and aggravation associated with my new academic surroundings, but instead I stuck with it. The initial difficulty gave me the best possible foundation upon which to develop my philosophical leanings.

We were able to garner eighteen papers with some participants from foreign countries. It was an exciting time in my life mingling with these professors from many different and varied institutions. Some who came to deliver papers were former teachers I had during my study years at Fairfield University. In all, the conference was a resounding success and I looked forward to participation in future conferences.

I made many friends at the conference but the most significant one was Ken Inada. Ken was a veteran of World War II and we had this in common. He fought with the all–Nisei 442nd Combat Regiment in Italy and France and wound up a hero. Ken told me of a Zen temple in New York City which sounded very interesting. The name is Shobo-ji and is on 63rd Street just off Lexington Avenue. The Roshi of the temple, whose name is Eido Shimano, is a friend of Ken Inada. I decided to attend services there and so called in advance for permission, which was given enthusiastically. When I arrived I changed into my robes and found my place, which had a paper place card bearing my name. Services were very meaningful to me at that time since I had not attended formal services for quite some time. The Shobo-ji temple is Rinzai Zen but I could not find much difference between Rinzai and Soto Zen.

The services started at 9:00 A.M. with recitation of a sutra, a transliteration of which was handed out at registration. It was then followed by a *kinhin* or walking meditation throughout the floor space of the temple in single file. Finally, this was followed by *zazen* or sitting meditation for forty minutes. At the conclusion of *zazen*, a vegetarian lunch was served while we sat in our places. This consisted of cooked vegetables and rice with tea. After lunch there was a final prayer for the dead and a reading of their names, which were provided on registration. The participants were a mixed ethnic group but generally all seemed to be serious zennists. People finally began leaving and I only had a small moment to convey Ken Inada's regards to Eido Shimano Roshi. I have since been back several times and usually go there on an *ad hoc* basis to remember the dead relatives of my family.

One day it occurred to me to call Dr. Shen of the Chuang Yen Monastery to tell him of Bill Paar's demise. He was very gracious on the telephone and invited me to visit him at the Woo-Ju Library on the monastery grounds. When I got there I was amazed at the various building placements, all surrounding the periphery of a lake, in the middle of which stood a statue of Kuan-Yin, the Goddess of Mercy. Her beauty in reposeful quietude gave rest to the eye and ear. I parked my car and went into the library where Dr. Shen, who amicably extended his hand in a forthright Western manner, greeted me. I bowed in *gassho* but took his hand as well to reciprocate the friendly gesture.

He was a short man with a rotund stature and small limbs. He had a round face with severely slanted eyes, which always seemed closed. His face was puffy, his neck thick and pink, and his chin was doubled. He was as bald as a knee, with a head that looked like a peanut. On his right cheek there was a big black mole as perfect as an elevator button. As best I could tell his age was probably in the late 70s. We talked for a few minutes in which I explained Bill Paar's death. I could hear him muttering — tsk, tsk — and hiss through his teeth with each sentence I spoke. He then told me in a soft spoken voice that Bill was a valued member of the Temple of Enlightenment in the Bronx but that he came to Chuang Yen frequently for meetings of the Institute for Advanced Studies of World Religions, which took place on the premises.

We then stopped talking as if being spent of words. There was a silence like the maw of sorrow. As if to break the silence, Dr. Shen offered to escort me around the area to tour the facilities. I felt honored by this courtesy and readily accepted. After inspecting the mechanical stacks of the library we got into my car and drove to the parking lot of the Kuan-Yin Hall.

The Kuan-Yin Hall is built in the style of architecture of the Tang Dynasty (618 A.D.–907 A.D.). It houses a statue of Kuan-Yin, the Goddess of Mercy and also has kneeling pads for services. Next door is the

Hall of the Great Buddha Vairocana. The building design is in Tang
Dynasty style as well. Inside the hall is a 37-foot statue of the Buddha —
the largest Buddha in the Western hemisphere, so they claim. Behind the
Kuan-Yin Hall is the Yin-Kuang Hall, which serves as the living quarters
for the monks. Around the other side of the lake between the Kuan-Yin
Hall and the Woo-Ju Library is the Tai-hsu Hall. This building is used
by Zen practitioners every Sunday morning for meditation. Lastly, in back
of the Dining Hall is the Memorial Terrace. This is where the cremated
remains of the deceased are held in urns, which have been placed in steel
niche with a nameplate on the outside surface.

It was an interesting tour and Dr. Shen told me of his plans for a
Seminary at Chuang Yen Monastery. One hundred acres of land has been
set aside for this undertaking. I have since become a regular patron of
Chuang Yen and have established a wonderful friendship with a female
monk whose name is Reverend Guna. I often go on Sundays to attend
Zen services in Tai-Hsu Hall. I also have brought many friends to Chuang
Yen who have heard of the "Big Buddha." During many of my visits, I
noticed whole Chinese families with their children and elderly relatives
would come from all parts of the metropolitan area and upstate New York.

I said goodbye to Dr. Shen after returning him to the Woo-Ju Library,
which incidentally, is named in memory of his wife (Woo-Ju Chu).

Gleaning the Buddha Fields

I found myself busy in preparation for the Second Field-Being Conference. This took place on the Fairfield University campus in August
1998. Coincidentally, the XXth World Congress of Philosophy was having its quinquennial meeting in Boston at the same time. Even though
this was a problem we decided to seize the opportunity and have a split
meeting—half in Fairfield and half in Boston. In this way we could get
exposure to a much larger audience. I began sending out letters to the
membership. By this time Beverly Kahn, one of my former teachers,

became Associate Dean and Orin Grossman became Dean. Both were good friends and I felt very comfortable discussing Institute plans with them. We not only received funding but also encouragement from both. In particular, I was very friendly with Dr. Beverly Kahn, whom I admired for her intelligence, interest, and ambition. Arrangements had to be made to house and feed about thirty or more participants for five days and then transport them by bus to Boston for five more days. Beverly was a great help in this regard.

Papers and abstracts were arriving almost daily for evaluation. While all of this was going on I received a phone call from my friend Maury who invited me to accompany him to his summer home outside of Austerlitz in upstate New York. I consented with the proviso that we stop for a short while in Livingston Manor on the way in order to visit the Dai Bosatsu Monastery. He agreed and so we met at the Marriott Hotel in Tarrytown where I could leave my car for the weekend. It was a two-hour drive but chatting with Maury seemed to make the time go faster.

I had called the monastery the previous day to get directions and make a reservation. I spoke with the head monk, who was most accommodating. When we arrived it was lunchtime so we were told to eat in the kitchen with the cook. In this way we did not interfere with the routine of the monks. The meal was simple vegetarian fare, which seemed to please Maury.

Dai Bosatsu, which means "Great Bodhisattva" in Japanese, is built in a style reminiscent of the Kamakura period (1185–1336). This type of architecture was designed to look like a distinctive Japanese monastery with the familiar curved roof and the Chinese beam-frame and bracket system known as *tou-kung*. The wooden portion of the monastery was made with imported *hinoki* wood. The floors were highly polished wood with white plastered walls, and heavy wood pillars typical of Japanese design. All in all it was a splendid sight and made me think of Japan and the Hosshinji Monastery where I spent my formative period of Zen gestation.

Dai Bosatsu is located within a Catskill forest of many acres and is completely surrounded by both deciduous and evergreen trees. It was a short walk to Beecher Lake where we could see a slight mist rising off the water. The water was mirror-like without a ripple. Unfortunately, we could not stay long but I encouraged Maury to sit *zazen*. We did this with the monks in the *zendo* for forty minutes. I was surprised to see only Westerners in the monastery but they acted in accord with traditional Japanese procedures and habitual practice. Afterwards I bade the head monk farewell with thanks and donated some money to the monastery. We were then on our way again to Austerlitz.

It was late afternoon when we arrived at Maury's summer home. I was daunted at the sight before me. Indeed, I was totally taken aback. I had always imagined a summer home to be of a cabin-in-the-woods variety or cottage type so familiar in films. This was reinforced by other summer homes I had visited in my travels. What I saw was a large conventional building that seemed to have been transported from Tremont Avenue in the Bronx. However, it was situated in a wood next to a pond which added an abundance of rustic charm. On entering, I observed all the amenities one would have in a suburban home. Maury installed me in a lovely room which had a comfortable feeling. I was beginning to feel at home and rested after our long trip.

Maury intended spending the next morning painting. I told him I would design and make a Zen garden for him near the front entrance to his house. Maury is a very early riser and when I got up I found him in the living room busily painting. We had a breakfast of cold cereal and fruit, after which I went out to face the day. The weather was cool and crisp with a crash of silence in the atmosphere. I felt an immediate tranquility being in the presence of such simple, primitive scenery. I began to have a dialogue with nature which culminated with the hawthorns and yews. In a rapture of delight, I told my troubles to their leaves in the belief that I was opening my heart to living creatures, who understood me. I went further into the woods in search of smaller yews and hawthorn bushes of about three feet in height. I found a whole group of them, which I proceeded to dig out while retaining a root ball. These were transplanted to the area designated for the Zen garden. Maury came out to help. Having found three suitable shrubs, I planted them as a backdrop for the Zen garden. I then looked for particular types of stones and rocks but unfortunately there were none of the specific type needed.

In Zen garden development one needs to place light-colored rocks at the distant point and dark-colored rocks in the forefront. In addition, a small stone lantern is usually eccentrically placed in the garden. This could carry a candle for lighting on special occasions. Also, it should be umbilically connected to the house by a flat stone pathway called an *ishidoro*. I was disappointed that I could not do more with the limited source of materials. I promised Maury that I would complete the garden on my next visit. However, I never returned due to travel pressures and many other business commitments. Maury told me on several occasions that the transplanted trees are living and thriving. Maybe one day I will be able to finish the job.

On Sunday we drove home to take up our daily activities. I had to get on with my two careers — chemistry and philosophy. On Monday, I received a call from Dr. Eileen Pennino of the Norwalk Community College. She is a professor of history and teaches an honors class called, "The Pacific Rim." She asked if I would be willing to give a volunteer lecture on basic Buddhism to her class, having heard about my lecture to the Lifetime Learners of last year. I decided to agree, thinking that it would add to my prestige with the powers that be at Fairfield University. In other words, I was using it to build my curriculum vitae in academia.

I entered Professor Eileen Pennino's class and was immediately introduced to the student body. The class was full with thirty-eight students, which were more than I expected. I lectured on Buddhism, beginning with an historical background and leading into Buddhist philosophy and theology. At the conclusion of my lecture, a question-and-answer period ensued, which frankly led to more understanding of the subject matter by the students. I was very impressed with the enthusiasm of the students.

I suddenly became very busy preparing for the second symposium of the International Institute for Field-Being. In developing the program,

Dr. Tong assigned me the role of commentator for the Buddhist concept of Dharmakaya. This was to be a presentation at the Boston venue. I was very excited at this prospect and started to search the literature to round out my knowledge and understanding of Dharmakaya with some additional facts.

The Dharmakaya (body of the great order) is the true nature of the Buddha, which is identical with transcendental reality, the essence of the universe. The Dharmakaya is the unity of the Buddha with everything existing. At the same time it represents the "law," the teaching expounded by the Buddha.

In Zen the three bodies of Buddha (sometimes erroneously confused with the Christian and Hindu Trinities), are three levels of reality, which stand in reciprocal relationship to each other and constitute a whole. The Dharmakaya is the cosmic consciousness, the unified existence that lies beyond all concepts. This substrate, characterized by completion and perfection, out of which all animate and inanimate forms as well as the moral order arise, is embodied in *Vairocana* (one of the five transcendent Buddhas).

It was a hot and sultry day when all the forty-eight participants gathered at the Dolan campus of Fairfield University for the second symposium of the Field-Being Institute. This was more than twice the number we had at the first symposium. In addition, there was the opportunity to renew friendships that I made at the first symposium. In particular, I was happy to see Ken Inada again. He recently retired from SUNY Buffalo and moved with his wife to Henderson, Nevada. She suffers from arthritis and they required a dry, arid, warm climate for her well-being. I always wondered how they could survive the severe winters in Buffalo, which start early and end late, leaving behind ninety inches of snow. I guess the old adage — you go where the work is — applies here.

Ken is a soft-spoken man of erect, slim stature which belies his age of seventy-six. He is a veteran of the Second World War, having fought in Italy with a Nisei battalion. More importantly, he is the translator of the works of Nagarjuna and is an exponent of Buddhist philosophy. Having

World War II in common, we became immediate friends and have corresponded by email and regular mail ever since. I told him of my friendship with Philip Yampolsky, whose place he took as editor of the Numata Center after Phil's demise.

The symposium at Fairfield University was successful due to the camaraderie established by the participants from disparate parts of the world. I was happy to meet with my newly acquired friends — Yong Huang of Kutztown University, Kwang-sae Lee of Kent State University, and John Li Schroeder of California State University. In addition to Daoism, John is an expert in kinesiology, the art of body movement such as Tai Chi. At the completion of our segment we all loaded into the bus, which was provided to take us to Boston for the XXth World Congress of Philosophy, taking place at the Marriott Hotel. I had arranged to stay with my daughter Suzy, who lives in Cambridge, and I looked forward to visiting with my two grandkids. All the others were staying at the Marriott Hotel.

The World Congress was immensely overpowering, with philosophers from every corner of the world to present and discuss the many problems besetting humanity. We, of the Field-Being Institute, had reserved a room for a roundtable discussion on Field-Being and Buddhism and were able to make many worthwhile contacts and attract several new members. I delivered my commentary on the Dharmakaya and found that I was nervous and most fearful that someone might ask a question which would challenge my limited knowledge. This did not happen and I found, much to my surprise, that I produced a modicum of interest in the subject matter, which lasted into the hallway.

The whole conference was very exhausting and after returning home I felt an urgent need to repose and renew, so I called my friend Mu Soeng at the Barre Center for Buddhist Studies to see if I could come up and visit. Mu Soeng provided me with my old room in the "farmhouse" where I could be alone for rest and contemplation. After a short talk about events in our lives I excused myself to eat dinner and then to my room to read and listen to music on my headset. I found myself dozing off and so prepared for bed. In the morning, at about 6:00 A.M., I rose, showered, shaved, and went to the *zendo* to sit *zazen* for forty minutes. When I finished *zazen* I made my way to the kitchen in search of breakfast.

As I walked into the kitchen I saw a small man wearing a gray knit hat, which matched his gray robes, sitting at the table eating. I made a *gassho* and said, "Good morning, my name is Al Shansky." He looked up with his full-moon eyes and replied, "Good morning, I am called Bhante. Come and join me. Try some of this lovely oatmeal." I sat next to him after spooning out several dips of the steaming oatmeal from the pot into my plate.

It was warm and somewhat lumpy but when I sweetened it with brown sugar and cinnamon it gave a smooth nut-like flavor. I noticed that Bhante had a completely shaven head after removing his knit cap. His head was round and smooth with deep-set round eyes and dark, thick, brooding eyebrows. His skin seemed hairless but was naturally bronze and slightly fleshy. I assumed from his appearance and speech he was of subcontinent descent, possibly Sri Lanka.

I told him of my feeling of boredom and ennui. He then responded with an invitation to join him at his monastery. He offered a one-room cabin, called a *kutis,* which was located on the premises of the Bhavana Society in a secluded forest near High View, West Virginia. This center offers Society members and friends rare, valuable opportunities to practice Buddhist meditation in an ideal setting. I immediately accepted, explaining that I would not practice *vipassana* meditation but would practice Zen meditation. He nodded in agreement and said, "As long as you emphasize a calm, centered awareness of mind and body leading to a fresh perspective on oneself, others, and life." He continued, "All that's needed is willingness, in the Buddha's words, to 'come and see' for oneself what this teaching is all about." Bhante (a term similar to Reverend) Henepola Gunaratana is the founder and president of the Society.

When I got there I was shown to the cabin which had a pot bellied stove but there were very few amenities and no furniture. The cabin, however, seemed very clean with a scrubbed wooden floor. This was going to be a real Spartan experience. I was told that meals would be provided in the dining hall or they could be taken to the cabin for solitary dining. I placed my sleeping bag on the floor in one corner and arranged my *zafu* and *zabuton* to face the west in accordance with good geomancy, also called *feng shui* (literally wind and water). *Feng shui* was originally practiced in China. Although not a religion, geomancy is an art which seeks to find places in the landscape in which complementary opposing elements are found to exist in a harmonic balance.

I decided to explore my surroundings. The area was completely wooded with oak and birch trees so thick that it seemed almost jungle-like. There was a high point which I began to climb to get a better view. When I reached the crest I saw what appeared to be a quicksilver lake, so I decided to descend from the diaphanous height of the mountain into the lake of fog. It was a lake surrounded by mountains and thick vegetation, shiny as a mirror but animated by the invisible whisper of a waterfall and birds flying overhead.

The next morning I awoke at 4:30 A.M.and went to the communal bathhouse to shower, shave and brush my teeth. All was silent but I noticed several monks busy at their toilet. I returned to the cabin and began my Zen meditation. Meditation is the art of seeing things as they are with awareness and wisdom. Usually we see the world and everything around us through the filter of our concepts or thoughts and through our mental images which we have collected in our daily life since childhood. Thus, these thoughts and mental images form the way we look at the world. Thought is both the source of human activity and human suffering. Thought is the root of greed, anger and delusion — the three sources of suffering in a human being.

We cannot simply suppress greed, anger, and delusion by keeping moral precepts, nor can we suppress them by maintaining calmness through some form of meditation based on concentration. Though these activities are useful to some extent, we need to go to the root of suffering: to let awareness see thought and break through the chain of thought — to go against the stream of thought. When we see things as they are, outside of thought, the mind changes its qualities completely. At the very moment of awareness, the mind immediately becomes fresh, pure and quiet. With this fresh, pure and quiet mind, we look at the world in which we live from a totally new dimension and then other wholesome qualities in life, such as love, compassion and wisdom, can come into being.

After sitting *zazen* for one hour, I alternated with walking meditation for twenty minutes around the outside of the cabin. In the cold, clear weather in the early morning, the sky had turned an ice-blue and the drab colors of the trees began to emerge. A magpie flapped and sailed among the dark oaks as I walked down to the dining hall for breakfast.

Apparently there was a retreat in progress and I encountered several people at the buffet table who had a zombie-like appearance. Talking is not permitted in the dining hall during retreat, but I was aware that people avoided eye contact as well. Most people looked down, averting confrontation, while walking and moving very slowly. In my experience with *vipassana* technique, this seems to be recommended procedure. Zen is a silent order, too, but eye contact is considered valuable as a friendly method of communication. Massive retreats have little meaning for me if there is no way for people to be involved with each other. For this reason I usually choose a solitary retreat where I am able to concentrate full time on meditation.

On my way back to the cabin I met a young man who was hiking up the trail to the mountaintop. I was following him because the cabin was in the same direction. He turned while waiting for me to catch up.

"Hi," he exclaimed. "Are you staying in the cabin?"

"Yes," I replied. "Would you like to see it?"

"Oh, yes, indeed," he responded exuberantly. He told me his name was Howard Sprake and that he worked as a law clerk in one of the government agencies in Washington. He said he became interested in Buddhism through readings but just started meditation instruction on this occasion. He admired my robes and my past history which I disclosed to him in conversation. We entered the cabin and sat on the floor while we talked. He kept asking me questions about Buddhism, which I was delighted to answer.

"I am wondering how meditation can lead to enlightenment," he naively asked. I was stunned by the question because it reminded me of a similar conversation I had in Hosshinji with Oscar the pilot (see Part 1). Why is it that people believe meditation will inevitably lead to enlightenment? Meditation is not an ineluctable process like night following day. Enlightenment is a learning process that takes much time and involvement. I answered him as best I could:

"The idea of enlightenment entails liberty, equality, rationalism, secularism, and the connection between knowledge and human well-being. In spite of the setbacks of revolutionary violence, political mass murder, and two world wars, the spread of enlightenment values has become the yardstick by which morals, political, and even scientific advances are measured.

"Different forms of meditation — breathing, counting, and mantras — are all with limited success. While these practices help to calm the mind, none led to deep understanding — to enlightenment. The aim of meditation is to attain direct insight into one's self— freedom from pain and suffering — and to attain a healthy mind, one that is stable and wise."

I stopped talking for a moment and noticed that Howard's eyes were beginning to glaze. I rallied my thoughts and said, "Shall I continue?" He responded by shaking his head affirmatively up and down.

"In Zen teaching, thought and awareness are two basic elements in a human being. When awareness is weak, thought drags us away into the past and future, forming a strong chain. Zen meditation stimulates, develops, and strengthens awareness to see thought and break through its chain. Through meditation, awareness becomes active and clear, and as a natural consequence encounters the process of thinking and sees thought clearly. It is very important in meditation not to suppress thought by any kind of concentration. If we do, though we might find contentment and joy, we will be unable to see the nature of thought. Rather, we should let thought flow freely and let awareness know and see it clearly. All we have to do is properly set up the mind and strengthen awareness. As a result, suffering is reduced and wisdom arises. The practice of Zen meditation, called *zazen*, can be carried out through our daily activities through a series of experiences by which the mind progresses stepwise towards the end of suffering.

"I know this is a long-winded explanation but I felt I should let you know the truth of what to expect from your involvement with Buddhism. Any quick and betoken method will militate against a positive effect. It won't be easy. Once you get started you will undoubtedly experience many failures. Just remember that failures are much more memorable than successes and so it will be constantly in your thoughts until you become an expert," I declared with conviction and assurance.

After the explanation, I felt I was riding a tiger much like the sages of ancient mythology. A Muslim holy man may ride astride a tiger as blithely as the Daoist sage Chang Tao-ling in his quest for enlightenment, or the Goddess Durga in the Indus Valley civilization, or the Buddhist ancestor Manjusri. I was fearful of falling off the tiger and thus being punished for my pontificating sermon.

I shook hands with Howard after we exchanged addresses and telephone numbers but I must confess there was no further undertaking. I packed up and looked for Bhante to say goodbye but I could not find him. So I went to the office building and left a donation check after being told that the retreats are offered free of charge in the spirit of *dana*, a Sanskrit word which means generosity. I then drove home.

The Third Symposium

I returned with a renewed spirit, ready to get involved with the third symposium of the Field-Being Institute. After consultation with Dr. Tong we decided to take advantage of the larger auditorium at the School of Business since we now thought that the next symposium might produce at least sixty papers. We were certainly growing and needed extra space for future presentations and accommodations. Dean Beverly Kahn was extremely resourceful in helping to secure this new venue for us. I applied myself with new vigor, sending out emails to everyone that I could locate using directories and other mailing list sources, such as alumni lists and organizational membership lists.

In very short order, we received some inquiries about our organization and the proposed third symposium. Also, our website engendered a significant number of requests for information. In addition, I had arranged for my youngest daughter Carol to play her flute to entertain us during the barbecue dinner on Saturday, August 14, 1999. She is a wonderfully accomplished musician. The Field-Being Institute was lucky to have her perform for their pleasure.

The Fairfield University campus is truly beautiful. The western section contains the Dolan campus, which is almost embedded in a thick, wooded area. The Campus flows with rolling green hills reminiscent of a sea of grass. In August the weather is warm and bright but nevertheless of salubrious quality. The grassed fields are in late verdure, decorated here and there with groves of floriferous and fragrant trees and shrubs, under cover and protection of pyramidal laurels and plumed, white birches, which now and then break through upon the sight from both sides of the roadway as we pass along, going up hill from the Barlow Road entrance.

As we enter the campus, the School of Business is on the left; on the right is the Bellarmine Pond, populated with Canadian geese with their white chin strap-looking necks, which come to feed on the succulent grasses surrounding the pond. Next to the pond is the Quick Center for the Performing Arts. Continuing up the hill on the left is the majestic, baroque-looking building called Bellarmine Hall, sitting on the campus' highest point, surveying all below like a captain of a ship standing at the forecastle.

Bellarmine Hall is the main administrative building of the University. Behind Bellarmine Hall is a lovely Zen garden, a shaded retreat, in a beautiful grove of maples and myrtles, where I sometimes sit in quiet meditation. We then passed the library on the right side, rolling downhill to a valley. After passing Bellarmine Hall we came to Donnarumma Hall, where my office is located. The parking lot of Donnarumma Hall abuts a wooded area wherein I have often seen deer with their faun ungulates as well as dark brown, wild turkeys on the ground and in the trees, and at times sea-green, miniature parakeets in flight fading to an azure spatter, reminding me of a Jackson Pollack canvas.

As the participants arrived they were assigned to sleeping quarters in the "townhouses," which are a form of condominium dormitory. There were forty speakers at this symposium. Among the speakers were Dr. Arjuna de Zoysa from the Open University of Sri Lanka and Dr. E. K. Altekar from the University of Poona in India. Both of these gentlemen presented papers on the interface of science and religion. I mention this because my paper, "Buddhist Shunyata, Process Theology, and Quantum Theory as Modes of Thought in Field-Being Philosophy," became part of the nucleus established by these two gentlemen on the philosophy of science from a Field-Being perspective.

At the conclusion of the symposium, we enjoyed a barbecue dinner on the patio of the business school. While standing about and talking, Fernando Alves, one of our student assistants, who asked if I believe in God, approached me. Actually, his question was, "Is there a God?" I answered as succinctly as I knew how: "Buddhism is a self-reliant religion and so has no need for a deity or a supreme being. Today many people are perplexed by the notion of God. Some have become agnostics or atheists because they reject outmoded ideas of God. Others were brought up to believe in God, but as they grew older were not sure that such a belief was reasonable in the modern scientific climate. Others hold on to faith but when challenged find it difficult to explain why they believe. Others have religious experiences, which make it impossible for them not to believe.

"Buddhism does not say that God does not exist. It merely says that Buddha is not a God and if you treat him as such you are looking the wrong way. One should look inwardly to correct problems that arise in life. Only you can help yourself. That is why I say that during meditation one should exercise the art of auscultation like a physician examining a patient with a stethoscope by listening to the sounds within the body."

He seemed to absorb what I was saying and every so often would nod his head in affirmation. Finally, he said, "But isn't it important to have faith and to lean on some outside source for support?"

I looked at him with profound strain and intensity and continued, "We all appear in this world as incomplete beings. There are all sorts of teachings available for that incomplete self. On the path to what we truly are, all sorts of things occur. When we really understand our nature, we understand that there is not any one single thing to be left out, avoided, or rejected. What Buddhism says is, when you manifest the true self, and then you have as your content everything that is good and bad. These are your very content; they are within you. What one has to realize is that, of course, we all want to be good people, but if one leaves out the devil, then one has just become a good fixated person. When we manifest a complete self, then we have as our complete content both the plus and the minus, both the good and the evil. That is why they say when one manifests true wisdom consciousness, the complete doing that is knowing, then there is neither God nor the devil."

Fernando left and I felt that he might have agreed with me. We rarely find that people have good sense unless they agree with us. I was hoping he understood my position as a Buddhist. It was not my intention to change his views. Fernando was born a Catholic and I was speaking from the Buddhist perspective. I was impressed when Fernando told me he was going to Japan to teach English to high school students.

After the symposium the group slowly disbanded with tearful good-byes in some cases. All went their separate ways. The next year was the beginning of a new millennium and offered hope and progress for our continuing search for happiness and satisfaction.

• PART 3 •

The International Institute for Field-Being

The New Millennium

The year became 2000 and the hope was for peace. It was once figured out that since the world began there has only been twenty years of total peace. That's a frightening assessment of mankind. We all profess world peace, but in my view we should strive for inner peace as well. Inner peace is the unique feeling that all human beings on this earth are seeking throughout their lifetimes. Inner peace is a state of being that we try to achieve through self-satisfaction, satisfaction with our lot in life, discovering who we are, and how we fit into this world.

Inner peace can only be achieved by dismissing all negative thoughts within ourselves; releasing the anger, revenge, hate, jealousy, envy, and other negative feelings that we possess. True inner peace is the peace we create within ourselves in our relationships to all human beings.

The time came to prepare for the Fourth Symposium of the International Institute for Field-Being. I began by notifying all the members of the Institute and placed "call for papers" notices in several philosophy journals and newsletters of the coming symposium. With the help of Dean Beverly Kahn, I was able to obtain the Business School auditorium as our venue once again. Indeed, Dean Kahn arranged for a Dean's reception for one of the evenings at the reception room of Bellarmine Hall.

We presented fifty-four papers with an additional eighteen audience participants, giving us the largest group to date. If this rate of growth continued we would necessarily have to arrange for concurrent sessions for paper presentations, requiring occupancy of the second auditorium as well at the Fifth Symposium in 2001.

Bellarmine Hall is a beautiful baroque building in Norman architectural style with Romanesque influence. Duke William I first introduced this style into England in 1066 after the conquest of England by a mixed French-Norman race. The present occupants, who converted it to the main administrative building of the campus, retained all of the period trappings such as the doors and walls. The foyer and reception room was to be used for the Dean's reception. This room has a terrace with a balustrade, which looks out on a field of carpet-like green grass surrounded by trees and flowering shrubs. Outside it was growing dark; the grass field surrounded the building with a guard of weeping willows and one could get lost in the labyrinths of high hedges and even higher trees, whose whispering voices were disorienting and could make anyone lose their way with the sound of rustling leaves. In observing this array, I felt what a very crude and clumsy clod I am — only of the earth, a minute speck among one hundred million stars — how can I write what is there? It is only to be written by the mind or soul, and that is why I strive so much to find what I call the alchemy of nature.

Dean Kahn arranged for a string quartet comprised of volunteer students to play background music for the guests as they munched finger food and slaked their thirst with a choice of many different kinds of beverages. The guests meandered into groups and talked about a myriad of subjects. It was at this time that I encountered Patel Gyopa, who approached me from behind and engaged me in a conversation about nature.

"I am very interested in nature and ecology," I said, "but I am afraid at the rate we are going, much of the rainforest in several countries will soon be gone and there is a real danger of speciation loss that can never be recovered."

While holding a glass of beer in his massive hand he replied, "I come from Calcutta, where the poor are evident everywhere. These people cannot get enough food to sustain life and yet we are more concerned with a few birds or trees than we are with people."

I looked at him as he spoke. Patel Gyopa was a very tall man, more than six feet, very dark, with both Indian and Negroid traces in his features—while his lips were thick, his profile was straight; while his hair was crinkly, his skin was smooth as sugar frosting, night-dark as a gypsy's. His eyes were green islands in a yellow sea. His broad, muscular shoulders spoiled the look of his neck, which was strong but longer than it seemed. Just as his arms were long and his devoutly proletarian hands were large, his torso was short, his legs long, and his feet bigger than a miner's shoes. He was powerful, awkward, delicate, and different. This man seemed so alien to the usual social profile of a good philosophical professor. He was a descendant of an English father and an Indian mother and was obviously someone who spent a good part of his life in menial labor.

He smiled with a trace of malice but more than anything else with self-irony, and said, "If you are interested in nature and ecology the best approach is through a study of complexity. Complexity explores a tough and topical problem of interest to scientists, technologists, and philosophers. It is the best introduction to the subject of nature that I know of. What do you think?"

"You may be right," I rejoindered. "But the overall lesson is that the management of our affairs within a socially, technologically, and cognitively complex environment is plagued with vast management problems and risks of mishap. In primitive societies, failure to understand how things work can endanger a family or, at worst, a clan or tribe. In the modern world, man-made catastrophes on the model of Chernobyl can endanger millions, possibly even risking the totality of human life on our planet." Since he seemed interested, I continued to explain, "Technological escalation is a sort of arms race against nature in which scientific progress requires more powerful technology for observation and experimentation, and, conversely, scientific progress requires the continual enhancement of technology." I paused for a moment then continued, "I am reminded of the movie produced by the famous Japanese film director, Akira Kurosawa. This film, called *Dreams*, was a series of eight vignettes, one of which was called 'Mount Fuji in Red,' depicting an accidental blow-up of the civilian nuclear reactors, leading to the complete devastation of the islands of Japan." The moral here is that we should fear human error or accident more than deliberate war.

The paper that I presented at the Fourth Symposium had the title, "Buddhist Motives in the Prose of Samuel Beckett." In this paper, I chose five of Beckett's novels —*Murphy*; *Watt*; and the trilogy, *Malloy*, *Malone Dies*, and *The Unnamable*— as examples of prose writing in which Beckett unknowingly uses Buddhist thought in the revelation of his characters and their experiences with an existential life. Beckett's novels are in fact an expression of pure dilemma, the dilemma of being human, which in this case can be simply put as "Clearly there is no God. And yet there must be."

Eastern philosophies resolve such existential problems by ruthlessly examining the mind — just as Beckett does. I have used my knowledge of Buddhism as a tool to understand the nature of the dilemma that Beckett's insightful observations of the human mind reveal: the nature of consciousness and personal identity; the meaning of existence and suffering; the truth of reality; time, change and transience; and the possibility of salvation. Buddhism uses this dilemma itself to effect an enlightenment that revolutionizes the mind and brings tranquility at last.

The paper was very well received and engendered many questions from the audience, particularly as related to existentialism. Dr. Tong told me later that my paper would be published on the electronic website of the Journal of the International Institute for Field-Being. I was grateful that my paper propagated so much interest among the existentialists in the audience. Dr. Tong is an expert on existentialism as he teaches a course in this subject with emphasis on Nietzsche.

After a while, I sat in the anteroom of the auditorium to rest and recover from my presentation. I was looking out of the window at the people milling about, having come from so many diverse locations.

"Excuse me," a woman said. "My name is Anjela Maldonado. I really enjoyed your paper. I am a professor of English Literature and Beckett is one of my favorite authors. May I join you?"

"Of course," I said with outstretched hand. "Please sit here."

I looked at her. Her face was as white as the moon, and her whiteness emphasized her thick, continuous, black eyebrows, which ran across her forehead and cast more of a shadow over the circles under her eyes, circles like the shadow of her immense eyes, as black as they say sin is black, although the eyes of this woman were swimming in a lake of omens. She was dressed in black, with long skirts and low-heeled shoes, her blouse buttoned up to her neck, and a black shawl nervously covering her back, tightly but carelessly wrapped, slipping down to her waist. Her disarray embarrassed her, as if it gave her a clownish air, and made her readjust the shawl over her shoulders, though not over her hair, which was divided strictly by a center part and gathered into a bun at the nape of her neck, where long, loose hairs had escaped as if a secret part of her were rebelling against the discipline of her costume. The loosened hairs were not as black as the tight hairdo of this pale, nervous woman, as if they were announcing something, antennas for some undesired news.

She began speaking slowly in a low tone almost as if she were revealing a long hidden secret. "I am a Catholic," she murmured with a susurration of breath, "And I find that I must carry my rosary beads with me at all times because I find them comforting and objects to focus on while I pray. I pray all the time. I revere these rosary beads as worship aids because they make the idea of God more concrete. I know that I can put my hands on them at any time as a tactile reminder of God." She opened her hand with a timorous movement and showed me a strand of 100 glass beads with a crucifix at one end lying in a pile in her palm. I was amazed at the sight and more so at her next comment. "I meditate on specific mysteries related to the life of Jesus while saying prayers on each bead."

I felt it necessary to reply, "I think it is wonderful that you have such a commitment. However, you should not be embarrassed. Plain strings of beads have been used in many religions as aids to open a path to the divine." I continued, "Muslim prayer beads are called *Mesbaha* from the Arabic word 'to praise.' Muslims touch each bead and recite the 99 names of Allah found in the Koran. The Hindu *Mala* are thought to be the oldest prayer beads. *Mala* means 'garland' in Sanskrit. Hindus use the beads to repeat mantras or to count breaths. Of course, the Buddhists have a *Mala* as well, which was adapted from the Hindu practice. The 108 beads of a Buddhist *Mala* represent the number of worldly desires or negative emotions that need to be overcome before reaching the state of nirvana; saying a prayer on each bead is supposed to bring purification."

She looked at me with a tranquil expression on her face. "Then you don't think I am foolish for depending so strongly on my rosary?"

"Not at all," I said.

She continued, "You see, it has become a habitual part of my life. I spent nine years of my life as a Roman Catholic nun. After leaving my order in 1978, I took a degree in English literature from Leicester University in London and now teach at San Ildefonso Bible University in San Antonio, Texas."

"You mentioned that you 'meditate on specific mysteries related to the life of Jesus.' Are you able to describe for me what kind of meditation you perform?"

She hesitated for a long moment, then proceeded to relate her meditation experience to me. "It doesn't matter where I am; I find a quiet spot and turn to the wall and allow the image of Jesus to whelm up and overtake me," she said in a quiet, deliberate way.

"That reminds me of a friend who claims he can meditate anywhere," I added with discretion. "My friend, Jamshed Shroff, a Parsi, anglicized his first name to Jim. Jim used to live in Riverside, Connecticut, and commuted every day to New York City where he worked as a synthetic organic chemist for the biotechnology firm, Forest Laboratories, Inc. Jim almost never got a seat on the commuting train so he decided to use his time while standing for 45 minutes to meditate. He found that standing meditation worked very well for him and he claims to have been refreshed when he got off the train. I believe him," I said, in order to reinforce her disclosure to me.

Suddenly, I was rescued by two approaching figures — Dean Beverly Kahn and her husband. I rose to greet them. "Hi Beverly, this is a lovely party. Thanks to you the Field-Being Institute is gaining a sophisticated reputation."

Beverly Kahn was a woman with a mother-of-pearl complexion and perfect facial symmetry accentuated by her hair, parted down the middle, with the sensual youth of her eternal figure. "Hi, Al," she said with a smile showing her pearl-white teeth. "I'd like you to meet my husband, George."

I grabbed his outstretched hand as I said, "I am delighted to meet you." I hastily responded, "This is Anjela Maldonado." For a few moments we all engaged in small talk, then we parted company. I was very tired and decided to go home. I couldn't help thinking of the *bon mot* given by Oscar Wilde, "Religions die when they are proved to be true."

Never the Twain Shall Meet

In mid-autumn, I received an invitation from Dr. Susantha Goonatilake of the Vidyartha Center for Science and Technology in Sri Lanka to attend the International Conference on Knowledge and East-West Transitions to be held December 11–14, 2000, at the National Institute of Advanced Studies on the campus of the Indian Institute of Science in Bangalore, India. The conference focused on the uses of Asian civilization knowledge for developments in science and technology. It apparently was my paper, "Buddhist Shunyata, Process Theology, and Quantum Theory as Modes of Field-Being Thought," which impressed Dr. Arjuna DeZoysa enough to recommend me as a speaker.

I had given this paper at the Third Symposium of the Field-Being Institute and I remember that Dr. DeZoysa had congratulated me at the time. I was most grateful to him for the recommendation. This would be my eighth trip to India and I was looking forward to being there at this time of the year when the weather is so pleasant. Naturally, it was to be an expense-paid trip and, of course, that made it even more delightful.

My journey to Bangalore was the longest and most burdensome trip I have ever taken from a starting point to a destination. I traveled for over thirty hours after making three airplane changes and finally arrived in Bangalore airport at 3:00 A.M. I never cease to be amazed at the immense activity which takes place at airports in Asia during the wee hours. There were people milling about everywhere. Naturally, no one came to meet me as promised so I was required to take one of the polluting put-puts which barely enabled me and my luggage a place to fit.

After riding a bone-crushing hour we arrived at the campus front gate which was locked and unguarded. I discovered a wall-phone at the side of the guardhouse and proceeded to make contact with anyone who would answer. Finally, after much ado, I found someone who kindly gave me directions to the NIAS dormitories. I was sorry to have woken the respondent but at the same time I was grateful to have been relieved of my anxiety and frustration, which was beginning to wear me down.

I arrived at the dormitory to be greeted by a sleepy individual who gave me a key after checking my name on a roster. He grabbed my luggage and, with a wave of his hand to follow him, we proceeded to my room. As I opened the door a noise within immediately told me that I disturbed the sleep of my roommate. I undressed in the dark and popped into bed exhausted from the travails of the journey.

The next morning I met my roommate, Dr. John Pickering. John is a professor in the Psychology Department of Warwick University in Coventry, England. After some preliminary discussion about future events and the location of facilities, John went out to a grassed area to perform his daily Tai Chi, while I showered and shaved and sat *zazen*.

I learned that there were fifty-seven papers to be presented. There were only eight Westerners among the group, of whom four came from the USA and four came from Europe. All the papers had a scientific motive with modification from different perspectives, such as history, language, or religion.

I went to breakfast in the dining room where I met Professor Anindya Sinha, who apologized for my difficulty last night. He thought I was arriving at 3:00 P.M. today. I showed him a copy of my letter indicating the 3:00 A.M. hour. His embarrassment was quite evident as he told me that the taxi charge would be reimbursed. I thanked him and proceeded to devour a wonderful English breakfast. While eating Dr. Sinha gave me an orientation lesson in the procedures of the conference together with a program and a booklet containing copies of the papers to be presented.

Sitting in the auditorium while listening to the speakers brought me to heights of understanding of which I was unaware. Some of these papers exposed a new dimension in the dichotomy of science and religion. Nature has secrets and it is the desire to uncover them that motivates the scientific quest. But what makes these "secrets" secret? Is it that they are beyond human ken? Do they concern divine matters? And if they are accessible to human seeking, why do they seem so carefully hidden? Such questions were at the heart of the papers being presented at this conference, in an effort to uncover the meaning of modern science. Some papers portrayed the struggle between the scientist and nature as the ultimate game of hide-and-seek, in which a childlike wonder propels the exploration of mysteries.

At lunchtime, I approached John Pickering with an invitation to join the Fifth Symposium of Field-Being, which was planned for August 2001 on the Fairfield University campus. He eagerly accepted and I felt good about his coming. Lunch consisted of typical Indian food with a lowered level of spice. I must say that I was grateful for the English-style breakfast we got every morning, since I find it difficult to eat too much of the Indian food, lowered spice notwithstanding.

I was able to convince four other members to accompany me by hiring a taxi to take us to Mysore. These members were Tej Prasad Gauchan and Min Bahadur Shakya, both from Nepal, and Anwar Nasim and Khalid Mahmood Khan, both from Pakistan. They all spoke English fluently but more importantly they all spoke Urdu, which was understood by the people in Mysore.

It was a four-hour ride to Mysore over some of the worst roadways I have ever experienced. We left Bangalore at 5:00 A.M. to arrive in Mysore about 9:00 A.M. The first thing we did was eat breakfast in an Indian "greasy spoon." I became most friendly with Anwar, who seemed very interested in me. I learned he was once married to a Canadian woman who died some years ago of breast cancer, causing him to eventually return to Pakistan, leaving his two grown sons in Canada. He has since remarried a Pakistani woman and invited me to visit him in Islamabad. I thought this might be possible on my way to the conference of the International Society of Chinese Philosophy in Beijing in July 2001.

After our morning excursion, Anwar asked our driver, "Do you know where there is a fast food restaurant?" The driver, not knowing the meaning of fast food, answered, "Yes sir, I know of an excellent fast food restaurant." Anwar looked at me as if to gain assurance and I said, "Let's go see this place." When we arrived at King's Court, I was dumbstruck by what I saw. This was no McDonald's. The doorway was made of rich, dark wood trimmed with architectural brass hardware. There was a turbaned doorman wearing white *jodhpurs* to greet us with proper obeisance. As we walked inside, a *maitre d'* seated us at an oblong table set with French service. Each place was set with Dresden china, knives, forks, spoons in proper order, and, to the right of each plate, a stiff linen napkin rolled up in a silver ring.

While looking at the menu, I was shocked at the prices. I hastily announced to the group that I would treat them all to lunch. This made a big hit, but I must confess that the prices were so low that my largesse was somewhat deceptive. The lunch for five people, which included entrée, desert, drinks and tip, came to just a little over fifteen dollars.

After a jovial lunch we drove to Melkote, a pilgrim center known for its handlooms. We spent most of the afternoon visiting a mosque and a Buddhist temple, then in late afternoon we started for home. It was a long and tiring day so we dispersed to our various rooms for rest and resuscitation. I still maintain email contact with my four comrades and I shall always remember the wonderful day we spent in Mysore together.

The next day I presented my paper, which brought forth many questions and much discussion from the audience. As I left the podium, I noticed an elderly man dressed in what seemed to be faded brown robes approaching me. He was totally bald. The extreme smoothness of his skull, bare as a baby's backside, contrasted brutally with his infinitely wrinkled face, crisscrossed by tiny lines running in all directions. A face that was an insane compass rose, its cardinal points not at north, east, south, and west but scattered in every direction, a cobweb with no symmetry. The wrinkles on his face were as uncountable as furrows in a field plowed for centuries and yielding poorer and poorer crops.

He held up his hands in a *gassho* gesture and said in a faint, crackling voice with a staccato accent, "Do you think we should study animal consciousness?"

I looked into his deep, sunken eyes and replied, "In answering this question, it must be assumed that behavior and consciousness in both animals and human beings result entirely from events that occur in their central nervous systems, and that there are no immaterial or supernatural processes underlying conscious, subjective thoughts and feelings." I stopped talking for a moment until I noticed his head nodding in assent.

So I continued, "We can also assume that consciousness has a function to play in our lives. These two important assumptions are enough to warrant an interest into how consciousness, as a functional, operational process, evolved in the animal kingdom and came to be such an important part of the mind." Once again, I looked at him and noticed a faint smile on his thin lips. He began blinking his eyelids as if to recognize my thoughts.

I slowly began talking again, "One point that must be remembered, however, is that we are unaware of most of the events that occur in our brains. But that component of central nervous system activity that gives rise to our conscious thoughts is of special significance because that is what binds us to a feeling of reality and makes us acutely aware of our existence. Animals possibly carry out much, or even most, of their behavior quite unconsciously, but insofar as they are conscious, their consciousness is an important attribute — from their own perspective and also from that of our own selfish one of trying to understand how we came to be what we are today."

He was somewhat short and slightly bent over, so he had to look up when he replied, "Thank you for your insight. My name is Sunil Goonasekera from Sri Lanka. I enjoyed your paper very much. I am very much interested in the concept of *intentional stance*, put forward by the cognitive scientist and philosopher, Daniel Dennett of Tufts University; maybe we can get together later and continue our discussion."

I took his hand and held it with its thick veins and old freckles and said, "Of course." Unfortunately, this never occurred since we all left at the end of the conference.

That night we were treated with two hours of entertainment in the auditorium, which was converted to a performance hall. A troupe of fifteen dancers and musicians were brought in from different parts of the country to perform original dances of their region, accompanied by live music. I was to leave the next day but shuddered at the prospect of my thirty-hour trip home.

Much Ado

After New Year 2001, I returned to Fairfield University to prepare for the Fifth Symposium of the Field-Being Institute (IIFB) on the Fairfield University campus in August as well as the International Society for Chinese Philosophy (ISCP) in Beijing in July. A vision of the future for me in 2001 entailed a period of tremendous amount of work. Now that I was committed to both conferences (IIFB and ISCP), I had to write a paper for each. I decided to write one paper on my life maturation through three philosophical changes for the ISCP. This could be considered a kind of philosophical journey, from the Marxism in my youth, through Existentialism in mid-age and Buddhism in finality.

The person who would understand the modern world must come to terms with Marx's ideas. The magnetic power of Marxism, unparalleled in the history of mankind, has drawn into its orbit peoples of different continents and races. Few will now deny that the communist movement, which invokes the name of Marx, has tarnished the ideal, which inspired his work. But the reaction against Marxism in America has finally led to a distortion in our conception of our own past and future. Marxist ideas have had an important part in shaping our contemporary political philosophy, and we would do well not to try to banish that chapter from our consciousness.

After Marxism, I was intrigued by Existentialism because it is one of the most exciting and enduring philosophies of our time. With its powerful emphasis on individual responsibility and the importance of passion and freedom, it provided me with a vision that was particularly appealing.

Existentialism is not a unified, confining system. Existentialism includes the religious existentialism of the Danish philosopher Soren Kierkegaard and his famous doctrine of the Leap of Faith. Existentialism also includes the warrior rhetoric and often shocking attacks on religion and morality by Friedrich Nietzsche. It encompasses the bold and profound approach to life advocated by Martin Heidegger. And Existentialism, while it is treated as philosophy, is developed significantly in literature.

The "absurd" view of life envisioned by the French-Algerian novelist Albert Camus is part of the existential tradition. And a major figure in existentialist thought is the French existentialist, Jean-Paul Sartre. He developed his radical, uncompromising notion of freedom in plays, literature, and, more technically, philosophical writings. And, of course, there are Fyodor Dostoevsky and Samuel Beckett who wrote without realizing the existential importance of their work.

In its 2500-year history, Buddhism has grown from a tiny religious community in Northern India into a movement that spans the globe. Buddhism originated in India, as a revolt to orthodox Hinduism, in the 6th century B.C.E., to its present-day status as a major world religion. The astonishing vitality and adaptability of a tradition has transformed the civilization of India, Southeast Asia, Tibet, China, Korea, and Japan and has now become a lively component in the cultures of Europe, Australia, and the Americas. More than twenty years ago, it became my opportunity to trace the evolution of this theology that is both familiar and foreign and to think in new ways about the definition of a satisfying and productive life. Thus, I titled my paper, "Marxism, Existentialism, and Buddhism: A Journey of Field-Being Ideas," to be presented in July 2001 at the International Society for Chinese Philosophy (ISCP) in Beijing, China.

As if I didn't have enough work, I was approached one day by Danke-Li, a Chinese lady who is a professor in the History Department of Fairfield University and a friend of Dr. Tong. She asked me if I would lecture on basic Buddhism to her class on Modern Japan. At first I was hesitant but, on reflection, I agreed to do this lecture because I felt it would cement my relations with the Dean and the Academic Vice President.

Danke-Li is a wonderful person who was kind and considerate to me ever since Dr. Tong introduced me to her. As I spoke with her I was aware of her graceful manners. Her hair was jet black; her face was a tawny-gold, the mouth small and red as a ripe fruit, teeth white and neatly aligned, erect of posture, a demure gaze, and clear eyes. Her smooth speech was modest, the body slender. She seemed to dominate in her dazzling grace all those surrounding her. I always got the feeling in our relationship that she treated me as an older uncle, which is a position of respect in the Chinese familial pantheon. At the lecture, I was surprised that many students asked meaningful questions, some about Buddhism and its comparison to Christianity. Danke-Li thanked me heartily as I left to return to my office. I did accept her gracious invitation to lunch.

Having acquitted myself dutifully, I returned to the business of the Field-Being Institute. In addition to writing my own papers, I had to arrange for a call for papers for the Fifth IIFB Symposium. I was able to contact all IIFB members throughout the world via email. By this method we received some commitments for the pending conference. We would probably have about sixty papers and an additional eighteen audience participants. I received an acknowledgement from John Pickering, whom I befriended in India. Also, because of the large number of papers expected, we have decided to have concurrent sessions. We employed six students to help with room monitoring and other needed tasks.

Together with our members from Asia and Europe, we at the IIFB had become truly international. It is with this thought in mind that we decided to have our future symposia in a foreign country. Dr. Tong had already solicited arrangements for the Sixth Symposium in Xi'an, China.

In addition to the work and problems associated with the two conferences (ISCP and IIFB) taking place this summer in July and August respectively, Dr. Tong and I were committed to act as delegates to the Center for Process Studies (CPS), commonly called the Whitehead Conference, at the Claremont Graduate School of Theology in Claremont, California, January 4–6, 2001. It was at the CPS meeting that we made contact with Michel Weber of Belgium, Franz Riffert of Austria, Jean-Marie Breuvart of France, and Helmut Maasen of Germany, all of who accepted our invitation to present a paper at the Fifth IIFB Symposium at Fairfield University in August.

These gentlemen are experts in process philosophy (Whitehead) and as such present a Western view of non-substantialism. Process philosophy is the doctrine that either what is is becoming, or that what is ultimately consists in change, or both. A process is a sequence of changes. Strong and weak process philosophy may be usefully distinguished. On the weak version it is sometimes maintained that each thing is always changing in every respect. On the strong version, there are only changes or, at least, the existence of enduring items logically depends upon changes, such that it is ontologically misleading to speak of what is or things that are.

The principles of the CPS meeting put us up at the Claremont Inn, which is a lovely, quiet, bucolic setting. The Inn had a shuttle bus and I was successful in making private arrangements with the driver to take me to the Hsi Lai Temple in Hacienda Heights. This is the temple made famous by Vice President Al Gore when he solicited donations for the 1996 Presidential campaign there.

Hsi Lai Temple encompasses 15 acres. The temple's Ming (1368–1644 C.E.) and Ching (1644–1911 C.E.) dynasty architecture is faithful to the traditional style of buildings, gardens and statuary of traditional ancient Chinese monasteries.

In 1967, Venerable Master Hsing Yun, the founder, established the Fo Guang Shan (Buddha's Light Mountain) Buddhist order, which is the largest monastery in Taiwan, encompassing over 600 acres. Fo Guang Shan is a Mahayana Chinese Buddhism monastic order. Mahayana in China has separated into eight different schools: Tian-tai, Pure Land, Ch'an, Hua-yen (Avatamsaka), Fa-shiang (Yogocara), Sanlun (Madhyamika), Dhyana, and Tantra. Fo Guang Shan belongs to the Lin-Chi Ch'an School. Hsi Lai Temple was built to serve as a spiritual and cultural center for those interested in learning more about Buddhism and Chinese culture.

I walked through the entire complex, inspecting all the buildings and gardens. This took about four hours and I wound up at the courtyard. The courtyard is used for walking meditation and I joined others walking over the geometric rectangles, which symbolize rice paddies. My driver was asleep in the shuttle bus when I approached to be driven back to the Claremont Inn.

Out of the Armchair

I was approached, once again, by Danke-Li to present a lecture to her class, Modern Japan, on the field of *ukiyo-e* prints. I had revealed to her that I had a sizeable collection of *ukiyo-e* prints in my possession and that these could represent pictures of life in old Japan.

The *ukiyo-e*, or "pictures of the floating world," which began to appear in the 17th century, are realistic representations of the actual world of the day. The idea that life is a floating world can be found in both East and West. For instance, it is stated in the Chinese classic *Chuang-tzu* that human life is adrift on the floating water called death, and Heraclitus, a Greek philosopher, said that all things were in a state of flux. This way of thinking became stronger in Japan than in China through the influence of Buddhism.

The term *ukiyo* originally was used in the Buddhist sense of the "transient and sad world." But when, after going through a period of incessant civil war, Japan became a society in which people could achieve success through ability, the term came to mean the "floating world" in which the fleeting pleasures of life were prized. In other words, the term came to be used in a worldly sense rather than in a religious one.

Ukiyo-e (floating world-picture) at first referred only to pictures of everyday life at the time, but later came also to include those treating historical or fantastic subjects, whether they were painted on sheets of paper or mass-produced by means of wood-block printing. At any rate *ukiyo-e* invariably represent the vital interests and concerns of the populace of the day, providing us with a good record of them.

My collection of several dozen *ukiyo-e* wood block prints by the most famous painters, such as Hiroshige, Hokusai, Sharaku, Utamaro, Chikanobu, and Shunsho, were accumulated over many years of visiting Japan. These depictions of Japanese life in the late eighteenth and early nineteenth century would make a valuable contribution to a class on Modern Japan.

My son, Richard, came to my house and with his 35 mm camera, took photographs of each of these prints as I placed them on an easel. The photos were then converted to slides and thus I was ready to lecture to Danke-Li's class with a carousel slide show.

Her class received the slide show with unusual enthusiasm. Of course, the pictures as art icons were beautiful in their own right. But, more importantly, the scenes they depicted — horsemen riding, farmers in the rice paddies, fishermen, scenes of home, courtesans, and kabuki scenes — all contributed to the interest of the students. Some scenes were familiar to some students, such as the Great Wave of Hokusai, which has been used in advertising and on calendars. But, generally the work was new and unknown to most of the students. At the end of the lecture, Danke-Li told me that she would try to get payment for me the next time she asked me to lecture. This made me feel good, but I vowed inwardly never to lecture again without payment.

Dr. Ed Grippe, assistant professor of philosophy at Norwalk Community College, has produced and coordinated an annual Great Ideas

Symposium commemorating the life of a great philosopher from a particular geographic area. This consists of a full day of lectures, seminars, and musical and theatrical performances. Dr. Grippe is a personal friend and a member of the International Institute for Field-Being.

Quite coincidently, I was asked by Dr. Grippe to present the very same lecture to a composite of students of the "intro" class and the Philosophy Club in the auditorium of the East campus. I agreed and was paid $200 for the lecture. The ice was broken; from now on I expect to be paid for lecturing.

With summer approaching Dr. Tong and I were preparing to leave for the 12th ISCP conference in Beijing. It was at this conference where I presented my paper, "Marxism, Existentialism and Buddhism: A Journey of Field-Being Ideas." Prof. Walter Benesch of the University of Alaska made a particular point of praising my paper in front of the audience. I was humbled by his remarks. After the conference a group of us, about twelve people, arranged to tour Xian and Dunhuang.

Xian, the capital of Shaanxi Province, is situated at the western end of a roughly equilateral triangle connecting Beijing and Shanghai. To the north of this city of about four million people lie the rugged Western Hills, dotted with ancient tombs. The chief interest in Xian is its archeological legacy. There are myriad tombs, temples and ruins in the area.

Among China's significant archeological finds of the 1970s were the thousands of life-size terracotta warriors and horses guarding the main entrance of the tomb of Qin Shi Huang Di (221–210 B.C.E.), the Qin Dynasty Emperor who unified China and linked together the segments of the Great Wall. A huge, hanger-like hall now protects it and next door is an IMAX theater, giving a realistic account of the war.

After three days in Xian, our group went on to Dunhuang, which is located in the Northwest desert corridor of Gansu Province near the Xinjiang border to the east and the Qilian mountain range to the west. This 2000-year-old town was once an important caravan stop on the Silk Road linking Central Asia and China. Today, it marks the site of one of the most priceless troves of Buddhist grotto art the world has ever known — the

Mogao Caves. Over a period of 1000 years, beginning in 366 C.E., literally hundreds of grottoes were carved out of the steep cliffs lining the Dang River. As in the grottoes later carved at Yungang (near Datong) and Longmen (near Luoyang), the main themes are the life of Buddha, various religious stories, and tales from Chinese folk mythology. It was my hope and intent to visit these latter two sites next year.

At about 5:00 A.M., during the period of incipient light, Sandra Wawrytko of the University of San Diego, Shohei Ichimura of the North American Zen Institute and I decided to climb up one of the sand dunes. When we reached the top we sat facing the East to watch the sun rise. An orange and yellow curtain hung in the night sky. It was a glorious display of color bouncing off the mountains until the light was too intense when the sun finally became visible overhead.

Afterwards we sat facing each other talking about ourselves in general terms. I became very friendly with both on this trip but, in particular, I had a close association with Ichimura-san because I was able to converse with him on occasion in my faulty Japanese and relate my interests in Zen to him. He has since sent me two texts of Zen writings, which he had translated. We then all returned to Beijing where I had a reservation at the Hotel New Otani Chang Fu Gong.

I had seen the Summer Palace and the Imperial Palace on previous visits, including the Great Wall and the Ming Tombs. Sandra Wawrytko returned to San Diego. I regret not having spent more time with her. She is the widow of Prof. Charles Wei-Hsun Fu of Temple University in Philadelphia. He was well known in the Department of Religion as a teacher of Chinese religions and philosophy. He died prematurely some years ago, leaving a serious vacuum in the status of Chinese religion in academia.

Into the Field

I returned to the States on August 10 and only had five days to prepare for the Fifth Symposium of the Field-Being Institute. It was at this time that I received the shocking news that Beverly Kahn was rejected for the permanent position of Dean and that a new Dean was installed. I went to Beverly to console her and express my sorrow at her leaving. I told her my favorite Dalai Lama saying: "Remember that not getting what you want is sometimes a wonderful stroke of luck." As it turns out this was somewhat prescient. She became Associate Provost of Pace University.

The Fifth Symposium was composed of concurrent sessions requiring people to make choices of the papers they want to hear. This is the first year we had eight "process people" speaking at our symposium and it made for a very congenial atmosphere. I chaired the Plenary Roundtable on Field-Being and Aesthetics and it was here that I gave my paper on Zen and art. In addition, I was a discussant in the session "Field-Being and Buddhism," as well as a speaker in the first concurrent session, chaired by my Bangalore roommate from England, John Pickering. I presented a paper, "Complexity, Reductionism and the Natural World."

Nota Bene

After a few months my life resumed. I received an email letter from Robert Magliola. Now retired from his professorships in Taiwan and Thailand, Robert Magliola continues as a consultant and interfaith retreatant of the Ling Chio Shan Buddhist Monastery in Taiwan and New York City. He invited me to attend services with him at the monastery's One Center at 10 Platt St. in lower Manhattan. I accepted and made a date to meet him there. Robert Magliola taught at universities overseas because he needed the money to provide full-time care for his sick and ageing mother who lived in Tom's River, New Jersey. She recently passed away in her mid–90s and so Robert retired and now lives in Tom's River.

When I arrived some people had preceded me into the temple. An amiable man, Sam Hsiao, who seemed to know to expect me, greeted me. I changed into my robes and shortly thereafter Robert Magliola arrived. We greeted each other and took up positions in the rear of the congregation. The Ling Chio Shan Temple is a Pure Land Buddhist temple, but Robert and I were able to do Zen meditation during the Chinese chanting of the other participants. I found the contrapuntal effect of the two disciplines to be quite wonderful. After the morning service, which took three hours, we partook of a vegetarian lunch. This is most unusual since Chinese culinary art depends to a great extent on meat, fowl, and fish, but you may be surprised to learn that tofu and beans along with mock chicken and mock duck made from flour go a long way in imitating meat and fowl. Services at Chinese temples on Sundays are usually accompanied by lunch where people gather to socialize and talk while partaking of the comestibles. It is an integral part of the service, which I find most friendly and even spiritual. I met and talked to several people who wanted to know all about me. I believe I made an important connection with these people. Most of the participants walked from Chinatown, which is nearby. Robert and I were the only Westerners.

As I left the One Center, Sam Hsiao shook my hand and invited me back. He gave me the phone number of the temple in order to check when services would be available and for me to make reservations.

Back to China

The beginning of another year, 2002, and preparations were being made for the Sixth IIFB Symposium to take place in Xian, China, at the Xiaotong University in August 2002. Xiaotong University is known as the MIT of China. It is a very large school devoted to science, engineering, and technology. It has a four-star hotel on campus where the participants will be housed. I had made five trips to China; 1980 with my son, 1983 with my wife, 1987 on business, and 2001 and 2002 for conferences. I have been to most parts of China and witnessed its growth into modernity over the past twenty years. I really love the country.

The total number of papers presented at the Sixth IIFB conference in Xian was 67 of which 38 papers were in Chinese and 29 papers were in English. The sessions were in concurrent format. Interestingly, some of the Field-Being members who were of Chinese descent and therefore bilingual attended the Chinese papers. The converse did not occur.

I chaired the 24th session wherein the paper, "Identity and the Doctrine of Karma in the Pali Nikayas," was presented by the Rev. Sammuk of the GaSup Sa Temple in Korea. I delivered my paper, "Zen Painting: A Field-Being Activity" at the 26th session, chaired by my friend, Prof. Wang Youru of Rowan University.

I had previously arranged for Prof. Curt Naser to accompany me to Luoyang and Datong. Now that the conference was over we made train reservations for Luoyang and the Longmen (Dragon Gate) Caves. Buddhism was introduced to Luoyang in 68 C.E. and one of China's first Buddhist monasteries, the Baimasi, was built here in 75 C.E. Carving in the Longmen Caves began in 494 under the Northern Wei and continued until the 7th century. The more than 1300 caves contain over 2100 grottoes and niches, several pagodas, countless inscriptions, and about 100,000 images and statues of Buddha. Together with the examples found in the caves at Dunhuang and Datong, the artwork of Longmen marks the high point of Buddhist culture in China.

Curt and I then returned to Xian for a day, which we spent visiting Hua Shan Mountain. We left at 9:00 A.M.for a two-hour ride to Hua Shan Mountain. The day was clear and warm and I was very apprehensive at my ability to perform considering my age. As early as two thousand years ago the Hua Shan was recognized as one of the five great mountains of China. It is about 45 miles east of the ancient city of Xian and is known for its sheer cliffs and precipices.

Hua Shan Mountain is about 6000 feet above sea level. A cable car took us up about 2000 feet to a starting point. Five peaks are most prominent: the North, South, East, West and Middle peaks. The South Peak is the tallest at about 6000 feet and is accessible only from the North Peak. Curt and I started the climb at the foot of the North Peak. The steepness of the step-path leading upward looks like a ladder hanging over the cliff.

It was worrisome, but we were there to enjoy the supreme beauty of Hua Shan and to test our mettle.

The path upward is almost perpendicular. Steps were cut into the rock face by Buddhist monks who climbed here through the centuries past. Iron chains have been installed for hand support. The path is only wide enough for one person to pass through at a time. This presents a problem when you encounter someone going down. Farther on is another flight of 570 stone steps. After we conquered this obstacle, the North Peak greeted us with open arms. We decided to rest at the teahouse on this terrace.

While resting there, we experienced what is known as a "white out." This is a phenomenon where clouds race in to the point where visibility is completely negated. After ten minutes of frightening blindness, we continued up the North Peak. I decided to try to meditate as I climbed but found my mind was too concerned about the danger of the height around me. Finally, we stopped at another terrace. Standing there, you get the feeling you can touch the sky and pick the stars. Clouds swirl around at your feet and the soughing of pines rises to your ear like the sound of the ocean.

It was a glorious climb but it was soon time to go down. Going up had been difficult but going down was painful and laborious. My legs felt like rubber bands and were troublesome in that it kept my mind from focusing properly. At last we descended and got aboard the cable car to take us down to the plaza. We then returned to Xian and the next day took the plane to Beijing. Curt and I rested in Beijing for two days, touring around the city by subway. We then arranged to take a train to Datong, the city of coal, of about a half-million people.

Datong is situated in northern Shaanxi Province on a dry, infertile plain. It is strategically located just south of the Great Wall and the border of Inner Mongolia. It was the Northern Wei conquerors that began carving the man-made caves at Datong in 460 C.E. known as Yungang caves.

In addition to Yungang, we visited the Hanging Temple at Mount Hengshan. It is built on a cliff face of Culping Peak. Because of its location and extraordinary structure, the temple has withstood earthquakes, storms and the effects of erosion. It is a perfect combination of natural beauty and human craftsmanship. We returned to Beijing the next day and continued our sightseeing for two more days. We then went home to pick up where we left off.

• PART 4 •

A Lonely
Buddhist Practitioner

San Francisco

After returning home from China at the near end of summer, I found myself in need of a rest before arranging for the presence of the International Institute for Field-Being (IIFB) at the American Philosophical Association (APA) meeting of the Eastern Division at the Philadelphia Marriott Hotel, December 26–29, 2002. There was one paper in particular which I enjoyed, "Buddhist Perspectives on Death."

It seems when the Buddha preached his *dharma*, one of the most contentious issues among his listeners was the subject of death, especially the question of whether or not there was an afterlife, or whether or not the soul was immortal. Many of his listeners seemed genuinely puzzled over the Buddha's teachings. As we know, when they approached him with these metaphysical questions, he was reluctant to provide a definite answer.

The notion of an eternal soul, or *tama*, originated around the fourth century, *tama* has some association with "breath" or "wind" and refers to a vital force or soul. However, the Japanese generally seem to be more interested in this life than in some afterlife. For example, an early practice was *tamayori*, literally meaning "calling the soul." This was calling the soul back into this life, so that death would not result, and was performed by calling the person's name. Today, cremation still occurs, which suggests that the journey will continue after death, not by the body but by the soul. There is often a family vigil that continues into the night and the following day. During this vigil a Buddhist priest chants a sutra to ease the soul's journey.

At the conclusion of the convention, I decided to visit with my sister and her husband who live in Newtown Square a small suburb of Philadelphia. Since the death of my mother and my two older brothers, she and I are the only ones left of our family nucleus. It was good to get together with them but I found an endless number of questions about Buddhism and my involvement.

After I took the train home to Connecticut, I made arrangements via email to visit Daigaku in the San Francisco Zen center after the New Year. I decided to stay for a week in the Zen center, starting on my birthday, March 26, 2003, to practice and also attend the American Philosophical Association (APA) meeting, which took place at the Westin St. Francis Hotel in San Francisco. Having planned on resigning my position as executive vice president of the International Institute for Field-Being (IIFB), I approached Dr. Tong, the president, during one of our morning talk sessions.

"Lik, I must tell you that I cannot continue with IIFB." I hesitated for an instant then continued, "I am resigning as of next month." I said this with some reluctance and hesitation.

He looked at me with wide eyes in surprise. "But why, Al? Is something wrong?"

With a quick rejoinder, I said, "No, no. I really enjoyed working with you. But I now feel that I would like to do some writing. I am too busy here with administrative duties to give it my full attention."

There was a long pause of silence. "All right, if that is what you want," he said, without remorse.

That's how it ended with no further conversation; no goodbyes; no farewell dinner; no "gold watch." I was a little miffed to say the least at this attitude. I worked without pay or compensation for more than six years.

Indeed, I paid my own way to all the conferences all over the world. I estimated that I had spent about $10,000 a year out of pocket for all the travel that I did on behalf of the IIFB. That's why I felt something that constitutes an equivalent or recompense for services rendered was due. Nothing was forthcoming. Yet, I have no regrets. I consider my work at the IIFB a continuation of my Buddhist training. I am grateful for all the friends and contacts that I made during that time. This proved to be very fecund later on.

I was very excited at the prospect of seeing Daigaku after so many years. We had kept in touch by email ever since he arrived in San Francisco from Japan, but now I was to see him in the flesh.

The San Francisco Zen Center is a former home for young Jewish single women who worked in the area at the turn of the twentieth century. The building was designed by Julia Morgan, who was the architect for Randolph Hearst's San Simeon castle. It is still visited by architecture buffs with special permission from the Zen Center. The San Francisco Zen Center was started by Shunryu Suzuki in the early fifties and some of his disciples are still there.

I landed at the airport and took the BART as well as a bus to the Zen Center on Page and Laguna streets. I registered at the front desk and asked for a room close to Daigaku's room. Daigaku was at work at the North American Soto Zen Headquarters in Japantown. We had arranged to meet in the evening when he returned from work. In the meantime, I made myself comfortable and rested from my long journey. At about 6:00 P.M., I went downstairs to the lobby and just as I arrived I noticed Daigaku coming in with his bicycle, wearing a helmet. He spotted me and we made a *gassho* to each other.

"Hiya, Al," he said.

"Hi, Daigaku."

We then shook hands and looked at each other for a long time without saying anything. He was sweating from his bike trip from Japantown, which is about two miles away.

"Al, let me wash up and I'll meet you in the dining hall for dinner."

"Okay," I nodded in agreement.

I got in the buffet line and filled my plate with food. I found a table and saved a chair for Daigaku. He arrived in a few minutes and we began chatting like two old ladies. Talking in American Zen dining halls is usually permitted in most places, whereas it is never permitted anywhere in Japan. After finishing our meal, we went to the courtyard to rest in the sun among the flowers.

After a while he said, "Would you like to see my room?"

"Yes, indeed," I replied.

So we went up to the third floor to his room. He sat on a cushion on the floor and I sat in his computer chair at his insistence. It was obvious that he still lived a rather Spartan existence.

"Tell me, Al, how are you really doing?"

"Well, for one thing, I resigned from the IIFB," I said with slow deliberation.

"Resigned?" He repeated with a querulous tone.

"Yes, I've decided it is time for me to start writing. It is something I've wanted to do all my life."

"What do you mean, write?" he asked with some consternation.

"I mean write books," I said, matter-of-factly.

"Okay, I understand. How about tomorrow? Would you like to see my office at Soto Zen Headquarters?"

"Yes, very much," I exclaimed.

"We can leave right after breakfast. *Zazen* and morning services precede breakfast so we will have time to practice," he added.

"That would be fine," I agreed.

"We can walk to Japantown where my office is located. It's only about two miles from here. Would that be all right?"

"Of course. I've been to Japantown on previous occasions. I always enjoyed being there."

"I remember from your emails that you will be attending the APA convention at the St. Francis hotel. When does that start?"

"It starts the day after tomorrow, so it won't interfere with my visit to your office tomorrow."

He seemed a little tired and weary and my eyes were closing, so I left him for the evening and returned to my room. I had no idea I was getting so tired, so I retired at about 9:00 P.M.

At 4:00 A.M. the wake-up bell rang through the hallway. I arose like a shot and made my way to the bathroom, after which I changed into my *samu-e* and appeared in the *zendo* downstairs for *zazen*. There were two forty-minute interludes of *zazen* then services were performed in the *hatto* on the first floor. After services, I went back to my room to change for a shower and dress for breakfast.

At breakfast, which consisted of fruit juice, oatmeal, toast and tea, I was able to continue my conversation with Daigaku. We continued speaking after breakfast while he made himself a sandwich and took a piece of fruit for lunch from the kitchen. I made friends with the *tenzo* (head cook) while Daigaku was preparing his lunch in a sort of bento. Afterwards we started out walking straight up Laguna Street to Geary where Japantown is located. Just on the edge of Japantown is the building housing the North American Headquarters of Soto Zen, as well as a Zen temple. I toured the office with Daigaku, a veritable modern office with modern, up-to-date equipment. This was a far cry from the primitiveness of the Hosshinji monastery. After a while we had some green tea and continued chatting.

Daigaku explained that his duties consisted of translating the many missives that come in from Japan in addition to translating the Hosshinji Newsletter into English. He also carries on correspondence via phone and email with inquirers and requests for information.

I could see I was taking up too much of his time so I left him. Since he had work to do, I promised to meet him for dinner once again. I made my way through Japantown, looking at all the statuary and monuments and doing mostly window shopping. Most of the stores were not opened yet, due to the early hour. I then decided to take the Geary bus to Union Square and pre-register for the APA conference at the Westin St. Francis Hotel. While there I recognized several people I had met at previous conferences. As I was walking through the hallway I chanced to meet Bill Cullinan of Temple University and an old friend from IIFB.

"Hey Bill. How're doing?" I shouted.

"Al! It's good to see ya," he responded.

"Where are you staying, Bill?" I inquired.

"I'm staying here at the Westin," he replied. "How about you, Al?"

"I'm staying at the San Francisco Zen Center," I stated with some pride.

"Really?" he said with a brightening of facial expression.

"Have you registered yet?" I inquired.

"Yes, I have and now I am going over to Chinatown to visit a Chinese Ch'an temple. Would you like to join me?" he said with a slight indication of breath.

"Oh, yes, very much. Shall we walk? It's only a short distance," I cautiously stated.

Indeed, the walk was uphill and somewhat arduous but Bill did not voice any objection. When we arrived at the Pi Mon temple we paused and rested before continuing inside. Bill seemed to be panting and gasping for air.

"Are you all right, Bill?" I wondered out loud.

"Yes, of course, I just need a little rest." He informed me by extending his hand.

We sat on the step entrance to the temple door for a few minutes in order to catch our breath before entering. When rested we entered the temple and bowed in *gassho*. Bill and I both selected and lit three pieces of incense sticks and then gestured to the seated Buddha three times. After that, we made supplication on our knees before the Buddha in Chinese style on the provided benches. We then withdrew from the temple with slight obeisance until we were outside.

"What now, Bill?" I asked.

"Al, we are in Chinatown, the Chinese culinary capital of the world. Let's eat. May I treat you to lunch at my favorite restaurant?" he exclaimed with enthusiasm.

"Yes, if you like. Where are we going?"

"It's called the Imperial and it is just around the corner."

When we arrived, a well-dressed man led us to a table. I could sense from the ambience that this was an expensive restaurant which was confirmed after perusing the menu. This occasioned me to say to Bill, "I would like to pay my share of the bill."

He frowned and said rather forcefully, "Nonsense, you are my guest."

The restaurant was filled with patrons, all eating and talking happily. I didn't mind the din because I was eating with gusto the many varieties of dumplings which came around on carts in bamboo steaming containers. A young girl was filling our cups with endless cups of tea. I love Chinese dumplings, which are called *dim sum* in Cantonese.

Bill and I have been friends since 1998, at the time the IIFB had a split session with the World Philosophical Congress in Boston. I had gone to a Tibetan Division session and sat down beside him. We began conversing and I invited him to hear my paper at the IIFB session that afternoon. He accepted and has been an active participant in the IIFB ever since.

Bill is a large, rather obese man who now sports a full beard reminiscent of Santa Claus. He has a somewhat mirthful and witty manner, especially when he talks about his travels. He has been to Tibet, China and Kyrgyzstan, studying Buddhist life in local culture. I find him a fountain of information and a joy to be with.

After lunch we strolled around visiting various tourist sights, including the Museum of Modern Art and finally wound up in the Yerba Buena Garden where we sat and talked some more. Bill told me his parents were dead and he wound up with their house in San Antonio, Texas. He did not live there since he was currently in Philadelphia near Temple University. He rented out the house to a minister and his wife. I have his email address, which we now use to contact each other before attending various conventions and professional meetings.

It was getting late so I bade Bill a fond goodbye and told him, "We'll meet at the APA tomorrow, Bill. Thanks for the wonderful lunch."

I took the bus back to the Zen Center to await Daigaku and dinner. While waiting, I browsed through the bookstore where I discovered some of Daigaku's calligraphy for sale. I knew calligraphy was Daigaku's hobby but I never knew he sold his work. I was told by the bookstore manager that Daigaku gives occasional classes on calligraphy at the Zen Center.

I was in my room reading when there was a knock on my door. I opened it to find Daigaku standing with a broad grin on his face.

"Come in," I said, with a *gassho*.

"Hi, Al. Wow, this is a beautiful room." He entered and looked around. I invited him to sit on the couch and he started speaking in a serious tone.

"I wanted to ask your advice on something," he said in a broody way. "I met a wonderful girl, Judy, with whom I find great *simpatico*, as they say in Italian. She and I have discussed the possibility of my moving in with her. I am considering a move into the first floor of Judy's house. It would be possible to make a temporary center there. Her house is in the Castro neighborhood and presently we are doing a one-day sitting in her attic (third floor) once a month. There are about ten people who come to these sittings and we probably cannot accommodate any more. Right now it's just an idea. For one thing, that apartment, which rents for $2000 a month, is her income. I could possibly give her $1000 a month and then try to make up the rest from those who are interested."

After much silent thought, I slowly tried answering him. "The idea of establishing a center in Judy's house sounds very exciting. It could be the beginning of a new facility for Soto Zen. Ten people are a good start. I know of Zen Centers that started with no more than ten participants. With your leadership it could blossom. Moving out of the San Francisco Zen Center to Judy's apartment could possibly work out but I would recommend moving slowly. By this I mean staying at the San Francisco Zen Center and your job until the membership has grown to a reasonable number. This would be difficult but at least you won't burn your bridges."

He looked at me with a glint in his eyes. "Thank you. I'll have to give it more thought. Now let's go to dinner."

After dinner we decided to go to a wine bar just a few blocks from the Zen Center to celebrate my birthday. After we were seated, Daigaku ordered a glass of red wine. I ordered an Orangina (a mildly carbonated, non-alcoholic orange drink).

He looked at me quizzically and remarked, "Don't you drink wine?"

I answered quickly, "No I don't. It is a sort of penance."

"I see. Do you mind if I do?"

"Of course not, but I am wondering why Buddhists drink alcoholic beverages if the Fifth Precept says 'do not partake of intoxicating beverages' and for that matter why they eat meat if the First Precept says 'do not kill.'"

He looked at me with a stunned expression as he hastened to explain.

"That's called *skillful means* in Buddhism. You may drink alcoholic beverages as long as you do not become intoxicated; and you may eat meat as long as you are not the slaughterer."

"I see. I did not mean to criticize. I really don't mind or care if you drink wine. In Hosshinji, Hanaoka-san used to drink beer, which he picked up in Obama. I am neither a teetotaler nor a vegetarian."

Later we walked back to the Zen Center and separated to our respective rooms.

The next morning I took the bus to the corner of Market and Powell and walked up to the Westin St. Francis. This is the route of the famous cable car, which I did not use. I met Bill Cullinan in the lobby and we attended several papers together. After much discussion with Bill, I found one in particular which grabbed my fancy. It was a comparison of cherry blossoms and the Japanese philosophy of impermanence.

The cherry blossoms, or *sakura*, bloom for less than one week out of the year. Of all the flowers, the Japanese can truly relate to the *sakura* for its beauty, all the more intensified by the fact that it is so transient. It dies away just after reaching its peak color and life. Its delicate blossoms are easily scattered by the wind or rain. The *sakura* reveals at least two immeasurable human truths for the Japanese: First, life is like the *sakura* in that what is of beauty does not last; second, the beauty of reality lies precisely in its impermanence. The *sakura* inspires the Japanese attitude of *mono no aware*, the "sadness of things," in which existence bears a "sad beauty." This is the way of being.

I found that practicing Buddhism at the San Francisco Zen Center for me was a remarkable replacement for the lack of a suitable temple near my home; albeit far away, being here almost reached Empyrean. I have found the practical aspects of Mahayana Buddhism, which stresses the unity of compassion and wisdom as exemplified by the Bodhisattva ideal, to be the perfectly ripened fruit of the whole vast tree of Buddhism.

Although I am quick to admit that the infrequent occasions that I go to Shobo-ji in New York City are very useful and suitable, the difference is that here at the San Francisco Zen Center, I practice *zazen* twice in the morning, go to daily services, and do *zazen* again at night before bedtime. It is an all-encompassing activity where one actually lives the practice.

To and from Connecticut

After an enjoyable week at the San Francisco Zen Center and spending quality time with Daigaku, I had to return home; and besides Daigaku would be traveling to Japan to visit with Harada-roshi at the Hosshinji Monastery. I promised Daigaku that I would return in the fall, perhaps September. We kept in touch by email. Now that I have resigned from the IIFB I was on my own in attending conferences. I made several attempts at writing and decide to begin with this memoir. Once started, I found it running smoothly as I began to narrate in my mind the many incidents of my Buddhist life. I wrote much of the summer of 2003 and spent a lot of time traveling to the homes of my children.

In April I visited my son's family in Holliston, Massachusetts, a suburb of Boston. On my return from an extended weekend, I found an email from Daigaku on my computer. In some sense I found it disturbing. While in Japan, the Roshi suggested to Daigaku that he find a temple in Japan in which to officiate.

I told him, by email, I thought this was the Roshi's ploy to keep him close by. I was convinced that the Roshi would like to see Daigaku settled in a local Japanese temple out of selfish motives to be able to call on him as a translator when the occasion arises. That was not all. In the next email he told me of an offer by a Mrs. Halifax of the Upaya temple in Santa Fe. It was an offer of very low salary, no fringe benefits and an indistinct possibility to become the Abbot. I tried to dissuade him as forcefully as I could with all candor. I could hardly wait until September to discuss these matters with him. I was convinced that he was becoming restless and in need of sound advice.

I arrived at the San Francisco Zen Center with great exuberance. It was good to be back. Miffen, the woman at the front desk, said, "Welcome back, Al. Are you staying a full week?"

I assented and was led to my room. She said to me, "You've arrived early this time. I think you can still get lunch."

I hastened downstairs to the kitchen and partook of a delicious lunch of salad, fish cakes and rice. I had nothing to eat for seven hours of travel and was very hungry.

After a light repast, I returned to my room to read and listen to music on my headset. I had brought along several tapes of classical music, which I enjoy. I spent the afternoon relaxing and napping. A loud knock on the door jolted me out of my oneiric state. I had no idea I slept for so many hours. I opened the door to find Daigaku waiting at the threshold.

"Al, did I wake you?"

"That's all right. I think I am suffering from time zone sickness. Come in. Come in. What time is it?"

He came in with long strides and deposited his large frame on the couch. "It's 5:00 P.M. I came home early to see you."

After a silent spell, he said, "How are you, Al? I see you got the same room as last time."

"Yes, I like this room. I'm becoming a regular guest here. I can foresee coming here at least twice a year."

"How is that?" he questioned.

"Well between the many conventions of the organizations to which I belong that use San Francisco as a venue and my additional desire to visit you I feel that it is very possible."

"That's wonderful, but what about your consulting business?"

I hesitated for a moment but then answered, "Oh, that is beginning to slow down. I don't believe I'll have many clients by the end of the year."

"Is that so? What will you do then?"

Once again I hesitated before answering, "I don't need the income any longer and so I will then spend more time on writing and pursuing Buddhist practice. I still haven't found a local temple or sitting group where I can say I truly belong."

He quickly interjected, "I think your interests are focused too much on Buddhist philosophy rather than Buddhist practice."

I looked at him and then nodded my head.

"You may be right. Philosophy did not cease for me to be an intellectual enquiry into the fundamental aspects of human existence, but it became, in addition, a matter of learning how to live in accordance with the principles that the Buddha revealed."

He looked me straight in the eyes with a flushed face. "What did Buddhism do for you?"

I quickly responded with assurance, "Above all, it showed how my view of myself had been mistaken. No longer could I believe that in my innermost self I was a separate individual. Life continued much as before, but my view of the world was slowly transformed the more I learned of Buddhism. I now believe at heart that we are all one despite anger, hate, and envy, however much these bad feelings intervene, there is always recourse to the one sure principle of Buddhism, that all are Buddhas, the universal spirit.

He looked at me strangely before commenting. "You are right, but isn't it obvious that the concept of consciousness follows, for what is the self if not consciousness?"

I took a deep breath before continuing, "Yes, everyone can easily identify with such an idea — that in themselves, beyond body and mind, lays a conscious self. In practice, of course, we often identify ourselves with the body, and especially with the mind. Buddhism, however, is concerned with overcoming the idea that each of us is a separate unit of consciousness and replacing it with universal consciousness."

He raised his hands to the top of his head and interlocked the fingers. "Wow, I find this conversation getting beyond me. But don't get me wrong; I really enjoyed it."

We both fell silent for a little while. I broke the ice by asking him a personal question. "Do you see much of Judy?"

"Yes, quite a lot. I saw her last night."

"Tell me more about her. I am interested in what she does with her time."

"Well, for one thing, she's an artist."

"Did you say an artist? What kind of artist?"

"She paints and sculpts."

"I see. It sounds great."

"Yes, she's a wonderful, talented girl."

"Where did you meet her?"

"I met her here at the Zen Center in one of our classes."

I was looking down but raised my head to ask another personal question. "I am sorry to continue this questioning but I am interested in your life. How did Judy feel about your going to the Upaya temple in Santa Fe?"

He looked at me and spoke with a rapid remark. "Oh, she was against it from the beginning. She didn't think it would be good for me either. I suppose between the two of you, I really gave up on Upaya."

For a moment I thought I detected despondency in his voice so I quickly replied.

"Daigaku, I think you are at a point in your life when you would like to put your Buddhist training to productive use. After all, you are a Buddhist priest and that sort of requires being established in a temple. Right now you are doing administrative work and lecturing and that is not all bad. You are making contacts and building your reputation. That means that eventually a good offer will come up, possibly as an abbot in a small but growing temple."

He hung intently on my words. "I hope so."

I continued with renewed enthusiasm. "Yes, I can see it happening.

But you must be patient and discretionary. Do not jump at the first thing that comes along."

He seemed to absorb all that I was saying.

"Okay, Al. Thanks for all your advice. I know you want the best for me. I'm not in a hurry. I hope you'll let me seek your advice in the future."

"Yes, yes, by all means. I want to help."

We shook hands and I noticed a smile growing on his face. I quickly remarked, "Now, how about going out for dinner tonight? You are my guest. What kind of restaurant would you like?"

He suddenly perked up and raised his head. "It sounds great. How about Indian food? I know of a nice Indian restaurant nearby."

We sat in the restaurant eating the hearty ethnic dishes that Daigaku ordered. I relished the Nam bread stuffed with Dal. We continued talking and to an extent discussed his future over many cups of tea. I felt it was important to bolster his state of mind with some sympathy.

"Don't feel bad about this turn of events. Always remember the saying attributed to the Dalai Lama—'it could be a stroke of luck that you did not get what you want.'"

He burst out laughing. "Isn't that the truth?"

I smiled and continued, "You'll see something very good is bound to come up in the future."

We left the restaurant and I walked him to the bus stop where he waited for the bus to take him to Judy's house. I continued on to the Zen Center. After a week of steady practice at the Zen Center, I returned home to Connecticut. I continued to do my writing and I prepared to go to the APA Eastern Division meeting at the Hilton Hotel in Washington, D.C.

It was there that I ran into Gereon Kopf whom I knew from the IIFB. Gereon is a sometime friend of Daigaku, who he met at Hosshinji. Gereon is also an expert in the Kyoto School of Japanese Buddhism. He gave a paper, "Unifying Power of Consciousness of Nishida Kitaro," the leading exponent of this philosophy.

Nishida criticized a number of philosophical positions that focus on only a part of the human psyche. For Nishida, the *Good* can be attained only when all faculties are balanced in a healthy synthesis. He called this the "unifying power of consciousness."

This unifying power of consciousness is the true "personality" existing deep within each of us. Realizing this personality is realizing the *Good*. Yet even though we tend to break consciousness down into disparate elements, such as intellect, will, and feeling, the true unity of consciousness is a pure and simple activity that comes forth of itself, unhindered by oneself; it is the original state of independent, self-sufficient consciousness, with no distinction among knowledge, feeling, and volition, and no separation of subject and object.

This is difficult and heady stuff but is a modern Japanese version of German philosophy, particularly Heidegger. I went up to the dais to congratulate Gereon. He extended his hand in a friendly gesture with a huge smile on his face. I was surprised because Gereon is sometimes known to be strident. He is a man of slight build with a ruddy complexion and an incipient tendency to baldness. He has a very heavy German accent when he speaks, which sometimes makes it difficult for me to understand him. He is a professor of religion and philosophy at Luther College in Decorah, Iowa. Coincidently, Daigaku is a graduate of Luther College.

I spoke as I approached him with outstretched hand. "Hi, Gereon. I really enjoyed your paper."

He grabbed my hand while speaking. "Thank you, Al. How's Lik?"

I was taken aback by this remark, particularly since I haven't heard from Lik since I resigned from the IIFB.

"I really don't know. I resigned from the IIFB and I understand Lik retired from Fairfield University and now lives in Las Vegas."

Back to San Francisco

After the New Year 2004, I decided to return to the San Francisco Zen Center to continue my practice and visit with Daigaku. Once again

I met with Daigaku at dinner. He told me he was holding a class on the book, *The Essence of Zen*, written by Sekkei Harada-roshi but translated into English by Daigaku. It was to take place that evening in the *hatto*. I was anxious to attend. It was there I met several people from previous visits. They all greeted me and were very solicitous. Was this because they knew I was a friend of Daigaku? Was I too suspicious of their motives? Daigaku is a natural-born teacher. He took the portion of the book devoted to the Key to *Zazen* as his commentary.

"In the Zen sect, the teaching is that by entering *samadhi* [intense concentration on consciousness], it is possible for you to awaken to the true Self since you forget the ego-self. Nevertheless, one man said that even this is not necessary, for the function of the Buddha will appear without *samadhi* and diligent effort. It is enough just to reach the wisdom of Buddha, the nature of Buddha as it is. This is enough. These are the words of Sekito Kisen, the author of *sandokai* [the merging of difference and unity], a sutra that is recited each morning in Soto Zen temples." Daigaku then went on to read and explain the one arrow of Sekkyo, a Buddhist parable.

At the conclusion of his lecture most people dispersed but I remained to speak and felicitate with him. He was anxious to admonish me for my many questions during the question period, which I took in good spirit. He then broached a new subject.

"Al, the Roshi is coming from Japan May 25th to give a Dharma talk at the Zen Center. I believe he will be accompanied by a large entourage. He will most probably visit several cities in southern California to give Dharma talks and I will accompany him to translate."

I excitedly commented. "Gee, that's great. I haven't seen him for ten years, since I left Hosshinji."

He gave me a studious look.

"Well you may not be able to do more than greet him. He will probably be feted and surrounded by the sycophantic temple hierarchy."

I then quickly responded. "Just to see him with a greeting would be enough for me. I know you will be very busy with the Roshi during that time but I am sure we can see each other for a small period of time."

I saw his shoulders rise and doubt spread across his face. The next day at lunch I sat next to a young man at the table who introduced himself to me.

"Hello, my name is Joe."

I turned towards him and said with a mouthful of food. "Hi, my name is Al."

He then began speaking hurriedly while eating. "I understand you're a friend of Daigaku."

I responded matter-of-factly. "Yes, we were in Hosshinji together."

He kept up his inquiry while we were eating. "Do you live in San Francisco?"

I immediately responded while shaking my head. "No, no, I live in Connecticut. I just came out here to visit Daigaku."

He then seemingly could not resist speaking in a proud manner. "I see. I introduced him to Melissa, who is a friend of my girlfriend."

I was somewhat startled by the statement but let it pass for the moment. We finished our lunch and as we stood up to leave he said, "Would you like to talk in the garden for a while? It is a lovely day and I feel certain empathy towards you, if you don't mind."

I agreed, since I have always had the capacity for participating in another's feelings. "Sure, that would be fine," I said.

In the garden we sat on a wooden bench and began a revealing conversation.

"My full name is Joe Shakarchi and I teach high school here in San Francisco but I am originally from New York."

I immediately inquired, "Shakarchi — is that an Italian name?"

He smiled as he explained, "No, it's Sephardic."

"Oh, then you are Jewish."

"Yes, aren't you?"

"Well, my birth religion is Jewish, but I also consider myself Buddhist."

He looked at me strangely, "Can a person be two things?"

I immediately answered without hesitation, "Why not? I had a friend, named Bill Paar, who practiced three religions, Lutheran, Methodist, and Buddhism."

He was silent for a long time but then continued in a labored voice.

"That's what I wanted to talk to you about. I have been practicing Buddhism here and also in Tassajara and Green Gulch Farm for a little while now and I still feel like an outsider. Why is that?"

I was stunned and a little daunted for a moment. "I don't know. Why did you start to look into Buddhism in the first place? Were you dissatisfied with Judaism?"

He lowered his head and spoke slowly, "I wouldn't say dissatisfied. I guess the problem starts with my atheism. The whole world is screwed up and God does not seem to be anywhere."

I dug deep into my own feelings for an explanation. "Well, I can't comment on that. I suppose it is different for different people. The Buddha confronted a different question — the universal truth of suffering — and he proposed a resolution to this question in light of empirically determined rational explanations. He remained reluctant to give any definite response to metaphysical questions concerning ultimate reality."

I rested to gather my thoughts and then continued, "If you are looking for anything more than what I just said you will not find it in Buddhism."

He looked up wide-eyed and studied me before he responded, "Do you really believe that?"

I didn't know how to answer his question, so I rattled on. "I'll tell you, I'm a product of the twentieth century, which gave us tremendous advances in science for the comfort of people but it failed society in not being able to resolve conflict and differences among the people of the world. Western religions talk about love but I have witnessed five major wars and a few horrible domestic skirmishes. It is quite apparent to me that religions have made less than a minor contribution in overcoming violence, hatred, greed, and ignorance. Sure, I believe it."

Shobo-Ji

I spent the next three months doing research at the Fairfield University Library and at home writing my memoir. Much of what I wrote was easy because it relied on my memory of events that took place in the early years of my Buddhist training at Hosshinji monastery. One Sunday I decided to visit and practice at the Shobo-ji Temple in New York. Having called in advance to reserve a place in the *zendo*, I felt confident that my practice would be fulfilling.

I found my usual place in the outer room next to the garden entrance. My place had a *zabuton* (mat) and a *zafu* (cushion) similar to mine at home. There was a place card in front with my name. As I was about to sit down a gentleman in monk's robes came in to water some plants. I recognized the Roshi of the temple, Eido Shimano.

"Good morning," I whispered.

He looked at me with a startled expression. "Good morning," he replied.

I quickly added, "I have regards for you from Ken Inada."

"Oh, thank you. Do you know Ken?"

"Yes, I do. I emailed him that I was coming here to practice."

"In that case when you email him back give him my best. Now, I must hurry we are about to begin."

Sitting *zazen* with other people in a temple is in some ways a desultory experience since many participants arrive late and others who arrive very early begin before the designated time. Nevertheless, it all ends after forty minutes at the sound of the bell when everyone rises to partake in twenty minutes of *kinhin* (walking meditation). This is an inordinately slow movement of the lined up participants around the circumference of the room. At the end of *kinhin* we all gathered in the main room, sitting on our *zafus* to hear the *teisho* (sermon) given by the Roshi at the conclusion of which we chanted a sutra in Japanese for the dead. This included calling out the names of the departed by the individual participants. I noticed that many of the participants were wearing a *zazen* robe of brown material whereas others were in civilian clothes. I wore my black robes, indicating that I was a member of Soto Zen. When the service ended, a light lunch was served by the monks to the participants while seated at their *zafu* places. This usually consists of a mixture of rice and vegetables to be eaten in bowls with chopsticks.

I said goodbye to Shimano-roshi who then invited me to attend O-bon at Dai Bosatsu Monastery in Livingston Manner, New York, in August. I thanked him and assured him I would be there. On my way out I stopped at the front desk to make the arrangements.

Indeed, I also made arrangements to return to San Francisco on May 25 until June 1, 2004, to see and hear Harada-roshi at the San Francisco Zen Center. When I arrived it was difficult to do much more than greet Daigaku this time because he was so very busy with the Roshi. The Roshi walked into the main hall with all of his attendants like a scene out of royalty. Daigaku was at his side explaining various matters to his ear as he leaned over. (Daigaku is more than six feet, three inches. The Roshi is no more than five feet, five inches.)

I was stunned to see that amongst his entourage was Doiku with whom I spent time in Hosshinji. I walked up to him with a *gassho* and said, "Hello, Doiku."

He looked at me with a stare of doubt. There was no salutation from him. He did not recognize me. There was no acknowledgement.

I stated again, "I'm Al Shansky from Hosshinji. Don't you know me?"

He looked at me with a blank expression and a shake of his head as he said, "I'm sorry."

He walked away and I looked at his retreating figure with distressful hurt in my mind's heart. This pain stayed with me for a long time. I never approached Daigaku about this but I did try to defend Doiku's action in my mind. There might have been a glimmer of faint recognition but he said nothing. It is true that I last saw him ten years ago. It is also true that he came across many people in his years at Hosshinji. How could he remember them all? Still, is that any reason to give me short shrift without deliberating a little longer and investigating a little further?

Everyone gathered in the *hatto* and sat on cushions to hear the Roshi's *teisho*. He spoke slowly in Japanese with incremental pauses for translation by Daigaku. The room was crowded with people hanging on every word spoken by the Roshi and Daigaku. It was obvious that this was a special event for the Zen Center membership. After the *teisho* people streamed out of the *hatto* and gathered in small groups in the hallway. I found Joe Shakarchi amongst a small group of familiar people.

"Hi, Joe. How are you?"

"Hi, Al. I see your friend Daigaku is fully engaged in his devotion to the Roshi."

Not knowing what to answer I just agreed with an assent of my head, "Yes, yes; this is due to his habitual pursuit of work."

Then he changed the subject and whispered in my ear with some intensity, "By the way, Al, I have some need of your advice. Can we go out to the garden where we can talk?"

"Of course we can."

We walked away from the maudlin crowd in the hallway and made our way to the garden. There were some people milling about in the garden, engaged in lively conversation, but we found a solitary, unoccupied bench close to the brick railing under an aspen tree.

"How's this?" I asked.

"Look's good," he answered.

We sat and he looked at me with wide eyes and a slight frown on his forehead.

"Al, I'm thinking of going to Japan to visit a friend, Simon, I have in Nagano. I'm wondering if you can give me some tips on other places to visit while I am there."

I was startled and looked at him questioningly, "Is that it? I thought you had some serious personal problem."

He lowered his head and mumbled, "I do have a personal problem."

I waited for him to speak. The silence was deafening. Finally, I said, "What is it?"

He looked at me with a slight muscular contraction of his eyes.

"The problem is that if I go to Japan, my girlfriend, Cynthia, threatened to relinquish our relationship."

"What do you mean?"

"I mean she doesn't want me to go and if I do that would be the end. She will leave me."

He seemed quite agitated and I detected some moisture in his eyes. His face was flushed like a red beet. He had an average stature of about five feet, eight inches and sported a close cropped beard with slightly balding head. Obviously, he was very excited as he said, "As it is, our relationship is somewhat tenuous."

So began a digression into fractals. What started out to be travel advice wound up as advice to the lovelorn.

"What do you mean?"

He thought for a moment then slowly replied, "Well she is a girl with many psychological problems. I have overlooked many of her foolish ways," he exclaimed with a determined set to his jaw.

"I see. Then there is nothing of value to save."

"I suppose not," he said under his breath.

I then posed a truism: "Why worry about something that would probably end even if you didn't go to Japan?"

"I know you're right. I guess I just wanted to hear it."

I placed my arm around his shoulder in a warm gesture as I said, "My advice is to go to Japan. Such opportunities don't come up very often. If Cynthia cares for you at all, she'll understand and wait until you return."

"Going to Japan is very important to me. I am a poet and I would like to visit with Simon so that I can review some of my poetry with him. He teaches English in a Japanese high school. Also, I would like to bring him one of my published books of poetry."

He hesitated for a moment then continued, "By the way, next year I am going to the Robert Bly poetry convocation in Maine. Are you familiar with that?"

After thinking a moment I responded with a measured comment, "I think I saw it once on TV."

He was excited as he started to tell about the Robert Bly gathering. "Well, a lot of diverse people come. There are some Hindus, Muslims, and Buddhists who share their poetry forms with the attendees."

"What kind of Buddhist poetry? That would interest me," I said.

"Well, mostly Japanese haiku poetry," he responded, but continued, "I like reviewing Buddhist experiences with these people. They always ask if Buddhism is a religion or a philosophy."

"What do you mean?"

"You must remember the famous story in Buddhist literature."

"Which story? There are so many."

"The first patriarch of Zen in China was asked by the emperor what was the ultimate and holiest principle of Buddhism. He replied, 'Vast emptiness, and nothing holy in it.' Another who was asked the searching question, 'Where is the abiding place for the mind?' answered, 'Not in this dualism of good and evil, being and nonbeing, thought and matter.' In fact, thought is an activity which divides. It analyzes, it makes distinctions, it criticizes, it judges, it breaks reality into groups and classes and individuals."

He stopped talking to catch his breath and I looked at him a long while before answering, "The aim of Zen is to abolish that kind of thinking, and to substitute not unconsciousness, which would be death, but a consciousness that does not analyze but experiences life directly. Although it has no prescribed prayers, no sacred scriptures, no ceremonial rites, no personal God, and no interest in the soul's future destination, Zen is a religion rather than a philosophy."

He looked at me questioningly. "I wonder."

I reiterated, "The doctrine of Zen cannot be analyzed from without; it must be lived."

"Yes, yes. You are right."

"Now, do you want me to recommend some places for you to visit in Japan?"

"Oh, I almost forgot."

"I have two places in mind. The first is Kyoto, where you can visit

Mt. Hiei and see the original temples of the Tendai sect from which devolved Honen and Shinran of the Pure Land sect. The second is Mt. Koya where you can see the origination of the Shingon sect of Kukai, after which you can take a boat to Tokushima on the island of Shikoku. If you want to you may visit some of the 88 temples around the periphery of the island."

"Okay, that seems great. I'll try and do some of that. Thanks."

After that we split up to go our separate ways.

O-Bon

I returned home after the experience of seeing the Harada-roshi and my meeting with Joe Shakarchi. I told Daigaku that I would not return for a while since I wanted to concentrate on my writing. He apologized for his business with the Roshi but promised to keep in touch with me by email. I felt a regretful note in his voice. My consulting practice was waning to such a degree that I made up my mind to arrange with my attorney to legally terminate the consulting business in the coming fall.

In mid-August I attended the O-Bon festival at the Dai Bosatsu monastery at Beecher Lake in Livingston Manor, New York, arriving Saturday in time for dinner. The participants were housed in a dormitory-like room with futons on the floor for sleeping. There were about twenty men in our room and close to an equal number of women in another room.

There was a dharma talk given by Eido Shimano Roshi after dinner who spoke about honoring the departed and the connection of families through filial piety. He spoke somewhat halting English but was easily understood. We then sat *zazen* while in the *zendo*. Almost all of the participants were Westerners, some of whom appeared to be dilettantes. When *zazen* was completed we went to the edge of Lake Biwa to sail the paper boats containing a lit candle, which were previously prepared.

Sleeping overnight was a chore due to the snoring, wheezing, and other night noises. I barely slept at all. Rising at first light was a pleasure, to get rid of the night din. I made my way to the lake and saw the misty fog rising off the water surface. There was a faint ripple in the water which caused a bobbing of some of the intact paper boats; others were flattened out like a white stain on the blue water.

I walked around the edge of the lake, enjoying the early morning air when I spotted a raccoon drinking water at the lake edge. I stopped so as to not frighten him. As I waited I noticed the many plantings of flowers and shrubs. The monastery building looks like it was transported from Japan and I learned later that a Japanese architect assisted in its design. With the rising sun, a bell sounded, meaning that all were to convene in the *zendo* for *zazen*. As I made my way to my sitting place, I noticed that some came in a dilatory manner. I was so tired from the lack of sleep the night before that I almost dozed off at my sitting place. After breakfast, I tried to locate Eido Shimano to bid him goodbye but he was nowhere to be found. I then left for the long ride home.

I just about finished writing my memoir when it occurred to me to start writing a fictional story about life in thirteenth-century Japan. I have always been intrigued by the fact that the four greatest sages of Japan all appeared in the thirteenth century: Honen of Jodo Shu (1133–1212), Shinran of Jodo Shinshu (1173–1262), Dogen of Zen (1200–1253), and Nichiren of Hokke (1222–1282).

So, I developed a fictional story of a young soldier who kills a prince in the famous battle of Dan-no-ura. Being filled with guilt and remorse he seeks solace by visiting the four sages over his lifetime to assuage his guilt. This became a device for the pronouncement of Buddhist philosophy. The book was written, titled the *Extinction of Illusion*, and published in 2006. Being familiar with the lives of these four sages through research, I decided to write another novella about the escapades of Shinran after his marriage to the nun Eshinni. Marriage was a disseverment of celibacy rules for monks and nuns at that time, so they were exiled to the wilds of northern Japan. Shinran and Eshinni, over their lifetime, propagated the Jodo Shinshu sect of Buddhism, which eventually became the largest sect of

Buddhism in Japan. This book was published in 2007 under the title of *Shinran and Eshinni.*

In December 2006, I attended the APA convention in Boston. This time my wife accompanied me. We were able to visit with my second daughter, Suzy, who works for MIT and lives in Lexington. We had a lovely time together, going to lunches and dinners in between my attendance at various sessions. One of the most important papers I heard was on Japanese neo–Confucianism featuring the philosophy of Chu Hsi.

Throughout his practical ethics, Chu Hsi provided a basis for underscoring the importance of relationships, for stressing the virtues of benevolence and righteousness. For the Japanese, the attraction of Confucianism lies precisely in its emphasis on human relationships. Chu Hsi's ethics and emphasis on relationships can be seen within the context of his teachings of *li,* or principle. In Chu Hsi's thought, *li* is both a moral and a natural law. In other words, because all things manifest Heaven's *li,* humanity participates in the creative power of heaven. Therefore, by obeying the will of Heaven, humanity sustains Heaven's creative power. This entails, for example, the reciprocity of affection and duties in human relationships, such as the father's affection and the son's devotion. By performing our duties we act according to *li,* and we participate in Heaven's design.

Confucianism is not Buddhism, but the relationship is quite evident if studied comparatively.

By this time I became very prolific with my writing. I started gathering notes for two upcoming books, one on the Henro pilgrimage which I made by walking and visiting the temples around the periphery of the island of Shikoku. I thought of titling it *The Philosopher's Walk* but ruled against it since there is a Philosopher's Walk in Kyoto, so instead I decided on *The Divine Walk.* A second book of my travels crisscrossing the Inland Sea is also a possibility, which would be titled *The Sea of Tranquility.* I find myself busy writing and researching. This had made me as happy as a lark frolicking across the countryside. But it was time to renew my spiritual self by returning to San Francisco and Daigaku.

My Birthday

Fortunately, there was another convention of the APA to take place in San Francisco on March 22, 2005, at the Westin St. Francis Hotel. I, of course, made arrangements to stay at the San Francisco Zen Center. This then would enable me to spend my day at the convention and still pursue my Buddhist practice in the morning and at night. The bus ride from the Zen Center to the Westin was only fifteen minutes, so I could go back and forth to take meals at the Zen Center.

Having emailed Daigaku before leaving Connecticut, I knew he would make time to visit with me. March 26 was my 80th birthday, so I invited Daigaku to celebrate my birthday with me. He, of course, accepted and I looked forward to the festivities.

When I met Daigaku in the Zen Center he introduced me to a pretty girl named Melissa.

"Hi Melissa. I'm happy to meet you." I made a *gassho* and continued speaking. "Have you been staying here at the Zen Center long?"

"No," she answered. "I have only been here a few months. Daigaku told me about you and I'm glad to meet you."

She bowed in *gassho* and we shook hands.

How can I describe her? She is petite but standing next to Daigaku one would describe her as small. She had a sweet, cherubic face with a small nose and classical cupid bowed lips. There was a slight dimple on both of her cheeks. Her skin seemed like soft fell with its milk-like appearance. She wore a constant smile on her face as if ready to laugh. I was immediately drawn to her genial nature.

"I hope you can join us for dinner this evening," I said, with great felicity.

"Oh, thank you. Yes, I would like that," she answered, with an almost childish exuberance.

So at 6:00 P.M. the three of us went to the Italian restaurant on the next block. It started to drizzle but we arrived before getting wet. After ordering we began to chat. I was on one side of the table and they were both seated on the opposite side. I had to smile inwardly because it seemed to me that I was being interviewed. However, the conversation was spirited and I could see that they cared deeply for each other.

"Have you been practicing Buddhism long?" I asked Melissa.

"Yes, many years here at the Zen Center and in Tassajara at Green Gulch Farm," she answered hastily.

They had ordered wine so Daigaku raised his glass and wished me a happy birthday. I had a Diet Coke but we all clinked glasses.

The next day after *zazen* and breakfast, I went to the APA at the Westin Hotel. I was anxious to attend the session on Tibetan Buddhism. The speaker gave an introduction to Tibetan Buddhism as a review, beginning with a summary of the Indian origins of Tibetan Buddhism and how it eventually was brought to Tibet. He explored Tibetan Mahayana philosophy and tantric methods for personal transformation. The four main schools of Tibetan Buddhism, as well as Bon, the indigenous religion, were explored in depth from a nonsectarian point of view. It was a systematic and wonderfully clear presentation of Tibetan Buddhist views and practices.

The next paper was even more to my liking because it presented one of the most important literary adventures of Nagarjuna, the originator of the Madhyamika School and the beginnings of Mahayana Buddhism. The paper was titled, "Nagarjuna's Letter to a Friend." The great Indian Buddhist master Nagarjuna (1st–2nd century C.E.) wrote his celebrated poem *Letter to a Friend* as a letter of advice to a king with whom he was friendly. Despite its short length (only 123 verses), it is a monument to the Indian Buddhist tradition. It covers the whole Mahayana path with unusual clarity and memorable imagery and it is for this reason that it is widely quoted by Tibet's great masters and scholars in the many commentaries they have written on the Buddhist path. The poem's condensed style and concentration of technical subjects, however, make it difficult for the average person to understand, and much of it required a certain amount of explanation for its message to be conveyed fully. The speaker's commentary provided such an explanation. I should like to add that the seminal text on Nagarjuna and the Madhyamika School was written by my friend Ken Inada. The book is now out of print and has become something of an iconic collector's item.

I must say that I find Tibetan Buddhism to be too flamboyant and almost directly opposite of Zen Buddhism, which is the most austere of the many sects of Buddhism. I have attended several Tibetan monasteries for services and found the blowing of horns, banging of drums, and clanging of cymbals overwhelming. Their monasteries are decorated in bright vivid colors of red and yellow, whereas Zen uses no color other than black and white or maybe sometimes gray. The only comparison I can make is that it reminds me of the Eastern Orthodox churches which deviate through flamboyance from the Catholic churches. I enjoyed the papers at the APA convention but after a one-week stay I returned home to take up my writing once again.

Philadelphia

After arriving home, I busied myself with preparing for the publication of my book, *The Extinction of Illusion*, which was scheduled to appear next year. I also continued writing my next book, *Shinran and Eshinni*. In November I went to the AAR convention in Philadelphia. I stayed at the Wyndham Franklin hotel. Before I left for Philadelphia, my attorney informed me that my consulting business was officially terminated. This was a sad time for me; after more than 35 years building a chemical consulting business it was all gone. But now I had ample time to continue my writing. I still had two clients for whom I promised to complete their work which should take place sometime next year.

I called my sister, Faye, when I arrived at the Wyndham Franklin Hotel and she graciously offered to pick me up the next night for a dinner at a restaurant close to her house in Newtown Square. I spent the day at the convention listening to papers and renewing acquaintances with people I knew from the IIFB and previous conferences. At 6:00 P.M. I was waiting outside the front door of the hotel when a large, black car rolled up. My niece, Ilene, jumped out and ran towards me with outstretched arms.

"Uncle Al, how are you?" she shouted.

We hugged and kissed. Ilene is a beautiful woman with a dark appearance and a cream-like complexion like her mother, glowing eyes and black hair. As I got in the car she introduced me to the driver.

"This is Harry, my fiancé."

He raised his hand as I said, "Hi, I'm Al, her uncle."

He mumbled a low, confused utterance. "Yes, yes, indeed, I'm glad to meet you. I've heard so much about you. It's like meeting a living legend," he said as he twisted in the front seat, reaching his arm backwards to shake my hand.

I laughed. "Glad to meet you."

We drove on with excited conversation until we reached my sister's house. I haven't seen her and her husband, Larry, in a few years. I have no excuses but it is true that I have been busy entering a Buddhist life and doing so much traveling. They all questioned me about Buddhism and why I took it up. Harry, a psychotherapist, in particular was interested in my Buddhist practice.

He began questioning me in a quizzical voice, "When you sit *zazen* do you feel a change in your demeanor?"

"What do you mean?" I countered with a frown on my brow.

"I mean, is there something like a personality change that occurs?" he explained as he looked at me with intense, penetrating eyes.

Then within the quietude I responded slowly, "I don't know. There is, of course, a very pronounced calming effect. All thoughts seem to be stilled within the first five minutes of sitting."

He pursued my answer with another question, "Well, tell me. How do you do that? You can't shut off thought."

After a slight repose I continued to explain. "Right now it is very automatic with me but when I first started I would follow my breath with a steady counting. This is the recommended procedure for novices. But it takes a lot of practice and does not happen quickly. Sometimes it takes years, but I believe one could become proficient in a few months of daily practice. It is true that thoughts come in to your head, but you don't dwell on them; you just let them go out. You must remember I have been sitting *zazen* for forty minutes a day for more than fifteen years without interruption."

He acknowledged my statement by bobbing his head up and down while muttering, "I see. I see," then in a forthright voice said, "I am very interested in *zazen*. Could you send me some literature on the procedure?"

He handed me his business card as I assented. "I do have something I could send you."

We then proceeded to the restaurant and had a lovely dinner spiked with very special family conversation. I wished Ilene and Harry much good luck on their pending marriage. After I was taken back to the hotel we all said a fond farewell with promises to see each other again in the near future.

The remainder of the convention was routine with nothing strikingly out of the ordinary and I found nothing different or distinguished in the remaining papers given. I did meet a lot of friends, whom I always bump into at these conventions, and this was pleasant.

I took the train home. To overcome my disappointment I returned to my manuscript. Shortly thereafter I submitted my completed manuscript, *The Extinction of Illusion*, to the publisher. As I said, it was released in early January 2006.

Eiheiji

On April 4, 2006, the Association of Asian Studies (AAS) was to have its annual convention at the Marriott Hotel in San Francisco. As a member, I intended going. What a wonderful opportunity to visit Daigaku and bring him a copy of my new book! When we met, we exchanged gifts. I gave him an autographed copy of my book and he gave me a framed calligraphy that he made. I was grateful and later on hung it in my den. He seemed pleased to have his name appear on the acknowledgement page.

I have dreamed about practicing in the Eiheiji Monastery in Fukui, Japan, ever since I became active in Buddhism. Eiheiji might be called the flagship monastery of Soto Zen Buddhism. It is the place where Dogen first started Soto Zen in the thirteenth century. In fact, I once thought of going there with my wife when we were traveling in Japan in October 1997. Unfortunately, we never made it but we did go to Hosshinji to visit Daigaku, who was there at that time.

This time I made up my mind to go, so I consulted with Daigaku as to procedure. "Daigaku, can you suggest how I might go to Eiheiji to practice for about a week?"

"Al, it's very easy. Just write a letter to the Rev. Kuroyanagi at Dai-honzon Eiheiji telling him that I recommend you to practice but be sure to tell him the preferred dates of arrival and departure so that they may be able to fit you in."

I did write the letter and hoped for the best. I spent the remainder of the week going to and from the conference at the Marriott. In addition, I went to the University of California — Berkeley for a one-day conference on Vietnamese Buddhism. It was very revealing to me that Vietnam, which is a Mahayana Buddhist country with a communist government, has taken up this religious practice again with vigor after the war. I made some new friends at the Asian conference after which I headed home.

One evening at home I received a telephone call from Kuroyanagi from Japan.

"Hello, this is Kuroyanagi. I am calling from Eiheiji in Japan. I am responding to your letter."

"Hello, this is Al Shansky. I am glad to hear from you."

"Shansky-san, we can certainly accommodate you between May 15 and May 22 for one week. Would that be satisfactory?"

"Yes, yes," I exclaimed hastily. "I would be delighted to accept those dates."

"In that case, I shall send you a blank application by email attach-ment. After you return it signed to us, you can make your flight plans and other arrangements."

"Thank you very much."

"Goodbye, please give my regards to Daigaku."

"Goodbye, I shall."

I hung up and felt very elated. I was finally going to Eiheiji. I imme-diately made flight arrangements to Osaka for May 9, 2006. When I arrived I took the train to Kyoto, where I stayed in my usual *ryokan* (Japanese inn) Hiraiwa. In Kyoto I spent a full day on Mt. Hiei visiting the origi-nal Tendai Buddhist temples. It was hard to believe that these temples were once occupied by Honen and Shinran, the promulgators of Pure Land Buddhism in the thirteenth century. I visited the Higashi Hongwanji tem-ple and the Nishi Hongwanji temple, the two most important Pure Land temples in Kyoto, Japan. I took photographs of both temples for inclu-sion in my next book, *Shinran and Eshinni*. I am very familiar with the city of Kyoto, having spent many wonderful days here on previous trips. After five days in Kyoto, I took the train to Fukui where I stayed overnight in the APA Hotel. The next day I took the bus to Eiheiji.

Standing in front of the entrance gate, I was awestruck by the size and imposing beauty of the edifice. People were going in and out of the gate. Because of their demeanor and dress, I assumed they were mostly Japanese tourists. I explained the purpose of my visit to the gatekeeper in broken Japanese mixed with some English. A monk was summoned who directed me to a small room, where I removed my shoes and placed them in a locker. He then gave me a pair of house slippers and asked me through gestures to follow him. We arrived at another room occupied by other vis-itors of both sexes.

I was the only Westerner. I sat down and waited with the others while listening to the buzz and whispers of their conversation. It was almost an hour of waiting before another monk came in and directed all of us to follow him through a long corridor at the end of which he placed the men in one room and the women in another room.

All of us placed our luggage in sequence on a table in the rear of the room. There were about ten men in my group. The idea is to use the luggage to dispense daily needs such as toiletries, underclothes, and sleeping garments. To the right was a closet which contained rolled-up futons to use for sleeping on the floor at night and kept rolled up and put away during the day when not in use.

While I was changing into my *samu-e*, an imposing-looking monk opened the *shoji* screen and headed straight for me. With a *gassho*, he said, "Welcome, Shansky-san. I am happy to meet you. Is there anything I can do for you? My name is Kuroyanagi."

I returned the *gassho* and replied, "No, I am fine. I am just getting settled. I am very glad to meet you and I am happy to be here."

He continued, "Tonight you will sit *zazen* and have your dinner at your sitting place, *o-ryo-ki* style. Then you will be led to the bath room for your ablutions; then off to sleep. The *zendo* is the next room where you will sit with the women as well. Do you have any questions?"

"No, I think you covered everything."

"Well, then, tomorrow after your lunch a monk will bring you to my office where we can have tea and chat for a while. At that time I shall introduce you to Hoichi Suzuki, who would like to meet you. He is retired but still an important adviser to our monastery."

After he left a young man from the group came over to me speaking very halting English, "Excuse, please. My name is Jogen. I am learning English in school. I do not speak well yet but if I can help you, please allow me."

"*Arigato*, Jogen. (Thank you, Jogen.) You are very kind. If I have any questions I will certainly come to you."

This kind gesture seemed to break the ice. After that the other men greeted me with recognition many times.

That night we all went into the *zendo* and found our places on the elevated platform and faced the wall in lotus position for the forty minutes of *zazen,* which began with a simple ring of a bell. At the end of *zazen* we turned around 180 degrees by sliding on our *zafus* while still sitting and faced the inner room. The *zafu* I sat on was the same as the one I have at home but there was no *zabuton*. Instead we were sitting on a *tatami* mat (course straw).

Having brought our *o-ryo-ki* bowls we were ready for dinner. *O-ryo-ki* bowls are nested concentric bowls which are placed in a line in front of one's folded feet. Chopsticks and a sponge-tipped stick are provided with the bowls to wash down the bowls. Monks came in carrying buckets of victuals. They placed boiled rice and vegetables in the bowls. Eating is done in a prescribed manner in which the utensils are used in a definite way with no deviations. We were supervised by a monk to correct any errors.

After eating we were led to the bath room where the men undressed and soaped up and washed by sitting on miniature benches at water spigot stations lining the lower walls of the bath room like a wainscot. All the men then went into the large soaking tub containing tepid water. This brought on a lot of jocosity and laughing. At the conclusion of toweling and dressing, we were led back to our dormitory-style sleeping room.

Everyone took out a rolled-up futon plus a pillow from the closet and spread it out on the floor. That spot became the individual's for the length of time one would be sleeping in the room. Lights were automatically doused at 9:00 P.M. I was so tired, I fell asleep as my head went on the way down to the pillow.

The wake-up bell rang at 4:30 A.M., at which time everybody rose and rolled up the futons to be put back in the closet. I dressed in my *samu-e* and brought along my *o-ryo-ki* bowls as I entered the *zendo* and sat in my place awaiting the others to arrive. At the bell *zazen* began for forty minutes. At the final bell *zazen* was over with a communal *gassho*. Everyone then faced around and placed the *o-ryo-ki* bowls in proper order in front. Monks came around with food for breakfast. After breakfast we all arose to line up in preparation for *choka* (morning service).

The line of people was led up a steep stairway which passed open areas on either side showing the mountainous terrain with plantings, trees and flowers. The long climb led to an immense room with hundreds of monks, citizens, and practitioners. We sat on the side in assigned places on the floor. The mentor for our group was a monk named Gakuryo. He was ordained recently and was originally from Hokkaido. He helped us with uncertainties as to behavior and performance. We chanted the *Sandokai* and watched the monks perambulating in *gassho* position as they walked in two rotating circles opposite to each other. It was a really beautiful sight.

The next day after lunch, I was brought to Kuroyanagi's office by a monk.

"Come in, Shansky-san. Make yourself comfortable. How was your lunch?" He indicated a chair with his extended arm as he spoke.

"Everything was wonderful," I said as I sat down on the embroidered seat of the provided chair. I inquired in a very low voice, "Excuse me, Kuroyanagi-san, but you speak flawless English. Tell me, where did you learn it so well?"

He immediately answered, "I lived for six years in California while I was a liaison officer for the Soto Zen Administrative Headquarters. I knew a little English when I arrived there but became most proficient after interacting with Americans."

Just then the door opened and a small, old man, who was slightly bent over, entered wearing black robes and a brown shawl on top. He had a small round, tawny face with a myriad of wrinkles that seemed to give him a perpetual smile. His eyes were an unusual gray color and they were constantly darting. He bowed very low with a *gassho* and said, in broken English, "Welcome, Shansky-san. I am happy to meet you. My name is Suzuki Hoichi."

I returned the *gassho* and said, "Suzuki-san, the pleasure is mine."

The three of us sat facing each other while a female attendant poured tea into the cups on a table between us. Suzuki and Kuroyanagi spoke Japanese to each other in a low voice and rather quickly, after which Suzuki directed his attention to me.

"I was told that you practiced at Hosshinji with Harada Sekkei Roshi."

"Yes, that's true."

Suddenly Kuroyanagi interrupted, "He is also a friend of Daigaku-san."

Suzuki looked up with a surprised expression, "Ah, I see. Daigaku is a wonderful man. He is now working at the North American Soto Zen headquarters in San Francisco."

"Yes, that's true. I visit him there quite frequently."

He continued, "I was told that you have made many trips to Japan."

"Yes, this is my twentieth trip."

"Ah, so, have they been for business or pleasure?"

"Some were for business and some for pleasure."

"Do you have a special place that you particularly enjoy?"

I hesitated and thought for a moment. "Well, I've been all over Japan, from Hokkaido to Kyushu and even traveled back and forth across the *Seto Naikkai* [the Inland Sea] but if I had to pick one place it would be Shikoku."

"Ah, yes, Shikoku is very beautiful."

I then stated with some pride, "I saw it all because I walked on the Henro pilgrimage."

"Ah, yes, the Henro pilgrimage is a wonderful thing to do. You have seen more of Japan than most Japanese people."

We all laughed. Then I hesitated a moment before speaking, "Suzuki-san, you have a very famous name."

"Is that so?"

"Yes, there is D. T. Suzuki, the philosopher, there is a violin-learning method called Suzuki method, and there is even an automobile called a Suzuki."

He looked at me wide eyed as he spoke with mirth, "Perhaps I am a reincarnation of the automobile."

We all laughed and began to chat in small talk as we sipped our tea. We arose and made *gassho* to each other at the conclusion of our visit. At the door, Kuroyanagi confided in me.

"I have made arrangements for Gakuryo to lead your group on an excursion to the top of the mountain tomorrow afternoon."

"Thank you very much for your many kindnesses to me, Kuroyanagi-san."

I left and returned to what is euphemistically called "work practice." This is nothing more than clean-up work, but I hasten to say it is a very necessary venture. Monasteries are self-sufficient societies and depend on the work of its members. If the contribution of its members falters, it could lead to deterioration of the monastery.

So I spent the week doing morning *zazen* followed by breakfast, morning service, and morning work. Then came afternoon *zazen*, lunch, and afternoon work, followed by evening *zazen*, dinner, and sleep. This may seem like a mindless routine, but it is not. It's a way to focus on the intuitive process in order to discover solutions to seemingly insurmountable problems such as self.

At the conclusion of my stay in Eiheiji, I said a tearful farewell to Gakuryo and then went to Kuroyanagi's office to bid him goodbye.

He placed a book of prayers, which we used at morning service, in my hand as he said, "Remember, human life is but a series of footnotes to a vast, obscure, unfinished masterpiece."

"Thank you for your kindness to me. I shall keep in touch with you," I blurted out.

"You are most welcome, Shansky-san. I hope you benefited from your stay here. Here is a present for you. I hope to hear from you in the future. Goodbye and have a pleasant trip home."

As he pressed the prayer book into my hand.

I was too choked up to thank him.

I took the bus to Fukui city where I immediately made the train to Kyoto. I stayed overnight and then took the train to Osaka for the airplane trip home. I felt real good, having accomplished my earnest wish to practice in the leading monastery of Soto Zen Buddhism. Can you imagine a Catholic praying in the Vatican? That's how I felt.

Academia

It took about a week to adjust my biology. One day I received a phone call from a dear friend, Ed Grippe.

"Al, how are you? What's doing?"

"Hi, Ed. I just returned from Japan last week."

"Wow, what luck! I have a proposal for you."

"A proposal — what do you mean?"

"As you know, Al, I am head of the philosophy segment of the Humanities Department at Norwalk Community College. Dr. Moores suddenly left for a position at Sacred Heart University, leaving his teaching post open. Would you like to fill it and teach Non-Western Philosophy this fall?"

"Would I? Of course I would! What's involved?"

"Non-Western Philosophy covers Hinduism, Buddhism, Daoism, Tibetan and Islamic philosophy. Can you handle it?"

"Yes, I can."

"Well, in that case, you will hear from John Alvord, Chair of the Humanities Department at Norwalk Community College."

"Thanks a lot, Ed. Have a good day."

I was reeling from the opportunity of this phone call. The next day John Alvord called me and set up an appointment to go through the particulars of the hiring process.

Thus, I became an adjunct professor of philosophy at Norwalk Community College to teach Non-Western Philosophy in the fall and World Religions next spring.

Dr. Ed Grippe, who I mentioned previously, is a professor of philosophy at Norwalk Community College and was an active member of the IIFB when I was executive vice president of the organization. That's how I came to know him. He gave many papers at our conferences and we had a personal continuous relationship. This opportunity came at a fortuitous time since I needed something to fill the vacuum left by the vacancy of my consulting business.

I am now a writer and teacher; not bad.

At Last

Having traveled the fabled outer reaches of the world, I only brought home ideas about the attainment of serenity. I am still troubled by the complexities of the Buddhist truth — the ultimate reality that would free mankind from the treadmill of life and death.

After this Proustian odyssey, which I am writing, I still have not answered the three questions that brought me this far — Who are we? Why are we here? What is the nature of reality?

It's all to do with selflessness; the realization that the object of your self-attachment is an illusion. What is the self? It may be the deepest mystery of philosophy, psychology, and neuroscience: How does the brain unite to create the self; the subjective "I"?

Scientific and technological advances now allow us to manipulate genomes directly at the level of single genes and their constituents, with speed and precision that far exceed what natural evolution has been able to achieve over the past 3.5 billion years. We already have in vitro fertilization and animal cloning; in the future human cloning and the exploitation of embryonic stem cells, among other capabilities, may be routine. At the same time, we are developing machines that will surpass the human brain in raw computing power and building an interconnected world of information-processing devices.

What is it about these phenomena that make us so uneasy — the shattering of the human self, as we know it? Eventually we must come to terms with the fact that genomes, computations, and mind are fluid, continuous entities, in both space and time. The boundary between the self and the world has begun to dissolve and ultimately may evaporate entirely.

Who could have predicted one hundred years ago the world in which we live today, let alone the shape of our spiritual inclinations as we speed through the next millennium? It sometimes seems to me that I evolved with the century: The teachings of Buddhism were tuned to the contemporary idiom, at the same time shaping it and responding to its needs.

Everyone today is responsible for his- or herself, home, health, income and spiritual well-being. Buddhism addresses this condition, focusing on the state of the personal psyche, the modern obsession.

Diversity and choice have displaced dogmatism and the security it brought. The present era offers man the right, for better or worse, to select what he wants from the various religions and philosophies of the world, adding some to his shopping basket, while rejecting others, at all times aware that his ultimate loyalty is only to himself and his own salvation. This emancipated, self-absorbed creature that I am, traveling alone across the spiritual landscape of the world, finds in Buddhism something that resembles the home I have longed for.

The mistakes of our ancestors have led us to desire a new beginning and a new understanding of God, free of past or misleading iconology. The motivation of present-day religion, in a predominantly secular western society, is enlightenment, whether it is attained on the psychiatrist's couch, the pew, the Buddhist mat or the plastic chair. Advocates of enlightenment are the modern-day prophets, though they can never teach the experience, but merely share their own realization of it in a comprehensible manner.

I have never experienced a life-changing epiphany, despite my years of meditation, but I have become fully aware of the conditions necessary for enlightenment. Buddhists call it *satori*— the moment of intuitive illumination when the mind and soul finally understand the basic truth of the universe. It is the instant of spiritual fission when the veil falls, when lives change.

Not yet; but I shall keep trying.

In the words of Teng Chingyang, written in the *Dharmapada*:

We are but passing guests from who knows where?

Say not thy home is here, thy home is there.

It suits me what I've got and what I've not.

The plum-flowers bloom here, there, and everywhere.

Epilogue

This story is true. It reveals a search for a life that transcends time and place. Part 1 starts in the late spring (May) through the summer and early fall (September). It is in reality a composite of this same season during the years 1992, 1993, and 1994. It was during those three occasions that I studied and practiced at the Zen monastery, Hosshinji Semmon Sodo, in Obama, Japan.

As of this writing, some of the characters mentioned in this narrative have left the monastery. Harada Sekkei Roshi left the monastery in June 2002 to become General Director of the new Soto Zen headquarters in Europe with an office in Milan, Italy, but after a year he returned to Hosshinji and took up his old post as Abbot. Daigaku Rumme, with whom I still maintain an epistolary relationship, has been at the Soto Zen North American Office in San Francisco since early in 2003. These changes were made at the behest of the Administration Headquarters of Soto Zen Buddhism in Japan.

Piyadassi returned to Ladakh for about two years after the untimely death of Sumano and then went to Korea to live in a Zen monastery for a short time. He then went to a culinary job in San Jose, California, and to my best knowledge he still resides there. We have spoken from time to time by telephone but we have not met as yet. Doiku, I understand, now has his own temple somewhere else in Japan and got married and became a Japanese citizen. I now know the finality of Taizan. He no longer remains elusive. I learned that he resides in Iowa City, Iowa. I spoke with him by telephone and learned that he is back in the construction business but still practices as a Buddhist. This seems to be a strange outcome for an ordained Buddhist monk. Yerney is home in Slovenia and did write his book, which he published in 2000 under the title, *The Power of Life*. We have corresponded via email to a limited extent. Hanaoka was, indeed, ordained as a monk and took up a post in a small village in Japan. Hosshinji now has the Roshi back full time.

Obama is a charming little fishing village and summer vacation spot on Wakasa Bay, north of Kyoto. I became very friendly with the merchants along the two main streets, which cut through the town and converged at the railroad station. I would visit with them on the one day a week we were permitted to leave the monastery grounds. On those occasions, I would go into town to shop for supplemental food, trinkets, and stationery and just to see how the world was managing without me. I also would visit with the fishermen and watch their boats come in with the catch of the day. People came from all parts of central Japan just to buy fresh fish. It reminded me of my youth in Sheepshead Bay in Brooklyn, New York, where I was born and did the very same thing.

Buddhism is the fourth largest religion in the world with about 400,000,000 adherents. It is fourth in line after Christianity, Islam, and Hinduism. There are many sects of Buddhism, such as Vipassana, Shin, Tibetan, and Zen. All these different sects have their distinctive methods of practice but they all believe in the teachings of the Buddha, called the Dharma. Zen ("Ch'an" in Chinese) seems to have discerned the essentials of the Buddha's teachings and spirit better than any other sect and to have developed their deeper implications more faithfully. For this reason, I became attracted to it.

Zen is not an independent Japanese entity. Dogen (1200–1253), who brought Soto Zen from China, stressed Buddhism so much more than Zen that he never explicitly used the Zen label. Zen and Ch'an are Japanese and Chinese translations for the Sanskrit word *dhyana,* meaning

208

208

meditation. Meditation is the common thread throughout all Buddhist sects including modern versions. But, how did it all begin?

Buddhism began in India (500–600 B.C.E.) as an evolvement from Hinduism. Myth has it that a young Prince of the Shakya clan named Siddhartha Gautama left his cloistered, opulent life and immediately became distressed and influenced by the suffering and despair of ordinary people outside the palace gates. Thus, he decided to lead an ascetic life in order to learn the ways of overcoming this deviation from the proper welfare of human society. After six years of unsuccessful investigation he sat under a bodhi tree (ficus religiosa) in the city of Bodhgaya in order to rest and contemplate. Suddenly, the answer came to him in full clarity. He became enlightened.

> *All life is pain and suffering.*
> *Pain and suffering is due to desires, grasping, and attachments.*
> *The way to get rid of pain and suffering is to give up desires, grasping, and attachments.*
> *The way to give up desires, grasping, and attachments is to follow the eightfold path.*

These four statements are called the Four Noble Truths and are a rudimentary part of every sect of Buddhism. Because Siddhartha Gautama was awakened to the truth he was called the Buddha, which means "the awakened one."

The eightfold path is a series of mindful conditions and a way of life subscribed to by every sect of Buddhism.

1. Right Views (understanding, knowledge): some intellectual orientation is needed if one is to set out other than haphazardly. It must, therefore, be agreed that the Four Noble Truths provide this orientation.

2. Right Intent (purpose, resolution): if we are to make appreciable headway persistence is indispensable.

3. Right Speech (do not use careless, idle and flippant words): always tell the truth. Approach truth ontologically rather than morally. Deceit is more foolish than evil. Do not use uncharitable speech such as false witness, idle chatter, gossip, slander and abuse.

4. Right Behavior (right conduct): the counsel is toward selflessness and charity. Use the Five Precepts:

Do not kill.

Do not steal.

Do not lie.

Do not be unchaste.

Do not drink intoxicants.

5. Right Livelihood (do not kill, do not be a soldier, do not be a slaughterer): for the layperson it calls for engaging in occupations that promote life instead of destroying it.

6. Right Effort (be ethical, use the precepts as a guide): there are virtues to be developed, passions to be curbed, and destructive mind states to be expunged so compassion and detachment can thrive.

7. Right Mindfulness (look at things truthfully): the Buddha saw ignorance, not sin, as the offender; more specifically the ignorance of our true nature.

8. Right Concentration (do proper meditation): the extirpation of delusion, craving, and hostility, the three poisons, will lead to a mind reposing in its true condition.

This eightfold path, especially the Five Precepts, is often referred to by unenlightened people as the "Buddhist Ten Commandments." Nothing could be further from the truth. Nothing in Buddhism commands an individual. All is an understanding, a suggestion for the way to a proper path.

At about the second century, a split took place in Buddhism, leading to two large bodies, Hinayana (lesser vehicle) and Mahayana (greater vehicle). The Hinayana was the more orthodox group, which did not want to change just to accommodate the laity. They called themselves Theravadin (teaching of the elders). They also preserved the original teachings and rules in a Pali Canon called the Tripitaka, which exists today in Sri Lanka. The Mahayana believed that it was unnecessary for the laity to practice in a monastery. Practice at home was fully condoned. As a result of the teachings of Nagarjuna (2nd/3rd century), the Madhyamika School was formed to preach and practice the middle path.

In the third century, King Ashoka made Buddhism the official religion of his kingdom in India, which covered most of the central portion of India. During this time there were several slow migrations taking place. The Hinayana went to Thailand, Myanmar (Burma), Sri Lanka, Cambodia, and Laos. The Mahayana went to Central Asia, Afghanistan, China, Korea, Japan, Bhutan, Sikkim, Bali, and Vietnam.

In addition, there were migrations of Tantric Buddhists taking place through passes across the Himalaya Mountains from India to places such as Tibet, Mongolia, Ladakh, Tuva, and Buryat. These were Mahayana Buddhists who called themselves Vajrayana (thunderbolt vehicle). This dispersion of Buddhism into other parts of Asia gave rise to many scriptures, said to number over ten thousand. In the Sung Dynasty (972 C.E.) a Chinese version of these scriptures was published consisting of 1521 works, in more than 5000 volumes, covering 130,000 pages.

Buddhist scriptures vary widely, and the quantity of them being so enormous, they have become segregated into different groups as they are favored by different schools of thought and practice. The T'ien Tai (Tendai) favor the more philosophical scriptures; the Shingon, the more esoteric; the Ch'an (Zen), the more intellectual and the Pure Land (Shin), the more emotional.

These scriptures are special transmissions. Think of Hinduism with its Vedas, Confucianism with its Classics, Judaism with its Torah, Christianity with its Bible, and Islam with its Qur'an. All would happily define themselves as special transmissions through their scriptures. Zen, too, has its text: they are intoned in its monasteries morning and evening. In addition to the sutras, which it shares with other sects of Buddhism, it has its own texts. The most important being the Shobogenzo.

There were two very important Japanese saints who brought Chinese Buddhism to Japan. Kukai (Kobo Daishi, 774–835) went to China to study Buddhism as a replacement for the Confucianism in which he was trained. He returned with Shingon Buddhism which he established in a monastery on Mt. Koya, east of the city of Kyoto. He and his followers were given permission to establish 88 Shingon temples around the periphery of the island of Shikoku. This is known today as the Henro Pilgrimage, where pilgrims can take up to two months walking the distance (about 750 miles) around the island visiting each temple.

The second saint is known as Saicho (Dengyo Daichi, 767–822), who brought back Tendai Buddhism, which was established on Mt. Hiei in Kyoto. This is where the great saint Honen (1133–1212) developed Jodo (Shin) Buddhism to be modified later on as Jodo Shinshu (true Shin) Buddhism by Shinran (1173–1282). Today Shin Buddhism is known as Pure Land Buddhism because of the invocation of the Nembutsu, *Namu Amida Butsu,* "Hail Amida Buddha," which is supposed to put one in the Western Paradise through faith alone as a form of salvation. Amida is a Bodhisattva who delayed his entry into Nirvana to help others reach that goal. Because of this reliance on Amida, Pure Land is often called Amidism.

The thirteenth century in Japan was the harbinger of modern Japanese Buddhism by including the teachings of four of the most important sages of Buddhist philosophy.

Honen (1133–1212)—founder of Jodo (Shin)
Shinran (1173–1292)—founder of Jodo Shinshu (true Shin)
Dogen (1200–1253)—founder of Soto Zen
Nichiren (1222–1282)—founder of Hokke Buddhism

Honen and Shinran's Shin philosophy devolved from Tendai Buddhism, which was established on Mt. Hiei. After much arduous effort the local populace gravitated to this form because they found entreaty with Amida Buddha by invoking his name, a simple matter that only relied on faith. Despite much denial, most people considered Amida to be a deity or at least a supreme figure. When Shin Buddhism was taken over by the Hongwanji temples, established by Shinran's grandson, the movement began to grow rapidly and eventually became the largest sect in Japan. There are many Shin temples throughout the world, particularly in the United States.

Zen, on the other hand, is not very large in population. In Japan there are about 9 million adherents divided among three sects: Soto Zen, Rinzai Zen, and Obaku Zen. Soto Zen and Rinzai Zen are very much alike with the only major difference residing in the treatment of *koans* (conundrums used to jolt the mind). Obaku Zen is a very small and minor sect and only caters to a group found near and around the city of Nagasaki. Some do not consider it a form of Zen at all since it is a blend of Shin Buddhism and Zen Buddhism.

Zen of the Soto and Rinzai sects is very popular in the United States and throughout Western Europe, Mexico, and in Peru and Brazil in South America. Zen is a very austere movement without the costly accouterments often found in Tibetan temples. It is a self-reliant religion which depends on years of practice through *zazen* (sitting meditation) to develop an acute sense of intuition.

Nichiren, during the thirteenth century, had a message of rebuke for other sects of Buddhism. Their belief in the Lotus Sutra as the true word of Buddha became a serious point of contention between followers of Nichiren and other Buddhist sects. But today there is a tranquil association of Nichiren, Zen, and Shin in all parts of the world.

I believe it is important that my readers become familiar with the way Buddhism came to America. In a country of such great religious diversity and one which claims to have more than a majority of Christians, it would seem that such an explanation would be desired and fitting. Buddhism arrived in the United States at the time of the World Parliament of Religions during the Columbian Exposition of 1891 in Chicago. The majority of the delegates and audience at the Parliament were Christians. But the non–Christian Asian religions were also very present.

On the third day of the Parliament, the Japanese Buddhist layman and translator Zenshiro Noguchi introduced most of the Japanese Buddhist delegation, including Rinzai Zen master Soyen Shaku, and representatives of the Jodo Shinshu, Nichiren, Tendai and Esoteric Schools. By the fourth day Horin Toki, a delegate, took great pains to differentiate the three Buddhist *yanas*, or vehicles, insisting all the while that the "truth of the three *yanas* (Hinayana, Mahayana, and Vajrayana) is the same, the difference being in the minds of those who receive it."

Soyen Shaku, the first Zen master in America, was matter-of-fact and down to earth. "Buddhism offers only one explanation, namely the Law of Cause and Effect. Buddhism considers the universe as having no beginning and no end. Our sacred Buddha is not the creator of the Law of Nature, but is the first discoverer of the law."

For the next fifty years or so, there was steady stream of Asian immigrants coming to the United States to escape poverty, pestilence, and inequities in their homeland. Most of these immigrants were from China, Japan, and Korea. They came to work on the railroads, in the canneries and mills and on the farms. They settled in ghetto-like areas called "Chinatowns" in Hawaii and on the west coast of the United States and Canada in the major cities such as Los Angeles, San Francisco, Seattle and Vancouver. In so doing they brought with them their indigenous religions and culture and Buddhism became very fertile. These new temples became study places for some of the local Asian people. The first Japanese Buddhist missionaries to reach the continental United States arrived in San Francisco on July 6, 1898; five years after the Parliament had closed. The two missionaries — Reverends Eryu Honda and Ejun Myamoto — had met with thirty young Japanese at the home of Dr. Katsugoro Haido and celebrated the founding of the Bukkyo Seinenkai, or Young Men's Buddhist Association. In September of 1906 a second group of Zen Buddhists arrived in San Francisco. This group was led by Sokatsu Shaku, a disciple of Soyen Shaku. Sokatsu had practiced hard for ten years at Engakuji Temple in Kamakura, Japan, before coming to the United States.

In the meantime, many universities had begun instituting departments of Asian Studies and departments of Asian Languages with heavy emphasis on China and Japan. One notable place was Columbia University in New York City, which had a group headed up by Professor William Theodore de Bary. His group consisted of Philip Yampolsky, who translated Japanese Buddhist literature, Burton Watson, who translated Chinese Buddhist literature, and Donald Keene, who translated Japanese literature. Among the students was William Francis Paar, who eventually, with other students, was placed in the military intelligence group during World War II because of their facility with Japanese and other Asian languages.

One of Sokatsu's students was a young artist by the name of Shigetsu Sasaki—later known as Sokei-an. Sokatsu and Sokei-an left Tokyo for San Francisco. After ten years Sokei-an left San Francisco and headed for New York City in 1916. He continued his Zen training and was authorized to teach Zen in 1928.

On May 11, 1931, Sokei-an and three others signed the incorporation papers for the Buddhist Society of America. This group grew slowly, with both Japanese and American adherents.

One of Sokei-an's students was Alan Watts, a young Englishman who at that time was living in New York City with his wife Eleanor Everett. They both attended Zen services at Sokei-an's apartment nearby. Alan Watts was an important contributor to the religions of Asia, particularly Zen and Daoism, by writing several best-selling books on these religious matters. There is no doubt that these books were responsible for generating great interest in Buddhism as well as other Asian religions.

In 1934 an American named Dwight Goddard founded an organization called the Followers of Buddha, an American Brotherhood. The Followers of the Buddha was an attempt to found an American monastic order. The American Brotherhood was not successful, but his book, *The Buddhist Bible*, became a bestseller and is still in print. It was not until the end of World War II that American Buddhism took hold.

In November of 1941 Sokei-an and the First Zen Institute moved into new quarters on East Sixty-Fifth Street in New York City. On December 7, Pearl Harbor was attacked. A few days later the FBI began to round up Japanese "security risks." On July 15, 1942, Sokei-an was taken to an internment camp. He was eventually released and died on May 17, 1945.

D. T. Suzuki began a series of seminars at Columbia University. At these seminars, the seeds of the so-called Zen "boom" of the late 1950s were sown. D. T. Suzuki was well known for his books, which were increasingly available in paperback. He had written a number of books for specialists, but most were essays addressed to the intelligent cosmopolitan in a humorous and direct style. His was a unique voice. No one else could speak of spiritual life with such a lively mixture of authority and informality.

Indeed, by the latter half of the 1950s, the idea of Zen had become so popularized that it achieved the status of a fad. In the 1950s the poets Allen Ginsberg and Gary Snyder with the writers Jack Kerouac and Philip Whalen became the leaders of the "beat generation" in San Francisco and Berkeley, California. Later on they were joined by Alan Watts. Watts made the West Coast his home and had begun to teach at the American Academy of Asian Studies in the early 1960s.

In the late 1950s, Eido Shimano became Zen master of the Zen Studies Society in New York City, which today is known as the Shobo-ji, a Rinzai Zen temple. I occasionally attend this temple. A number of Americans who received monastic training in Japan began to open temples in the United States. Two Americans, notably Robert Aitken and Philip Kapleau, made a great impact on the Zen scene in America.

In the early 1960s, Shunryu Suzuki was responsible for starting the San Francisco Zen Center, Sokoji, which today has several associate temples in the Bay area, including Tassajara and Green Gulch Zen Farm as retreat centers. I have practiced at the San Francisco Center many times.

In Minneapolis, Katagiri Roshi started the Minnesota Zen Meditation Center on Lake Calhoun, where I received my initial training in meditation. Unfortunately, Katagiri Roshi died of cancer in 1991. Many of his disciples over the years had gone to Hosshinji monastery in Obama, Japan, as I did.

In Maine, Walter Nowick, after many years, had become dharma successor of Zuigan Goto-roshi. In Boston, the Cambridge Buddhist Society continued. In New York, the First Zen Institute of America and Eido Shimano's Zen Studies Society continued to expand.

In Philadelphia, Dr. Albert Stunkard organized a Zen group. In Washington, D. C., another Zen group was associated with the Zen Studies Society. There was also the Washington Buddhist Vihara, a Theravadin group.

In Rochester, Philip Kapleau's Zen Meditation Center of Rochester continued to grow. I practiced at this center once. In Chicago, the Reverend Gyomay Kubose, a Shinshu minister, established a *zazen* group.

In San Francisco was the San Francisco Zen Center in which over a hundred and fifty people were sitting *zazen* and attending lectures in the fall of 1966. In Hawaii, Robert Aitkin's Diamond Sangha continued to grow with several satellite centers on other islands and a strong relation to San Francisco. In Los Angeles, a group under Maezumi-sensei established permanent quarters.

As can be seen from the foregoing catenate the establishment of Buddhist centers was growing and well established from the 1960s to the 1980s. But there was more to come.

One of the most important expositions of Buddhism in America is Tibetan Buddhism. In 1950 the Chinese invaded Tibet, forcing the fourteenth Dalai Lama (Tendzin Gyatso) to flee into exile with hundreds of thousands of refugees to Dharamsala in India. The world was aghast at this unprovoked aggression but did nothing. Today there are many Tibetan refugees in America who brought their version of Buddhism with them. They established many temples on the East Coast as well as the Midwest.

The Dalai Lama became very popular through speeches at universities and conventions and with the support of Hollywood personalities such as actor Richard Gere. The Dalai Lama has been received by heads of state all over the world offering sympathy but he has only gained publicity from these excursions. This, however, caused many curiosity seekers to pursue this form of Buddhism with compelling wonderment.

Another very important impact on the Buddhist scene is Vipassana, known as Insight Meditation. Jack Kornfield and Joseph Goldstein met at the Naropa Insitute in Boulder, Colorado, where I practiced Shambhala meditation. They both studied intensively in Southeast Asia and are products of Theravadin Buddhism. They started the Insight Meditation Society in Barre, Massachusetts, which now houses a large complement of buildings, including the Barre Center for Buddhist Studies and the Forest Refuge. Jack Kornfield also established Spirit Rock Meditation Center on the West Coast in the Bay area. These venues have become very popular through exposition on television and are of great interest to the serious student as well as the laity as retreat places. It is very obvious, by this time, that the most popular Buddhist sects in America are now Zen, Shin, Vipassana, and Tibetan. They attract many thousands of people who feel they gain some benefit by attending one or more of their sessions.

What is it that would attract such a large group of people who come out of a different birth religion to Buddhism? The answer probably lies in the differences between Buddhist philosophy and practice and the practice of birth religions, which rely heavily on entreaty with an unseen God and prayer for sustenance. In Buddhism there is no God, no soul, and no hereafter. All is self-reliant. It can be said that Buddhism is really a course of instruction designed to render one the ability of self-realization and the primacy of moral merit and personal excellence. It is interesting that Buddhism is not a proselytizing religion. It has no missionaries. People come of their own accord.

Having said all of the above, I should like to take this opportunity to recognize the four American monks that I encountered during the three times that I stayed at Hosshinji: Ryubu Whitney, Taizan Shaeffer, Doiku Griffin and Daigaku Rumme. They have all been of great help to me while I practiced and learned Zen. For this, I shall be eternally grateful to them. I hope they will understand and forgive the minor attributes I ascribed to them in this story. It was only done to emphasize the nature of our relationship and the importance of Zen practice. It was not intended to besmirch or denigrate anyone.

In particular, my friend and mentor Daigaku has been a consistent source of wise counseling. I am truly beholden to him for his concern, effort and help. We maintain a correspondence on an *ad hoc* basis, which hopefully will continue for years to come.

In October 1997, I returned to Hosshinji with my wife to visit Daigaku. We only stayed a short while but it was good to see Daigaku again after a three-year hiatus. My wife had accompanied me to Japan on several previous occasions but I believe this visit was important in that it revealed to her the seat of my Zen experience and learning.

Finally, I should like to state that Zen has become an integral part of my life. I practice *zazen* every morning without fail for forty minutes at which time I renew my vows in Japanese and English. Even though my psyche is bombarded daily by events, I try to maintain a reasonable connection with Buddhist teachings.

Part 2 covers a period where I no longer have the guidance of a Zen Master. Like the Ronin or a former Samurai warrior, I am forced to roam the earth without a master. Zen is the radical approach to Buddhism. Historically, Zen arose as a Buddhist sect resulting from a blend of Buddhism and Daoism. What Zen has done for me is to clarify and liberate my state of consciousness. Zen offers me a way of experiencing life directly, a way of learning who I am and how I want to live. While in the Hosshinji Monastery, I studied with a Japanese Zen Master, Harada Sekkei Roshi, and was helped with advice by a mentor, Daigaku Rumme through the formal approach. Now that I have left the monastery, I am involved in an individual study program without a Zen Master.

When asked about Zen Masters and teachers, my friend Bill Paar always had this to say: "The old fox can learn more from the young fool than the young fool can ever hope to learn from the old fox." Gee, but I really miss Bill. Our time together was so short. We hardly knew each other. Still, I am concerned about a solitary system, even though Nietzsche said, "Remember this and know that any system of liberation may work once, for one individual."

May I take this opportunity to divulge that the character of Alice did not exist in the form described in the Kagyu Thubten Choling Monastery in Wappinger Falls? I did meet a woman there who I thought was terribly confused and flighty. I chose to use her as a common foil for some of my critical thoughts. She was what is called in the vernacular parlance a flake.

I would also like to take this opportunity to disclose that Dr. Tong and I did attend the 11th International Society of Chinese Philosophy (ISCP) in Taipei, Taiwan in July 26, 1999. This was my sixth trip to Taiwan, with the only main difference being that I went to the top of Ali Shan Mountain during a misty rainy morning. I chose not to reveal this in the chronology of this story since I did not believe the circumstances would contribute much to my views of Buddhism. I was able, however to make friends with Prof. Alan Fox of University of Delaware and Prof. Dan Lusthaus of University of Missouri — Columbia who were avowed vegetarians and taught me to appreciate vegetarian fare as a component of Buddhist life.

In Part 3, I met the character Anjela Maldonado at the Fourth Symposium of the Field-Being Institute. She was, indeed, a former Catholic nun who had a lot of trouble adjusting to civilian life. As a result, we had many conversations regarding her dilemma. I felt some of these thoughts would be appropriate in this story.

In 1996, the strange triple life I led for the next six years began in earnest: chemist, essayist, and lecturer. Yet I always had the feeling with my entry into philosophy that I was a fraud. I am sure some of my associates regarded me as not professional as a philosopher. In certain senses, of course, this was true. I never earned a living solely as a philosopher and I had neither a Ph.D. in philosophy with all the grounding that would have provided nor the detailed understanding of other disciplines that professional philosophers were expected to have, although they might specialize in only one group. And yet, I must confess, that my colleagues accepted me if for no other reason than ostensibly as an oddity.

Once seen as an exotic faith, Buddhism has attracted Westerners seeking more satisfying spiritual lives in our multicultural society, due in part to celebrity converts, motion pictures, and the popularity of the Dalai Lama. A radically different form of this ancient faith is emerging that borrows liberally from varied Buddhist traditions in Asia and is far more egalitarian than Eastern practices.

The study of Buddhism enables me to scorn death; it raises me above earthly concerns by speaking to me of the things of the spirit; it refines all my feelings; and that reasoned, almost philosophical courage is much finer than physical courage or the boldness of the senses, for it is in reality the courage of the spirit.

Like Franz Schubert's *Unfinished Symphony*, this work must end at this point. This should not be an enigmatic case because like Schubert's

Unfinished Symphony, the two surviving movements are the most dramatic and personal statement of the *lacrimae rerum* in symphonic literature. It seems clear that Schubert disowned the work whereas I consider this work a prequel of things to come.

Index